Education and Democratic Citizenship in America

EDUCATION
and
DEMOCRATIC CITIZENSHIP
in
AMERICA

Norman H. Nie

Jane Junn

Kenneth Stehlik-Barry

THE UNIVERSITY OF CHICAGO PRESS
Chicago and London

Norman H. Nie is professor of political science at the University of Chicago. Jane Junn is assistant professor of political science at Rutgers University. Kenneth Stehlik-Barry is a doctoral candidate in political science at Northwestern University.

The University of Chicago Press, Chicago 60637
The University of Chicago Press, Ltd., London
© 1996 by the University of Chicago
All rights reserved. Published 1996
Printed in the United States of America

05 04 03 02 01 00 99 98 97 96   1 2 3 4 5

ISBN: 0-226-58388-0 (cloth)
0-226-58389-9 (paper)

Library of Congress Cataloging-in-Publication Data

Nie, Norman H.
    Education and democratic citizenship in America / Norman H. Nie,
Jane Junn, Kenneth Stehlik-Barry.
        p.   cm.
    Includes bibliographical references and index.
    ISBN 0-226-58388-0 — ISBN 0-226-58389-9 (pbk.)
    1. Political participation—United States.   2. Citizenship—United
States.   3. Education—United States.   I. Junn, Jane.   II. Stehlik
-Barry, Kenneth.   III. Title.
JK1764.N54 1996
306.2—dc20
                                                            95-26657
                                                            CIP

For our parents, who saw to our education

Lucille and Ben Nie
Sue and Robert Junn
Patricia and Leo Barry

Acknowledgments

The research process that lies behind a book like this one entails a tremendous amount of work, considerable money, and the assistance of many people. In our case, we hope the product justifies the work and the money. Here, we would like to thank those who contributed their ideas and time.

We begin, however, by acknowledging a profound debt of gratitude to our families, especially to Carol Nie, David Champagne, and Janis, Cassiopeia, Leila, and Thea Stehlik-Barry, for their love and understanding.

We give special thanks to three colleagues and friends, without whom we could have neither started nor completed this book: Sidney Verba, Kay Schlozman, and Henry Brady. With them, one of the authors designed and conducted the 1990 Citizen Participation Study. The first part of the book is based on these data. The survey was a community effort among us, and is the mainspring of many of our subsequent ideas. Our collaboration continued after the data were collected, and we thank them for the detailed comments they provided on the successive drafts of our manuscript. We owe a special debt to Henry Brady, who challenged us to improve our analysis of the over time data in an early draft of Chapter 8. His detailed critical comments revolutionized our thinking about how to provide a convincing test of the competing education models.

Many other colleagues volunteered their time. In particular, we wish to thank M. Kent Jennings and Robert Shapiro for their detailed and insightful reviews of more than one of the drafts. Their comments and suggestions have helped strengthen the analysis and argument tremendously. Lutz Erbring provided extraordinarily detailed comments and suggestions through several versions of the entire manuscript. Although we did not always take his advice, we hope the improvements he suggested show in the analysis, and we are certain it is a better book for his advice. Finally, we owe a great debt to the late James S. Coleman, who after reading a draft of Part I several years ago, urged us to test our hypotheses from the cross-sectional data in the most stringent way, by using the model to make retrospective predictions with survey data over time. The analysis he pressed us to do is now in Chapter 8. Without his insight and encouragement, we would have never made the effort to assemble and analyze the over time data from the General Social Survey and the National Election Study, which became essential to testing the validity of the argument. We wish he could be here to see what we came up with.

We owe special appreciation to Ira Katznelson for his astute and extensive comments on Part I of this book, many of which we have incorporated. We also wish to express our gratitude to Michael Dawson, Mark Hansen, and Adam Przeworski, who gave us careful readings on drafts of both parts of the manuscript and offered important suggestions. Other colleagues at the University of Chicago and Rutgers University made contributions at one time or another throughout the time we were writing the book: Jon Elster, Andy Farkas, Jim Fearon, Dedi Felman, Simon Jackman, Richard Lau, Edward Laumann, Anne Nie, Lynn Sanders, and Steven Walt. Sometimes this help was freely volunteered, but on other occasions we were not above corralling those we thought could help us with a problem. In addition, we benefited from the comments and questions of participants at various conferences and seminars at which we presented our ideas: the American Politics Workshop at the University of Chicago, the Midwest Political Science Association, the New York Area Political Psychology Seminar (at Columbia University's Center for the Social Sciences), and the American Political Science Association.

Intensive empirical analysis cannot be done without good research assistants. Jean Jenkins' phenomenal SPSS expertise and good humor made running and documenting the complex analysis of the over time data in the second half of the book almost fun. We thank her for her dedication, her hard work, and the important substantive contributions she made to the analysis. We also give special thanks to Jonathan Kochavi. In addition, we are very lucky to have had the able assistance of Julie Alig, Linda Andes, Robert Boatright, Stacy Bosshardt, Rachelle Brooks, Sharon Caldwell, Jonathan Gould, Erica Grevemeyer, Emily Horowitz, Wei Hsin, Grace Huang, Su Kwak, Brenda Marshall, Betsy McEneaney, Imran Siddiqui, and Daniel Slotwiner. Each made a special contribution, and each is greatly appreciated.

Little in this world runs without money, and empirical social science is certainly no exception. The 1990 Citizen Participation Survey was an ambitious and expensive undertaking. Members of 15,000 households were surveyed by telephone to obtain information on their levels of political activity, interest, and knowledge, as well as information on their demographic characteristics. Over 2,500 of these respondents were later selected and interviewed in person at greater length. The Spencer Foundation, the National Science Foundation, the Hewlett Foundation, and the Ford Foundation generously supported the research. Later, the Spencer Foundation provided the authors with additional funds to support work on Part II, enabling us to expand our scope. We owe special thanks to John H. Barcroft of the Spencer Foundation for providing us with the extra support needed at a crucial time. We are grateful to them all and hope they judge the product worthy of the investment.

We wish to express a special debt of gratitude to the universities and enterprises where we work. First, we extend our appreciation to the Division of the Social Sciences and the National Opinion Research Center (NORC) of the University of Chicago. The division provided a home and significant financial support for the project over many years. NORC both did the fieldwork for the Citizen Participation Study and administered a number of our grants. It is also the home of the General Social Survey, whose director, Tom W. Smith, has been extremely helpful to us in guiding our use of the data and its bibliography. Martin Frankel, Chief Statistical Scientist at NORC, provided helpful counsel in the development of the sample weights for the 1990 Citizen Participation Study data. Many thanks are due also to Patrick Bova, the librarian of the Paul Sheatsley Memorial Library at NORC, who assisted us in data and literature searches throughout the project. Julie Antelman and Mary Westbrook of NORC helped us through the morass of paperwork. Our friends in the Department of Political Science at the University of Chicago—Kathy Anderson, Lorraine Dwelle, Heidi Parker, and Mimi Walsh—helped us through administrative problems. Rutgers University, Jane's institutional home, has been generous with release time and research support to an unusually accommodating degree for a junior faculty member. In particular, we thank Richard Wilson and Phyllis Moditz of the Department of Political Science at Rutgers for facilitating the leave time.

SPSS Inc. has made extraordinary contributions to the project and to this book. SPSS played an important role in preparing this book for publication; its desktop publishing experts shaved months off the amount of time it typically takes to prepare an academic book. Bob Gruen, director of SPSS publications, facilitated the process by giving his time and expertise. Yvonne Smith and Bonnie Shapiro found extra time in their hectic publications schedule to edit the text, create the graphics, and put the manuscript together. We are very grateful to them for the superb work they did. Patricia O'Neil and Bonnie Melton provided valuable assistance with proofreading and graphics.

SPSS also subsidized the participation of one of the co-authors, and we thank Sue Phelan for providing Ken with some time to work on this book. SPSS has also generously given computer hardware and funds for travel and research assistance. We thank Eileen Brady and Bob Brinkman for keeping our records straight and Tony Babinec for answering our statistical questions. Last but certainly not least, Jack Noonan, president of SPSS, and Edward Hamburg, senior financial officer, have consistently maintained that it is good for the company to have the founder and chairman of the board using the product on a daily basis. We are grateful for the largess that follows from those beliefs. SPSS was invented and designed to study exactly the kinds of questions we wrestle with in this book; the management of SPSS has clearly honored its roots.

Finally, we would like to thank John Tryneski, senior editor at the University of Chicago Press, for his enthusiastic endorsement of this project. Publishing a book with an academic press should always be this easy.

At a historical moment when serious thought is being given to eliminating or curtailing governmental support for research in the social sciences, we would like to give testimony to the immense value of the two ongoing data collections which form the backbone of Part II of this book. Without the General Social Survey and the National Election Study, which are both supported primarily by the National Science Foundation, we would never have been able to provide as definitive a test of our hypotheses regarding the differential impact of relative versus absolute education on democratic citizenship. To the founders of these two immensely important data-gathering enterprises, and to those who carry their work forward, we wish to record our thanks. The continuity and quality of these data collections are essential for social scientists and policymakers to investigate social and political processes and trends in the United States, for they are the only two ongoing noneconomic studies of political and social behavior and beliefs. Even in a time of severe budgetary constraint, we can ill afford to be penny-wise and pound-foolish.

Norman H. Nie
Hailey, Idaho

Jane Junn
New Brunswick, New Jersey

Kenneth Stehlik-Barry
Chicago, Illinois

Contents

Figures and Tables

FIGURES

APPENDIX FIGURES

TABLES

APPENDIX TABLES

1

Education and Democratic
Citizenship in America

Enlightened Political Engagement

This book is about the relationship between formal education and democratic citizenship. We consider a question that has preoccupied political philosophers, theorists, and political scientists for centuries. How and to what extent does formal education influence citizenship in democracy? The enormous scope and consequence of such an inquiry make the present consideration of this question but a partial formulation both in definition and explanation. We focus on the causal processes of education as formal schooling for a particularly important set of citizenship characteristics in the contemporary American democracy. In particular, we consider the ways and the extent to which education influences how knowledgeable citizens are, how attentive they are, how regularly they vote, how active in politics they are beyond the vote, and, finally, how tolerant they are of the free expression of unpopular political views.[1]

We concentrate on this set of citizenship characteristics and on their relationship to formal education for several reasons. While perhaps not all-inclusive, these characteristics are, nevertheless, necessary conditions for democratic citizenship. Furthermore, a deeper understanding of how formal education influences what citizens know, how much attention they pay to politics, and how politically active and tolerant they are has important implications for both democratic theory and educational policy. Political theorists continue to

---

1. Education does not influence all political attitudes and behavior. For example, neither the strength of partisanship nor confidence in institutions is strongly related to educational attainment.

place great hope in the importance of education for the development of the democratic citizen.[2] In many ways, we see this work as following in the tradition of Almond and Verba's classic, *The Civic Culture*.[3] Our task is, however, narrower in the range of explanatory factors we consider, yet deeper in the sense that we consider in detail one particularly critical determinant of democratic citizenship: formal education.

The causal roots of democratic citizenship are important because the qualities and expectations of individual citizens comprise a critical element of what has been called the "cement of society".[4] Democracy requires relatively little punitive or physical coercion for legitimacy; there are no secret police, domestic passports, or national lists of citizens in American democracy. The method of social governance for the majority of citizens is, in essence, noncoercive, voluntary, and compliant. Thus, each time we witness a transition of power from one regime (administration) to the next without troops, tanks, or protests in the streets, one wonders where such allegiance—such social cement— comes from. How does the American democratic system of government maintain order amidst the vast freedom given to and taken by citizens? Put in another way, what stops those who are powerful or skillful in politics from seizing ultimate power at any given time? While Americans today may not live up to Tocqueville's nineteenth-century characterization of us as continuously engaged and active citizens, we are, nevertheless, among the most active citizens of democracy anywhere in the world. The range of possible actions that can be taken by citizens of American democracy is vast and incorporates simultaneously the pursuit of self-interest as well as allegiance to norms.

How education influences both the pursuit of self-interest in politics as "political engagement" and the comprehension and support of the rules of the game as "democratic enlightenment" is the focus of our study. The notion that formal educational attainment is the primary mechanism behind citizenship characteristics is basically uncontested. A half century of empirical evidence in American politics points to the consistent and overwhelming influence of "the education variable" on various aspects of democratic citizenship. Formal education is almost without exception the strongest factor in explaining what citizens do in politics and how they think about politics. From early empirical

---

2. See, for example, the series of articles in the "Symposium on Citizenship, Democracy, and Education" in *Ethics*, 1995.

3. Almond and Verba, 1963.

4. See Elster, 1989; Gramsci, however, was first to coin the phrase.

studies of political behavior and attitudes, formal educational attainment has been identified as the chief explanatory variable.[5] Philip Converse described the overwhelming significance of formal education in this way:

> There is probably no single variable in the survey repertoire that generates as substantial correlations in such a variety of directions in political behavior material as level of formal education.... But the true domain of education as a predictor has to do with the large class of indicators of popular involvement and participation in politics. Whether one is dealing with cognitive matters such as level of factual information about politics or conceptual sophistication in its assessment; or such motivational matters as degree of attention paid to politics and emotional involvement in political affairs; or questions of actual behavior, such as engagement in any of a variety of political activities from party work to vote turnout itself: *education is everywhere the universal solvent, and the relationship is always in the same direction.*[6]

But why is education the "universal solvent"? How do higher levels of formal education make citizens more active in politics and more tolerant of the political beliefs of other citizens, for example? While study after study over the past 50 years has *identified* formal education as a critical determinant of democratic political behavior and attitudes in the United States, few have provided an *explanation* of exactly why and how education influences political behavior and attitudes. Missing from the great body of political behavior research is a more systematic explanation and empirical investigation of exactly why education is such a powerful explanatory variable and how education influences different types of behavior and attitudes in distinct ways.

The explanatory linkages that do exist on the relationship between formal education and citizenship vary from the role of education in creating social and economic status and resources to the impact of education on verbal cognitive ability, civic norms, and political motiva-

---

5. Lazarsfeld et al. (1944, p. 42) stated, "Formal education is, of course, a direct creator of interest." Campbell, Gurin, and Miller (1954, p. 192) called education "a particularly crucial control variable." Berelson et al. (1954, p. 25) declared "Better-educated people have more political interest than the less-educated." Key (1961, p. 329) wrote "Education not only tends to imbue persons of a sense of civic duty and a sense of political efficacy; it also propels them into political activity." Campbell et al. (1960, p. 252) wrote of education, "...no other social characteristic employed in our research bears such a strong relationship to turnout in presidential elections." Dahl (1961, p. 316) stated, "Widespread adherence to the democratic creed is produced and maintained by a variety of powerful social processes. Of these, probably formal schooling is the most important." Wolfinger and Rosenstone (1980, p. 102) identify one of their core findings as "the transcendent importance of education."

6. Converse 1972, p. 324, *emphasis added.*

tions. Wolfinger and Rosenstone provide perhaps the clearest and most comprehensive theoretical account of how formal education influences voting turnout.[7] The common explanation in the political science literature for why education is such a powerful predictor of other forms of participation embraces Wolfinger and Rosenstone's contention that education lowers both the material and cognitive costs of participating. It is reasoned that people with higher levels of education have better-paying jobs and more financial resources, and can therefore more easily absorb the financial costs of contributing money to politics, for example. It is also argues that people who have been in school for more years absorb civic values and develop interest in politics, which then facilitates increased participation. These loosely-structured resource and socialization arguments represent the extent of the theoretical explanation to the question of exactly how education influences various citizenship characteristics.

Our theory of the causal processes underlying the impact of education on characteristics of citizenship incorporates a more traditional view of the rational citizen, along with an alternative view of political life distinguishing higher-order motivations of human activity beyond self-interest.[8] These two perspectives are important to our understanding of how formal education influences citizenship because we see citizens in relationship to government as neither *homo economicus*, driven exclusively by simple individualism, or *homo sociologicus*, constructed solely by social forces. Rather, we see citizenship as a zone of transactions between the state and civil society, where the issue is not private versus public interests but, instead, the terms of their intersection. We use elements of these two compelling theories of human behavior because they are well suited to the question at hand, and they are equally important in organizing the story that the data tell. Our idea of the democratic citizen incorporates both of these perspectives, for

7. In their book *Who Votes*, Wolfinger and Rosenstone (1980, pp. 35-36) state: "Education, as we have argued, does three things. First, it increases cognitive skills, which facilitates learning about politics....Thus, education is a resource that reduces the costs of voting by giving people the skills necessary for processing political information and for making political decisions. Second, better-educated people are likely to get more gratification from political participation....Finally, schooling imparts experience with a variety of bureaucratic relationships....This experience helps one overcome the procedural hurdles required first to register and then to vote."

8. These are exaggerated characterizations of two divergent theories of human behavior, and their juxtaposition does not describe any scholarship in particular. Rather, the emphasis on the extremes underscores the opposition of two fundamentally different sets of assumptions.

either alone cannot fully account for the range of characteristics that define democratic citizenship. While theories of rational choice are elegant, alone they are inadequate explanations of democratic citizenship. Instead, a critical underlying assumption evident throughout this work is the observation that all citizens are members of the political community. Citizenship is collective behavior, by definition. The interpretation and justification of what is in our interest and what we value, both individually and collectively, is therefore bounded by this connection.[9]

The empirical evidence for our argument comes from a recent survey of Americans, the 1990 Citizen Participation Study,[10] and from two on-going surveys of the political behavior and attitudes of American citizens, the General Social Survey and the National Election Study, which have been repeatedly conducted over the last 20 years. In Part I of the book, we develop a model about the two distinct effects of formal educational attainment on democratic citizenship. We begin by describing empirical measures of two dimensions of citizenship with data from the 1990 Citizen Participation Study. We organize a diverse set of characteristics considered to be qualities of citizenship into two dimensions—democratic enlightenment and political engagement. We do not claim that these two dimensions comprise an exhaustive understanding of citizenship, for there may be additional dimensions as well as other individual indicators of the two dimensions that we identify. In addition, while our model of democratic citizenship as enlightened political engagement is built from data from 1990, the concepts of political engagement and enlightenment are general theoretical constructs that may accommodate additional factors. The first dimension, political engagement, is composed of behaviors and cognitions that enable citizens to pursue and protect self-interest in politics. Not all interests can win in a competition of conflicting preferences and interests and, in fact, not all views can even be heard. The political outcomes of the democratic process are by definition scarce goods, and political engagement is a competitive pursuit in what amounts to a zero-sum game. The second dimension is democratic enlightenment, which signifies those qualities of citizenship that encourage under-

9. See, for example, Etzioni (ed.), 1995; and Walzer, 1992.

10. The 1990 Citizen Participation Study, conducted under the principal investigation of Sidney Verba, Kay Lehman Schlozman, Henry E. Brady, and Norman H. Nie, is discussed in detail in Chapter 2 and in Verba, Schlozman, and Brady, 1995.

standing of and adherence to norms and principles of democracy. Unlike political engagement, which is essentially competitive, democratic enlightenment is basically consensual in nature. Enlightenment signifies an understanding of and commitment to the rules of the democratic game and tempers the unbridled pursuit of self-interested political engagement.

The model that we develop from the 1990 data will show that formal education influences political engagement by allocating scarce social and political ranks that place citizens either closer to or further from the center of critical social and political networks that, in turn, affect levels of political engagement. The rank to which individuals are assigned is the result of the impact of education on a long train of life circumstances, including occupational prominence, voluntary associational membership, and family wealth. For political engagement, formal education works as a sorting mechanism, assigning ranks on the basis of the citizen's *relative* educational attainment. Relative education is not the absolute number of years attained but the amount of education attained compared to those against whom the citizen competes. As the aggregate amount of absolute education in the population changes over time, the relative significance of a given number of actual years of education will vary. This results in interesting and counterintuitive predictions about changes in political engagement over time.

Education has an entirely different effect on democratic enlightenment and develops, instead, cognitive proficiency and sophistication in individual citizens. The influence of education on social network position matters here not at all. Rather, formal education encourages cognitive development and enables citizens to understand the long-term trade-offs necessary in democracy. In this way, more formal education adds continuously to the extent to which citizens exhibit characteristics of enlightenment in an additive or cumulative fashion. As aggregate amounts of education in society increase, so should levels of democratic enlightenment.

In Part I, we develop a more comprehensive theory about the causal linkages between formal education and individual-level political cognitions, behaviors, and attitudes. Education is the driving force in the development of citizenship qualities through two distinct pathways— the first, to political engagement through network centrality and the second, to democratic enlightenment through cognitive proficiency.

Because the 1990 data include such a rich set of measures of the dependent and intervening variables, we are able to both specify and test these more complex education models.

Our theory of the effects of education on political engagement as a relative sorting mechanism versus an additive mechanism is at odds with the conventional wisdom in political science of the "simple education-driven model,"[11] and what we call the absolute education model, or AEM. The predictions from the relative education model provide unexpected and counterintuitive answers to the question: what happens to the characteristics of democratic citizenship when average levels of education change over time? Raising these questions requires little conjecture or imagination, since one of the most striking changes in the United States over the last century is the substantial and monotonic increase in formal education attainment among its citizens.

It is in these over time predictions from our theory of how and why formal education affects democratic citizenship where our argument diverges most from previous studies and is, therefore, where we believe its most significant contributions lie. In Part II of the book, we will demonstrate that for both dimensions of democratic citizenship, the traditional absolute education model provides an inadequate explanation of both the direction and magnitude of change in political engagement and democratic enlightenment over time. With regard to political engagement, the AEM predicts change in the wrong direction; and for enlightenment, the conventional wisdom underpredicts the magnitude of change. Both predictions based on the absolute education model are incorrect because a critical explanatory variable—the educational environment—is omitted from the specification of the model. Exactly how and why this is the case will become clear as our story unfolds. But first we turn to a fuller exposition of our concept of democratic citizenship as enlightened political engagement.

11. Converse, 1972.

Part One

Education and Citizenship in the
United States, 1990

2

Enlightened Political Engagement

Characteristics of Democratic Citizenship
and Their Relationship to Education

A central assumption of this book is that democratic citizenship has two important dimensions that are necessary conditions for the maintenance of democracy. Implicit in this is the companion assumption that individual citizens and their characteristics matter. Political engagement, the first dimension of democratic citizenship, signifies the capability of citizens to engage in self-rule and encompasses behaviors and cognitions necessary for identifying political preferences, understanding politics, and pursuing interests. Democratic enlightenment, the second dimension, signifies the understanding of democratic rule through knowledge and acceptance of the norms and procedures of democracy. As such, enlightenment indicates the recognition of a shared destiny with others in the political community. Throughout the history of the United States, debates over citizenship have revolved around who would be granted the right of self-governance, along with the concomitant responsibility to the political community. The "quest for inclusion," as termed by political theorist Judith Shklar,[1] has been fought around these two dimensions of citizenship—the right to engage in self-rule and the acceptance of the procedures and principles of democracy. Some of the most significant political struggles of the twentieth century—for example, the women's suffrage movement, the civil rights movement, and immigration reform—have involved the political incorporation of groups of new citizens. Political opponents of the inclusion of these new groups have frequently argued that women, blacks, and other nonwhites either do not possess characteristics of

1. Shklar, 1991.

political engagement and democratic enlightenment or are incapable of developing such qualities.[2]

While political theorists dispute the prominence of one dimension over the other, one thing remains virtually uncontested: education is strongly related to characteristics of these two dimensions of citizenship, affecting both the capacity for self-rule and the acceptance of democratic rule. Indeed, a common theme throughout western Enlightenment political philosophy is the importance of education in developing the cognitive and moral qualities necessary for citizenship in a democratic polity.[3] These writings had important influences on nineteenth- and twentieth-century American theorists, such as John Dewey[4] and University of Chicago scholar Charles Merriam.[5] Contemporary political and educational theorists, such as Amy Gutmann, continue to echo the theme of the importance of democratic education.[6] Likewise, current policymakers place great hope in, and responsibility on, the process and institutions of formal education to promote democratic citizenship in America. The continued importance of education to citizenship is illustrated by the extent to which government directs public education in the United States: federal departments define goals, states appropriate funds and set standards, municipalities and local governments hire teachers and run schools, and citizens contribute tax dollars to the maintenance of the public education system.

While there are many hypotheses about why education is important in preparing citizens for democracy, there is common agreement that education provides both the skills necessary to become politically engaged and the knowledge to understand and accept democratic principles. With education, citizens become better able to understand the

2. See, for example, Takaki, 1990; and Phillips, 1993.

3. The vital importance of education to democracy is discussed in the writings of John Locke, particularly in *Some Thoughts Concerning Education* and, less explicitly, in *Two Treatises of Government*. On Locke, see, for example, Tarcov, 1984. In *Emile*, as well as in the *First and Second Discourses*, Rousseau, while somewhat skeptical of the likelihood of success of civic education, nevertheless placed significant responsibility on education to contribute to the development of citizens. And John Stuart Mill, without being explicit about the ways in which education would accomplish these goals, argued in *Considerations on Representative Government* that education would promote knowledge and intelligence among citizens. See also Thompson, 1976.

4. Dewey's most significant writing on education and democratic citizenship is *Democracy and Education*, 1916. For discussions of Dewey's educational and political philosophy, see Steiner, 1994; Daminco, 1978; and Somjee, 1968.

5. Merriam (1931, 1934) authored a series of studies exploring the nature and determinants of democratic citizenship, in which formal education figured prominently.

6. Gutmann, 1987, 1995.

political world, their stake in it, and the implications for the political community. In this chapter, we examine the two dimensions of democratic enlightenment and political engagement by identifying characteristics of each. Using data from the 1990 Citizen Participation Study, we analyze the following seven characteristics of democratic citizenship: political participation, voting, political tolerance, attentiveness to politics, and three types of political knowledge—knowledge of democratic principles, knowledge of leaders, and knowledge of other current political facts. These characteristics are conditions necessary for democratic citizens to know what their interests are and how to act on them as well as to understand that the interests of all citizens are fundamentally linked by virtue of their membership in the political community.

We begin with a discussion of the concepts of enlightenment and political engagement and then consider empirical measures of the characteristics of these two dimensions of democratic citizenship in the 1990 Citizen Participation Study data. The final section of the chapter documents the relationship between formal educational attainment and the seven characteristics of democratic citizenship.

The 1990 Citizen Participation Study was a comprehensive and unique data collection, aimed primarily at documenting the extent and determinants of Americans' voluntary participation in social and political life. While we do not take advantage of many of the features of the 1990 Citizen Participation Study in this book, we do rely on the comprehensiveness of the study in developing a model of the effect of education on democratic citizenship. Respondents were queried about their participation across a broad spectrum of political and social activities, along with their level of political knowledge, attentiveness to politics, and beliefs about democratic values. In addition to these characteristics of democratic citizenship, the 1990 data included numerous variables that link education to characteristics of citizenship, such as measures of verbal cognitive proficiency and social network position, along with organizational affiliation, occupational prominence, and a wide range of demographic information, including formal educational attainment.[7]

DEMOCRATIC CITIZENSHIP AS ENLIGHTENED POLITICAL ENGAGEMENT

The two conditions necessary for democracy are political engagement and democratic enlightenment. The idea that citizens must be capable of self-rule—of identifying and pursuing their own political interest—is often discussed within the context of a model of citizen as *homo economicus*, driven by simple individualism, rationality, or self-interest. Alternatively, the idea that citizens must recognize the collective enterprise of democratic government, and in so doing accept the rules and outcomes of the democratic process, is frequently discussed within the context of the model of citizen as *homo sociologicus*. This model views citizenship as a construct of the collective relationship between citizens and the political community, rather than characterizing citizenship as atomistic.

Both explanations have considerable merit, and both carry even greater scholarly baggage. The tension between the two models is a familiar theme throughout political theory and is perhaps best exemplified in the persistent conflict between "liberals" and "communitarians."[8] While the discussion above conflates the ontological issues of the identification of factors that account for social life and the advocacy issues concerning the primacy of individual rights versus community life, we invoke the two traditions neither to take a side nor to inform the theoretical debate.[9] It is not our objective to develop a theory of citizenship.[10] Rather, we utilize the distinction between liberals and communitarians as a heuristic for disentangling the two dimensions of

7. The 1990 Citizen Participation Study data are unique in that the study was conducted in two stages. In the first stage, over 15,000 randomly selected individuals representative of the adult U.S. population were asked in a telephone survey about the extent of their voluntary social and political activity, along with some basic demographic questions. This large sample of individuals was interviewed in order to obtain sufficient numbers of two types of respondents that were oversampled in the second stage of the study: African-American and Latino respondents and those active in a range of social and political activities—in particular, in activities that are relatively rare. In the second stage of the study, some 2,500 of those interviewed in the first screening stage of the study were selected for reinterview. A disproportionately large number of activists and minority respondents were selected for interviews in the second stage. For additional description of the 1990 Citizen Participation Study, see pp. 31–33 and appendixes A and B of Verba, Schlozman, and Brady, 1995.

8. Contemporary "liberal" statements include Rawls, 1971, 1993; Dworkin, 1977; Macedo, 1990; and Galston, 1991. "Communitarian" responses include Walzer, 1984; Sandel, 1984; and Etzioni (ed.), 1995.

9. See Taylor, 1989.

10. See Kymlicka and Norman, 1994, for a comprehensive discussion of recent work on citizenship theory, and the essays in Beiner (ed.), 1995. See Thompson, 1970, for an analysis of the history of citizenship in democratic theory. See also Pocock, 1992.

political engagement and democratic enlightenment. Thus, the notion of democratic citizenship as enlightened political engagement adopts ideas from both the classic liberal political tradition as well as ideas from the communitarian, or participatory-republican, perspective. While we agree with the liberal notion that individuals will seek to exert and protect their interests in politics, we disagree with the companion contention that the public arena exists solely as a forum in which self-interest is either won or lost. On the other hand, while we agree with communitarians that democratic citizens must recognize that their individual fate is intimately bound with that of their fellow citizens in the political community, we are not convinced that from this realization the construction of the common good necessarily follows.[11]

The argument for democratic citizenship as enlightened political engagement rests on the idea that the two dimensions are, on one level, theoretically distinct but are also intimately connected to each other in terms of shared determinants. As will become clear in the data analysis to follow in this and subsequent chapters, the empirical measures of the characteristics of engagement and enlightenment—political participation, voting, political tolerance, attentiveness to politics, and the three types of political knowledge—are strongly interrelated.

Political Engagement

In order for democracy to function, individual citizens must first be able to identify and understand their preferences and political interests. Engagement in politics entails surveillance of the current political landscape and requires attentiveness to and knowledge of politics. Citizens must then also be capable of pursuing and protecting their interests by electing and petitioning representatives in democracy. Thus, one necessary condition of democratic citizenship is more instrumental in nature, with the citizen motivated to action by the rewards or benefits derived from politics.

Benefits may be particularistic as well as collective, and, as such, the motivation to seek these rewards can be narrowly self-interested as well as more altruistic.[12] Rewards from engagement are therefore broadly understood. Benefits from political engagement might include expressive benefits such as the desire to affect public policy, along

---

11. See Mansbridge, 1980, for an analysis of the tension between "adversary" and "unitary" democracy.

12. See Jencks, 1990; Mansbridge (ed.), 1990; and Elster, 1990, for discussions of varieties of altruism, the limits of self-interest, and altruism versus self-interest.

with more intangible rewards of psychic gratification.[13] Benefits can also include the reward of supporting organizations, parties, and candidates for office, which can be enlarged by the individual's estimate of his or her impact, or by the closeness of the election.[14] Engagement characteristics of citizenship thus include the capacity to formulate considered policy preferences—self-interested or otherwise—and to act on one's own behalf (or on behalf of groups of citizens) to seek political goals.[15]

This view is not uncontroversial, particularly within the context of classic statements of rationality and political participation, which argue for narrowly defined rewards. Under circumstances where the benefits from participation are collective, rational citizens motivated by self-interest have no incentive to invest time and energy; they can simply "free-ride."[16] However, as Verba, Schlozman, and Brady argue, "narrow versions of rational choice can be salvaged by enlarging the theory to specify a much wider range of benefits that can enter the utility calculus of the potential activist."[17] They analyze data from the 1990 Citizen Participation Study and demonstrate that citizens who participate in politics report a wide range of benefits and gratifications significant enough to outweigh the cost of taking part.[18]

Our definition of political engagement comes close to the notion of autonomy, understood as authorship of one's life in the social context, with a bundling of identity and interest, where people are capable of choosing their own actions. Political engagement is like autonomy in the sense that autonomy implies the ability to be self-governing.[19] This suggests that each citizen is the best judge of his or her own interest, understood as "whatever wants or desires a citizen expresses in the political

13. On expressive benefits and involvement in organizations, see Schlozman and Tierney, 1986. On gratification from fulfilling a citizen's duty of voting, see Riker and Ordeshook, 1968. On expressive benefits versus instrumental benefits, see Fiorina, 1976.

14. On the benefits from group loyalty, see Fiorina, 1976; and Uhlaner, 1989. On the enhancement of benefits of electoral participation by the closeness of the election, see Ferejohn and Fiorina, 1975. See also Aldrich, 1993.

15. We would like to thank Sidney Verba, Kay Schlozman, and Henry Brady for suggesting this clarification and wording for this point.

16. For classic statements of the rationality of participation and the free-rider problem, see Downs, 1957; and Olson, 1965. See Schlozman, Verba, and Brady, 1995, for a lucid discussion of the rationality of participation, pp. 99–105.

17. Verba, Schlozman, and Brady, 1995, p. 104.

18. See Chapter 4 in Verba, Schlozman, and Brady, 1995, for a fascinating analysis of the reasons activists report for participating in various activities, and pp. 127–132 for the reasons for political *inactivity*.

19. See Christman, 1988; Haworth, 1986; and Meyer, 1987.

process in which claims are made; or if he is not engaged in such processes, whatever wants or desires he would be likely to express were he so engaged."[20] In this way, our understanding of the political engagement dimension of democratic citizenship is broader than the "engagement" discussed in Verba, Schlozman, and Brady (1995), and somewhat narrower than the "civic engagement" described in Putnam (1995a, 1995b). Verba et al. characterize political engagement in psychological terms, as interest in politics and public affairs, efficacy, and political knowledge.[21] While the political knowledge and attentiveness characteristics are included in our political engagement measure, we exclude efficacy and include political participation and voting.[22] Putnam describes "civic engagement" in his work on social capital beyond the political realm, as "people's connections with the life of their communities, not merely with politics," adding that "[c]ivic engagement is correlated with political participation in a narrower sense, but whether they move in lock-step is an empirical question, not a logical certitude."[23]

While the three notions of political engagement differ in important ways, they share a common determinant in formal educational attainment. Putnam identifies education as having a strong relationship with his measure of civic engagement, noting that "[e]ducation, in short, is an extremely powerful predictor of civic engagement."[24] Verba, Schlozman, and Brady also identify education as chief among the explanatory variables of participatory behavior and their notion of engagement.[25] We will argue that formal education is important to the characteristics of political engagement because it sorts individual citizens into positions in the social and political hierarchy that facilitate political engagement to a greater or lesser degree.

20. Thompson, 1970, p.13.
21. Verba, Schlozman, and Brady, 1995, p. 16, Chapter 12.
22. Measures of both internal and external efficacy are available in the 1990 Citizen Participation Study data. Internal efficacy is more closely related to the political engagement dimension of citizenship described here, but we did not include it because it signifies a self-perceived rather than objective capability of citizens to be heard in politics. All of the measures of political engagement that we include are measures of behaviors and cognitions—actual political activity, discussing politics, knowing elected officials, and so on. External efficacy may be more closely related to the democratic enlightenment dimension, but we did not include it because it does not signify a commitment to democratic values and principles. Instead, it is more a measure of the respondent's assessment of the responsiveness of current representatives.
23. Putnam, 1995b, p. 665.
24. Putnam, 1995b, p. 667.
25. Verba, Schlozman and Brady, 1995, pp. 15–21, chapters 12 and 15.

Democratic Enlightenment

Political engagement is but half of the understanding of democratic citizenship. To think of democratic citizens as solely autonomous actors in pursuit of political interests would be inaccurate. Rather, citizenship is also collective behavior, and membership in the democratic polity implies a necessary shared connection with others in the community. As such, the political community enforces the rules and norms under which political interaction in democracy takes place. Democratic enlightenment entails adherence to norms, including the recognition that one has shared interest—collective interest that may sometimes contradict and override one's individual preferences. The democratic value of procedural fairness is another aspect of enlightenment and means that all citizens have a right to political interests (selfish and otherwise) and that all citizens are allowed the chance to express and pursue them.

It is clear that these democratic values are enforced by members of the political community. What is not clear, however, is the extent to which these social norms operate because of what Jon Elster terms "everyday Kantianism" (using justifications of long-term outcomes) or because of the "blind, compulsive, mechanical, or even unconscious" adherence to these norms or values.[26] Democratic norms may in fact have a kind of "grip on the mind"[27] that makes these social norms operate at a deeply internalized, if not unconscious, level.

As we will argue in subsequent chapters, formal education is important to the development of enlightened democratic citizens because it fosters the recognition among individuals that their fate is controlled in fundamental ways by the actions and policies of democratic government. At the same time, education encourages in citizens both the recognition that their fate is intimately connected with that of their fellow citizen and the recognition that the goals of fairness and equality are important to the long-term stability of the democratic system. These are the characteristics that underscore the notion of democratic enlightenment.

While of significantly less dramatic appeal, our hypothesis about the role of education in encouraging enlightenment is perhaps not unlike an example Elster describes of strong Kantianism. During World War II, residents of a small French village gave refuge to Jews notwithstanding the knowledge that, if caught, they too would be executed. The motivation for this action was described in the thought of a Protestant pastor in the village: "During the war years he did not spend pre-

26. Elster, 1989, p. 101.
27. Elster, 1989.

cious time and energy investigating the effects of his actions on any political theory he might hold. He chose to do without intellectual systems and without fear-filled predictions. He decided simply to 'help the unjustly persecuted innocents around me'....With his sophisticated mind he put his sophisticated mind aside."[28]

Just as formal education is important to political engagement by enabling citizens to recognize and pursue political interests, education, in its effect on democratic enlightenment, also limits the harmful pursuit of this self-interest. In the absence of democratic values and norms, and with democratic citizenship as political engagement only, the practice of democracy would be more akin to unbridled freedom. And, while it is clear that there are other constraints on the individual exercise of liberty, democratic enlightenment works to harness the freedom of political engagement and imbues the practice of citizenship with a sense of responsibility. Thus, democratic citizenship as enlightened political engagement means that citizens are capable of pursuing political preferences within the framework of a polity in which there are shared interests in protecting both the normative goals of fairness and equality and the democratic process of free expression. The data from the 1990 Citizen Participation Study will help to disentangle these two dimensions and the different effects education has on them.

While we discuss democratic citizenship in the terms above as enlightened political engagement, it is important to acknowledge that there are also competing visions of citizenship. Among the most significant challenges to the liberal-democratic construction are those considering citizenship within the context of race and ethnicity and racism in America.[29] A second critical reading of democratic citizenship as enlightened political engagement might come from those who question the legitimacy of the more conventional understanding of *political* and *public*, as well as challenge the notion of universal citizenship.[30] In addition, while few in number, there are other definitions and empirical investigations of citizenship.[31]

28. Elster, 1989, quoting Hallie, pp. 194–195.

29. See, for example, DuBois, 1989 [1903]. For a contemporary analysis of race and citizenship, see Dawson, 1995; Hanchard, 1990; and Foner, 1988. See also Rogers Smith, 1988, 1993; and Stevens, 1995.

30. For an outstanding review of recent feminist constructions of citizenship, see Jones, 1990. See also Dietz, 1992; and Pateman, 1992. For a critique of the idea of universal citizenship and an argument for "differentiated citizenship" and cultural pluralism, see Young, 1989, 1990.

31. See Conover, Crewe, and Searing, 1991 and 1993, for a report of an innovative research design. See also Almond and Verba's classic 1963 empirical investigation of citizenship, *The Civic Culture*.

A second important qualification is that our idea of democratic citizenship is silent about the extent to which citizens of democracy should possess the qualities of enlightened political engagement. No requirements on the desirable levels of political participation, attentiveness, or political knowledge, for example, are imposed. Rather, we leave the debate over what levels of these qualities are desirable in democracy to theorists with a broader set of normative concerns. On one extreme are those who argue that citizens make good choices with little information and that democracy functions pretty well without much citizen activity.[32] However, others may suggest that higher standards and a broader range of citizenship characteristics are necessary.[33]

CHARACTERISTICS OF ENLIGHTENMENT AND POLITICAL ENGAGEMENT

We describe the two dimensions of enlightened political engagement as the capability of identifying and acting on political interests and the recognition of democratic principles and the rights of all citizens to hold and express interests. We will use data from the 1990 Citizen Participation Study to examine how these two concepts are operationalized. We include seven characteristics of democratic citizenship: participation in difficult political activities, regular voting, political tolerance, political attentiveness, and three types of political knowledge—knowledge of democratic principles, knowledge of leaders, and knowledge of other current political facts. Some are attributes of political engagement only, some are elements of democratic enlightenment only, and others characterize both dimensions. Table 2.1 displays the logic of the relationship between the seven measures of democratic citizenship and summarizes our hypotheses about their relationship to enlightenment and political engagement. The table also specifies how each attribute was measured using data from the 1990 Citizen Participation Study.[34]

32. See, for example, Mueller's argument for the minimal (political) human being. Mueller, 1992, p. 983.

33. See, for example, Barber, 1984.

34. Appendix A presents the exact wording of all the questions used in the analysis, along with the distribution of each of the measures.

TABLE 2.1 Attributes of political engagement and democratic enlightenment

ATTRIBUTE	ENGAGEMENT	ENLIGHTENMENT
Knowledge of principles of democracy: Fifth Amendment, democracy versus dictatorship, meaning of civil liberties		Understand the nature and principles of democratic government
Knowledge of leaders: U.S. representative, both U.S. senators, state representative, head of local schools	Know the relevant players of the game, who to petition, and who to watch	
Knowledge of other current political facts: Majority party in Congress, more spending on NASA or social security, voting age, primary election reforms	Know what is at stake in politics	Familiar with current political issues and "rules of the game"
Political attentiveness: Discuss local and national politics, interest in local and national politics, attention to newspaper stories on local and national politics	Recognize one's interests, and find out who opposes or supports those interests and why	Watch for threats to the system
Participation in difficult political activities: Contact officials, campaign work, serve on local board or attend meetings, informal community activity	Pursue political interests	
Voting: Regular voting in local and national elections	Elect officials representing one's political interests	Engage in a behavior to express solidarity with the system
Tolerance: Tolerance of the expression of political viewpoints		Appeal to procedural fairness and recognize the legitimacy of competing interests

The first three sections of Table 2.1 detail three types of political knowledge—knowledge of the principles of democracy, knowledge of leaders, and knowledge of other current political facts. The 1990 Citizen Participation Study included a battery of 12 factual questions on political knowledge. Since the earliest public opinion surveys in the 1940's, there has been some controversy about how to best measure political knowledge among citizens. Notwithstanding disagreement regarding the boundaries of a definition of political knowledge, there is consensus on the central importance of the individual's ability to understand and retain concrete political facts. The idea of political knowledge as factual knowledge has gained wide acceptance within political behavior and political cognition research.[35]

Each of the three types of political knowledge is measured in a simple additive scale of the number of right answers. Knowledge of the principles of democracy is measured by three questions on whether respondents correctly identified a constitutional guarantee of the Fifth Amendment, knew the difference between democracy and dictatorship, and could identify the meaning of civil liberties. Knowledge of this type is fundamental to the structure and meaning of the American democracy. The correct answers to these questions do not change with successive elections, policy shifts, or even institutional rearrangements. Knowledge of the principles of democracy is an abstract understanding because it requires a conceptual apparatus to understand the relationships between things. Thus, knowledge of the principles of democracy characterizes the enlightenment aspect of democratic citizenship. It signals that citizens understand the basic tenets of democratic government, underscoring their ability to recognize that their interests are linked with those of their fellow citizens. Figure 2.1 shows the percent-

35. In a comprehensive work on political knowledge, Delli Carpini and Keeter argue that measuring political knowledge in the mass public with a battery of factual questions is the best approach. See Delli Carpini and Keeter, 1996, pp. 10–16. See also Delli Carpini and Keeter, 1993. Luskin also supports the measurement of political knowledge through factual questions about politics, "...because they are more direct than abstractness-based measures, I suspect that information-holding measures represent the best *single* existing approach." Luskin, 1987, p. 890, *emphasis original.* Zaller concurs in the assessment of the desirability of measuring political knowledge with factual questions. "Political awareness is, for both theoretical and empirical reasons, best measured by simple tests of neutral factual information about politics. The reason, in brief, is that tests of political information, more directly than any of the alternative measures, capture what has actually gotten into people's minds, which, in turn, is critical for intellectual engagement of politics." Zaller, 1992, p. 21. See also McClosky and Zaller, 1984, for factual questions on political knowledge. Some of the items used by McClosky and Zaller were selected as models for political knowledge questions in the 1990 Citizen Participation Study.

age of the population who can correctly answer between zero and three questions about the principles of democracy. The data show that more than a third of all respondents answered all three questions on the principles of democracy correctly, and almost half got two of the three questions right. Only a small proportion—less than one-fifth of the population—could answer fewer than two of the items correctly.

FIGURE 2.1 Distribution of knowledge of the principles of democracy

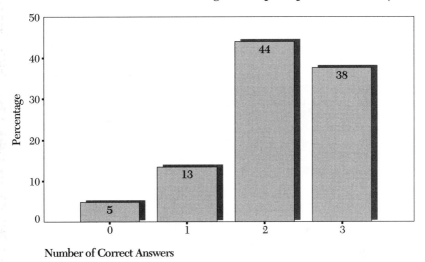

Number of Correct Answers

The second type of political knowledge measures the ability to name elected officials and political leaders. This is measured with an additive scale of the number of correct answers, scored from 0 to 5. In the 1990 Citizen Participation Study, citizens were asked to name their representative to the U.S. House of Representatives, their two U.S. senators, their representative to the state legislature, and the head of the local school system. Figure 2.2 shows the proportion who can correctly identify between zero and five political leaders. One-quarter of the respondents could name none of these political leaders. On the other end of the scale, 16% could name four or five leaders. In contrast to knowledge of the principles of democracy, this second type of knowledge does not remain constant over time. Unlike the guarantee of the Fifth Amendment, elected officials can change every few years. Knowledge of leaders thus requires continuous monitoring of the political arena, and the incentives to update this information are more instrumental in nature. Citizens must be able to identify their elected officials and leaders so that they know whom to watch and whom to petition. They must know which representatives and groups share or oppose their beliefs. Individuals cannot express their preferences and interests in politics if they do not know who represents them. Thus, knowledge of leaders characterizes political engagement rather than enlightenment.

FIGURE 2.2 Distribution of knowledge of leaders

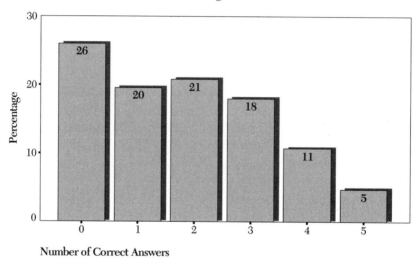

Number of Correct Answers

The third measure of political knowledge is knowledge of other current political facts. The measure is based on four questions about current political facts: Which political party has more members in the U.S. House of Representatives? Did the federal government spend more money on NASA or social security? How old do you have to be to vote for president? Who was mainly behind the increased use of primary elections in the United States to choose candidates? The distribution of this measure is shown in Figure 2.3. This third type of political knowledge is not as well developed and is measured with less accuracy than the measure of knowledge of the principles of democracy and knowledge of leaders. Nevertheless, knowing these other current political facts indicates that the citizen knows what is at stake and who holds political power, which is a characteristic of political engagement, as well as has an understanding of the democratic "rules of the game," which is a characteristic of enlightenment. Thus, knowledge of other current political facts characterizes both political engagement and democratic enlightenment.

FIGURE 2.3 Distribution of knowledge of other current political facts

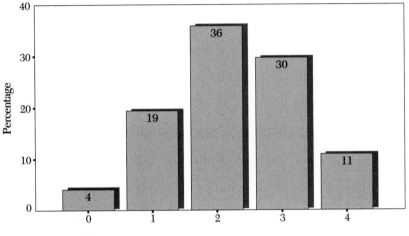

Number of Correct Answers

Closely related to these three types of political knowledge is the fourth characteristic of enlightened political engagement, a measure of political attentiveness. Figure 2.4 shows the percentage of the population for each level of attentiveness in the 1990 Citizen Participation Study data. This measure combines interest in politics, frequency of discussing politics, and attention to politics in the newspaper. Respondents were asked how much attention they pay to stories on national and world politics and public affairs and, in a second question, how much attention they pay to stories on local politics and community affairs. They were also asked how interested they are in community politics and local affairs, as well as national politics and public affairs. A third set of questions on the extent to which individuals discuss local and national politics was administered. The measure of political attentiveness combines these six measures in a simple additive scale.[36]

36. The questions in the attentiveness scale measured discussing politics, interest in politics, and paying attention to stories on politics in the newspaper in ordinal-level scales. Responses on each of the six items were rescaled to between 0 and 1 and then summed. See Appendix A for the exact wording of the question and the coding categories.

Being politically attentive indicates that citizens recognize their need for political information in order to effectively pursue their interests in politics and implies on-going surveillance of political events. In this sense, attentiveness is a characteristic of political engagement because following and discussing politics helps citizens recognize political preferences and pursue and protect interests by identifying those who support and oppose them. However, attentiveness is also a characteristic of the democratic enlightenment dimension of citizenship in that citizens can watch for threats to the democratic system. By being attentive to politics, citizens understand not only what they have to win or lose in the political world but also the constraints under which the political game is played.

FIGURE 2.4 Distribution of political attentiveness

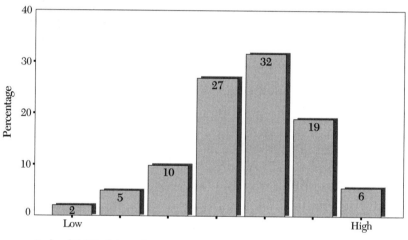

Scale of Political Attentiveness

A fifth characteristic of democratic citizenship as enlightened political engagement is participation in difficult political activities. This behavior is most clearly a characteristic of the political engagement dimension, for in order to pursue political preferences and interests, citizens must be prepared to act in politics. Difficult political activities are those requiring a substantial commitment of time and energy. Respondents in the 1990 Citizen Participation Study were asked whether they had contacted government officials, taken part in campaigns for candidates or parties at the local or national level, served on a local community board or council or attended meetings, and whether they had taken part in informal political action in the community. These four activities constitute the scale of difficult political activities. Figure 2.5 shows the distribution of the political activity measure. Taking part in any of these activities demonstrates a desire to pursue political interests. However, only a small proportion of the population takes part in three or four of the difficult activities, and half participate in none.

FIGURE 2.5 Distribution of participation in difficult political activities

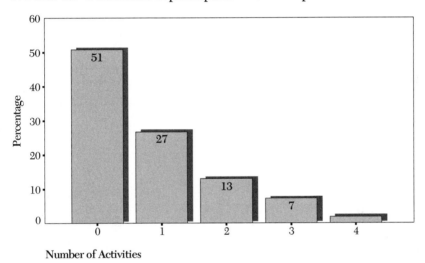

Number of Activities

The sixth attribute of citizenship is regular voting in local and national elections and characterizes both political engagement and democratic enlightenment. For both presidential and local elections, respondents in the 1990 Citizen Participation Study were asked in what proportion of all elections in which they were eligible did they vote. Unlike the more difficult activities of contacting government officials, campaign work, attendance at local council meetings, and informal community activity, the political activity of voting is less demanding. Voting requires much less time, effort, and information than the more difficult acts of political participation. Likewise, voting conveys less information to government than is transmitted through contacting offi-cials or participating on local boards, for example. Nevertheless, voting officials in and out of office represents a clear effort among citizens to exert their preferences in deciding which leaders will best represent their interests. At the same time, the act of voting is also a characteristic of the enlightened democratic citizen in that voting is a behavior that expresses solidarity and support for the democratic system. Voting is thus a characteristic of enlightenment as much as it is an immediate instrumental means of electing candidates who support one's political interests. The enlightened citizen may well understand that voting in any given election is a very limited tool for expressing preferences and may be equally aware that one vote has only the very remotest of probabilities of influencing the outcome. However, he or she also understands that the political community at large has an enormous stake in maintaining a viable system of electoral accountability as one of the most important checks against corruption and the abuse of power by political elites. Voting is thus a characteristic of both political engagement and democratic enlightenment and, as such, is driven by both self-interest and social norms. Figure 2.6 displays the percentage of the population in each of the voter turnout categories.[37]

FIGURE 2.6 Distribution of voting turnout

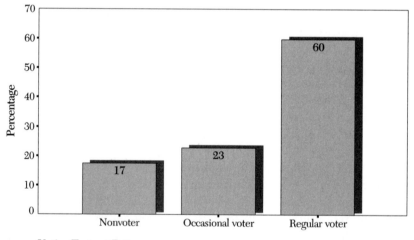

Voting Turnout Pattern

37. The questions on voting in presidential and local elections asked respondents about the regularity of their voting since they became eligible to vote. There were five response categories: never, rarely, some, most, and all. The measure of regular voting shown in Figure 2.6 was created by rescaling the categorical responses to between 0 and 1 and taking the sum of the two voting measures. See Appendix A for the exact wording of the question and distribution of the variables.

The seventh and final attribute of democratic citizenship operationalizes the notion of tolerance. Tolerance is the belief that all citizens have the right to express their political views, regardless of how dangerous or repugnant those views may be. Attitudes of tolerance have been studied widely, and while the measurement, trends, and determinants of these beliefs are much in dispute, there is consensus on the definition of political tolerance as "a willingness to permit the expression of ideas or interests one opposes."[38] As such, tolerance signals a fundamental commitment to the rules of the democratic game and, in this sense, is a characteristic of the enlightenment aspect of democratic citizenship.[39] Tolerance was measured in the 1990 Citizen Participation Study with an updated subset of the original questions from Samuel Stouffer's classic 1955 study of Americans' attitudes toward civil liberties.[40] Respondents were asked if they would allow someone who is against all churches and religion and someone who advocates doing away with elections and letting the military run the country to make a speech in their community. Two additional questions were asked on whether a book written by someone arguing that blacks are genetically inferior and a book in favor of homosexuality should be taken out of the local public library. The measure of tolerance is a simple additive scale of these four questions, and the percentage of citizens giving between zero and four tolerant responses is shown in Figure 2.7. The vast majority of Americans are tolerant, with almost half giving a positive response to all of the questions and two-thirds saying yes to three or more of the questions. Tolerance is a characteristic of the democratic enlightenment aspect of citizenship, where a high degree of tolerance signifies the recognition of the importance of allowing all in the political community the right to express their views, regardless of the content. Citizens who are committed to tolerance are in effect declaring their support for the protection of a free and open society. In the absence of this freedom, the system is weakened, for intolerance of the expression of political interests by one group of citizens means that the interests of any citizen may be deemed inappropriate and thus

38. Sullivan, Piereson, and Marcus, 1982, p. 2.

39. See Gutmann, 1995, p. 567.

40. Stouffer, 1955. There are at least two alternative ways to measure political tolerance. Sullivan, Piereson, and Marcus (1979) suggest a content-controlled measure of tolerance, while Gibson (1992) and Gibson and Bingham (1982) suggest a multiple-indicator approach, which poses conflicts among values. We chose to measure tolerance with the Stouffer items because of the proven reliability of these measures, the availability of a long time series of these items in the General Social Survey (administered by the National Opinion Research Center), and the brevity of the questions. See also Sniderman, Brody, and Tetlock, 1991, p. 123.

silenced. Support of tolerance underscores the recognition that intolerance raises the possibility that all citizens may lose the right to political expression and political engagement.

FIGURE 2.7 Distribution of tolerance

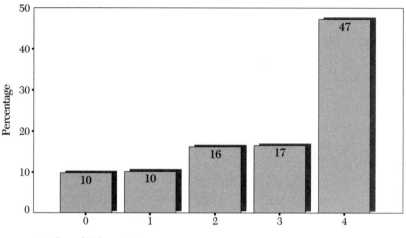

Number of Tolerant Responses

It is the combination of all seven of these attributes of political engagement and enlightenment that defines democratic citizenship as the capacity for self-rule and the acceptance of democratic norms and procedures. Some attributes, such as participation in difficult political activities and knowledge of governmental leaders, are more clearly indicators of political engagement only, in that they enhance the capability of citizens to pursue political preferences and interests. Likewise, knowledge of the principles of democracy and tolerance are characteristics of democratic enlightenment only, in that they reflect an understanding of shared interest with other members of the political community to protect the rules of democratic governance. However, other attributes, including attentiveness to politics, knowledge of other current political facts, and regular voting play dual roles in characterizing both enlightenment and political engagement. A point of clarification is necessary. While we argue that the two dimensions of political engagement and enlightenment are distinct, we are not arguing that they are orthogonal. Rather, characteristics of each of these aspects of democratic citizenship are empirically related to one another. Next, we will consider the relationship between these seven attributes of enlightened political engagement and years of formal educational attainment.

EDUCATION AND ENLIGHTENED POLITICAL ENGAGEMENT

Data from the 1990 Citizen Participation Study support perhaps the best-documented finding in American political behavior research: the strong positive relationship between formal educational attainment and political behavior, cognition, and attitudes. From the earliest empirical studies of civic involvement and electoral participation, formal educational attainment has been identified as the strongest and most consistent positive influence on the characteristics of citizenship. More recent works in political behavior, such as Wolfinger and Rosenstone's *Who Votes*, and Verba, Schlozman, and Brady's *Voice and Equality*,[41] echo the earlier findings of the significance of education in explanations of political behavior. Tom W. Smith reports that education is the most frequently used variable in the General Social Survey.[42] As an explanatory variable of social and political behavior, formal educational attainment is unrivaled.

The 1990 Citizen Participation Study data provide no exception and show that education has a positive and substantial effect on each of the seven attributes of democratic enlightenment and political engagement. Well-educated citizens display substantially greater levels of understanding of the principles of democratic government, have a much better ability to identify incumbent local and national leaders, and can more frequently give the correct answer to questions about current political facts. The well-educated pay much closer attention to political life; they report discussing, reading about, and being interested in politics in much larger proportions than their less educated counterparts. It is not surprising, then, that the more educated citizen is much more likely to participate in political life, including those difficult activities of contacting public officials, working on political campaigns, serving on local boards, and working with others in the local community. Those with higher levels of formal education are also much more likely to vote in both local and presidential elections than their less educated counterparts. Education is also strongly related to

41. Wolfinger and Rosenstone, 1980; and Verba, Schlozman, and Brady, 1995.
42. Smith, 1995, p. 215.

tolerance. Those with higher levels of educational attainment are much more likely to say that they support the right of public expression for those with unpopular political views.

TABLE 2.2 Correlations between attributes of enlightened political engagement and education

ATTRIBUTE	CORRELATION
Knowledge of principles of democracy	.38
Knowledge of leaders	.29
Knowledge of other political facts	.37
Political attentiveness	.39
Participation in difficult political activities	.29
Frequency of voting	.25
Tolerance	.35

Table 2.2 presents the bivariate correlations between formal educational attainment and the seven attributes of enlightened political engagement detailed above. The data demonstrate a substantial, positive, and consistent relationship between education and characteristics of citizenship. Education is most strongly related to political attentiveness, knowledge of the principles of democracy, knowledge of other current political facts, and tolerance, with a correlation coefficient above or equal to 0.35. Education is also strongly correlated with the other attributes of knowledge of leaders, participation in difficult political activities, and voting, at 0.25 or above. The magnitude of these relationships is as strong as any other well-documented relationship between education and its social outcomes, such as income or occupational prominence. The consistency of the relationship between education and all seven attributes is also important; education is strongly related to each of the characteristics of enlightened political engagement, and to a surprisingly parallel degree.

It is important to note that the analysis presented here of the data from the 1990 Citizen Participation Study includes only those respondents who were age 25 and older at the time of the survey. We place this restriction on the data to limit the analysis to those likely to have completed their formal education. Respondents between the ages of 18 and 24 are excluded because formal education—in particular, college and graduate education—may not yet be completed. While some individuals continue their education beyond age 24, the vast majority of people have left school by the time they reach 25 years of age. The United States Department of Education reports that in 1990, 57.2% of 18- and 19-year-olds and 28.6% of 20- to 24-year-olds were enrolled in school, while only 7.7% of 25- to 34-year-old citizens were enrolled in school.[43] Among those between 18 and 24 years old in the 1990 Citizen Participation Study, 20% report being in school full time. Including only those 25 years old and above obviously reduces the size of sample; 9% of those interviewed in the 1990 study were less than 25 years old. However, the remaining sample of 1282 weighted respondents is a high-quality representative sample more than adequate for the tasks at hand.[44]

The relationship between educational attainment and the seven characteristics of enlightened political engagement can be seen in greater detail by comparing the level of these attributes by levels of education.[45] Figure 2.8 shows this pattern for the three types of political knowledge. From the figure, it is clear that knowledge of democratic principles, knowledge of other current political facts, and knowledge of leaders all increase monotonically with the amount of formal schooling. The solid line represents the proportion of correct answers across the three questions on the principles of democracy. From its placement above both the dashed line (representing knowledge of other political facts) and the dotted line (showing knowledge of political leaders), it is clear that Americans can more frequently give the correct answers to factual questions on democratic principles than to questions on the other two types of political knowledge.

---

43. Snyder (ed.), 1993, pp. 16–17.

44. While a total of 2,517 interviews were completed in the second follow-up stage of the 1990 Citizen Participation Study, the effective sample size in our analysis is significantly smaller. Recall that the 1990 study was a two-stage survey that utilized a strategy of stratified sampling in order to oversample political activists and minority Americans. The first adjustment we made was to remove 29 cases that were invalidly selected for a follow-up interview. The second adjustment was made in order to achieve a representative and unbiased sample of the U.S. population for statistical analysis. It was necessary to account for the fact that disproportionately large numbers of certain types of people were interviewed and, therefore, that it was easier for those who were in groups targeted for oversampling to get interviewed. The formula for calculating a weight variable that adjusts the sample to be representative of the U.S. population as well as adjusts the effective size of the sample to account for the selection bias is detailed in Appendix B.

45. The data in Figure 2.8 to Figure 2.12 show education in a continuous form as years of educational attainment, with the exception of those having below six years of education. These respondents, because of their small number, were combined into one category of six years or less.

FIGURE 2.8 Relationship between education and three types of political knowledge

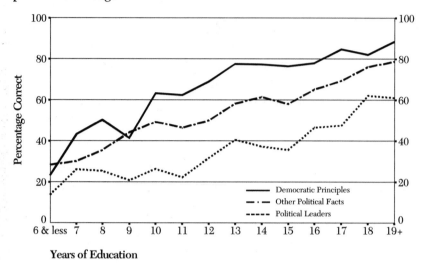

FIGURE 2.9 Relationship between education and political attentiveness

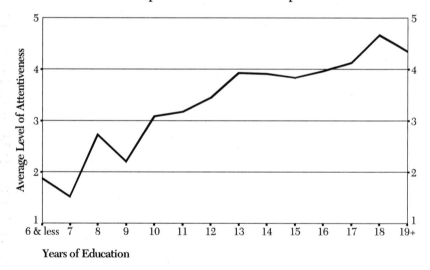

Figure 2.9 shows the average level of political attentiveness by education. The data show a steady and monotonic increase in political attentiveness as educational attainment increases. Those with some college education score an average of 4 or more on the political attentiveness scale. On the other hand, those respondents with less than a high school education are half as attentive to politics.

Figure 2.10 and Figure 2.11 show the relationship of participation in difficult political activities and voting turnout to educational attainment. Figure 2.10 reveals that those with less than a high school education take part, on average, in less than one of the difficult activities of contacting officials, working on political campaigns, serving on local boards or attending meetings, and working with others informally in the community. Alternatively, those with a college degree and beyond are more than twice as likely to participate in difficult political activities. Out of the four difficult activities, however, even very high levels of education encourage only a bit more than an average of one difficult act. This distribution underscores the extent to which these activities are indeed difficult activities to perform.

FIGURE 2.10 Relationship between education and difficult political activities

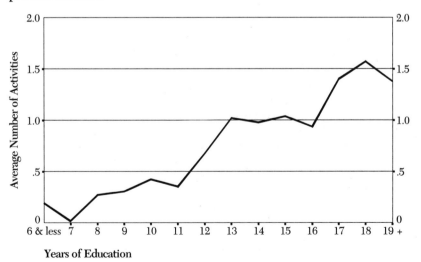

The relationship between educational attainment and voting turn-out in local and presidential elections is shown in Figure 2.11. Voting increases in a substantial manner across the entire range of educational levels, except for spikes at 7 and 18 years of formal schooling.[46]

FIGURE 2.11 Relationship between education and voting turnout

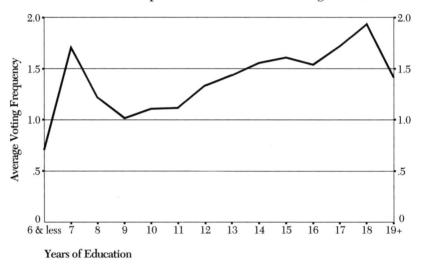

Years of Education

Finally, Figure 2.12 shows the relationship between tolerance and formal educational attainment. The data show a steep increase in toler-ance with each additional year of education, with the exception of nine years of formal schooling. For those with a high school education or less, the average score on the tolerance scale is around 2. However, for those with a college degree or more, the mean score is well over 3.

46. The spikes are likely an artifact of small sample sizes: 12 weighted cases with 7 years of education and 19 weighted cases with 18 years.

FIGURE 2.12 Relationship between education and tolerance

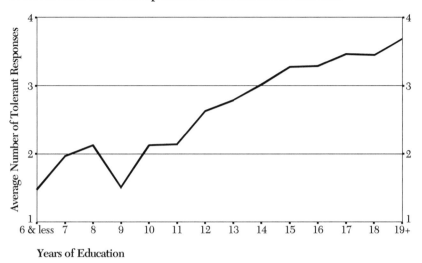

Years of Education

CONCLUSION

The data from the 1990 Citizen Participation Study show a consistent relationship between formal educational attainment and all seven attributes of democratic citizenship in terms of magnitude, direction, and basic shape. Education has a strong and positive influence on the three types of political knowledge, political participation and voting, attentiveness to politics, and tolerance. The findings do not diverge from the conventional wisdom that education is important to democratic citizenship.

However, in this chapter we also argued that democratic citizenship has two important and distinct dimensions. Democratic enlightenment represents those characteristics, such as tolerance and knowledge of the principles of democracy, that signify a basic understanding of and commitment to democratic norms, procedures, and outcomes. Political engagement, on the other hand, signifies the capability of citizens to pursue their preferences in politics and is characterized by attributes such as participation in difficult political activities and knowledge of leaders.

How can it be that the direction and magnitude of the relationship between formal educational attainment and characteristics of political engagement are so similar to the relationship between education and attributes of enlightenment, especially when we argue that political engagement and enlightenment constitute two distinct dimensions of citizenship? In other words, how can one variable have such different patterns of influence? In the next chapter, we address this question and begin to analyze the complex influence of education on democratic citizenship by examining the separate pathways that formal education takes to enlightened political engagement.

3

What Links Education to Enlightened Political Engagement?

Cognitive and Positional Pathways

The data in Chapter 2 make it clear that the relationship between educational attainment and all seven of the attributes of enlightened political engagement are positive and strong. However, what is the mechanism that links education so strongly to this set of behaviors and cognitions? While recognizing the overwhelming importance of formal educational attainment in a half-century of empirical research, political science has only vague and fragmentary notions as to why the more educated citizen is more likely to exhibit characteristics of democratic citizenship.

In this chapter, we argue that there is not one single pathway through which formal educational attainment influences all of the attributes of enlightened political engagement. Instead, there are two theoretically and empirically distinct mechanisms linking education to democratic citizenship. The first runs through the cognitive outcomes of education; the other, through the impact of education on the positional life circumstances of individuals.[1] Educational attainment takes a cognitive pathway in its influence on attributes of democratic enlightenment through its effect on the development of verbal cognitive proficiency, and a positional pathway to political engagement through its effect on the placement of individuals in social networks.

Education is one mighty variable, with well-documented importance to a host of outcomes in social, economic, and political life. However,

1. Education may have other influences on different outcomes. See, for example, Michael, 1972. However, we address here only the effects of education on characteristics of the two dimensions of democratic citizenship.

sociologists and economists disagree over the prominence of one function of education—as a developer of cognitive capabilities—versus the second function—as a stratification mechanism. For example, economists study the significance of formal education in the development of "human capital" as knowledge, skills, and analytic capability, and its consequences for productivity and income earnings.[2] Sociological studies of social mobility, status attainment, and stratification demonstrate a strong positive correlation between years of education and occupational position and earnings but are more concerned with the impact of education on status and inequality than on the development of human capital.[3]

We borrow insights from each of these traditions and argue here that education works through both cognitive and positional pathways to influence characteristics of enlightened political engagement. We begin by examining the cognitive outcomes of education and identify a measure of verbal cognitive proficiency that is relevant to political life. We next consider the second pathway education takes to characteristics of democratic citizenship and discuss in detail our measure of social network centrality. While the data will show that the effect of education on the cognitive pathway is largely direct—unmediated by intervening educational outcomes—the influence of education on social network centrality takes a more circuitous route. For this second pathway, the analysis will show that a series of positional outcomes, including occupational prominence, family income and wealth, and voluntary associational membership, are what link years of formal schooling and social network centrality.

THE COGNITIVE PATHWAY: EDUCATION AND VERBAL COGNITIVE PROFICIENCY

We are interested in the cognitive pathway through which formal educational attainment influences attributes of democratic citizenship. The verbal cognitive proficiency of citizens represents their capacity to understand political events and analyze the implications. As such, an appropriate measure of the cognitive effects of education is one that captures the capabilities that are important to the words and language of politics. Political struggles in democracy are waged in public arguments,

---

2. Becker (1993, p. 17) has identified education and training as "...the most important investments in human capital." On human capital more generally and on the relationship to income, see Schultz, 1960, 1961, 1971; Mincer, 1958, 1970, 1974; Becker, 1993; and Becker and Chiswick, 1966.

amidst the rhetoric of political debate. Because politics is largely concerned with the utilization and manipulation of language, *verbal cognitive proficiency*, as opposed to mathematical or spatial ability, is the most relevant aspect of cognitive ability in relation to democratic citizenship.

Formal education has a dramatic impact on the ability of individuals to gather information on a variety of subjects, organize facts meaningfully, and efficiently process additional and related knowledge. In short, education enhances cognitive proficiency and analytic ability. This argument is, in fact, one of the main justifications for general education. Becker and economic theorists studying human capital have argued that education is a capital investment essential to increasing earnings and productivity, for example.[4]

Formal education not only provides individuals with the specific competence necessary to perform duties within a given profession but also enhances more generalizable skills that are applicable to understanding the political world. Of particular importance is the ability to integrate and organize information about government and politics.

3. Classic empirical works on education and social stratification include Blau and Duncan 1967; Lipset and Bendix, 1959; Eckland, 1965; Sewell and Hauser, 1975; and Sewell, Hauser, and Featherman (eds.), 1976. Meritocratic and functional theories of stratification posit that formal education provides skills that are necessary for success in performing the tasks of occupations—tasks that have become increasingly more demanding with the introduction of new technology. Within this tradition, measures of intelligence have been identified as a critical intervening variable in the process of status attainment. See especially Duncan, Featherman, and Duncan, 1972; Duncan, 1968; and Herrnstein, 1971. Strong critiques of meritocratic theories have been articulated by Bell, 1972; Olneck and Crouse, 1979; and Krausz and Slomczynski, 1985.

    In contrast to the functional and meritocracy-based theories of social stratification, the importance of education in status attainment has also been interpreted as the result of the organization of society around an educational credential system. Rather than acting as an agent of change, more education and degrees simply convey information about past performance of individuals or their preexisting status. In effect, educational attainment confers credentials on those already preselected to achieve high status. As Collins (1979, p. 7) has argued, "The educationocracy...is mostly bureaucratic hot air rather than a producer of real technical skills." Other critiques of stratification as a function of meritocracy argue that meritocratic arguments are at best partial explanations of the complex process of stratification. Jencks et al. (1972), for example, show that while almost half of the variation in occupational position is due to education, a good portion of the variance is left unexplained. Another competing claim is that education is a mechanism that reproduces hierarchical structures of class relations in capitalism. According to this view, education is the primary legitimator of the ideology of capitalism and works to reproduce domination that already exists in society by conferring upon the highly educated the rewards of a high position in the preexisting social and economic hierarchy. Education, broadly conceived, is therefore designated as the central reproductive mechanism for inequality. See Bourdieu, 1990; Bowles and Gintis, 1976; and Cole (ed.), 1988.

Liberal democratic theorists, such as Rawls, have argued that formal education teaches citizens, among other things, "...knowledge of their constitutional and civic rights...."[5] Knowledge and understanding of political information strengthens the ability to draw connections and make sense of political principles. Education is commonly identified as a mechanism for developing the ability of citizens to engage in critical and moral reasoning.[6] Contemporary political theorists echo this theme and argue that formal education has an important role in teaching both the competence and traits necessary for political deliberation in modern liberal democracy.[7] In addition, research in political science has identified the importance of education in developing the cognitive abilities relevant to weighing political alternatives and consequences and choosing among them.[8] Other scholars, such as Sniderman, Brody and Tetlock, have documented differences between educational groups in support for "principled" political tolerance and have shown that those with higher levels of formal educational attainment are much more likely to support democratic values.[9]

The 1990 Citizen Participation Study included a potent and well-validated measure of verbal cognitive proficiency, known as the vocabulary test from the General Social Survey.[10] Respondents were asked to identify the meaning of 10 words from a set of choices. Figure 3.1 presents the distribution of the 10-item test.[11] Ten percent of the survey population in the 1990 Citizen Participation Study could answer three

4. See, for example, Becker, 1993.

5. Rawls, 1993, p. 199.

6. Classic examples include Kant, 1900; and Durkheim, 1961, chapters 17 and 18.

7. See Gutmann, 1987, chapters 2 and 6; and Gutmann, 1995. See also Macedo, 1990; and Galston, 1991.

8. See McClosky and Brill, 1983, for a discussion of the (cognitive) requirements of political tolerance, pp. 17-18. See also Sniderman, Brody, and Kuklinski, 1984, for an analysis of the different effects of educational attainment on patterns of policy reasoning and political values; and Kuklinski, Metlay, and Kay, 1982.

9. Sniderman, Brody, and Tetlock, 1991, pp. 128-134.

10. See Thorndike, 1942; Thorndike and Gallup, 1944; and Alwin, 1991, for an in-depth discussion of the vocabulary test as a measure of verbal cognitive proficiency.

11. This measure was created as an additive scale of the total number of correct answers. For the small number of respondents who did not attempt to answer any of the vocabulary questions, their score on the overall measure was imputed from interviewer assessment on three measures: the ability of the respondent to understand the questions on the survey, the respondent's general level of information about politics and public affairs, and the degree of interest in the interview that the respondent displayed. This imputation was made for only those few respondents who refused to answer the vocabulary questions. See Verba, Schlozman, and Brady, 1995, for a similar analysis.

or fewer items correctly on the vocabulary test, while 29% identified the meaning of eight or more of the words correctly. On average, the entire sample of respondents was able to correctly identify 6.3 words of the 10-item vocabulary test.

FIGURE 3.1 Distribution of verbal cognitive proficiency

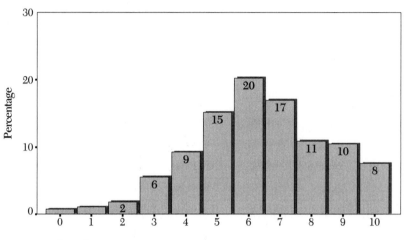

Number of Correct Answers

FIGURE 3.2 Relationship between education and verbal cognitive proficiency

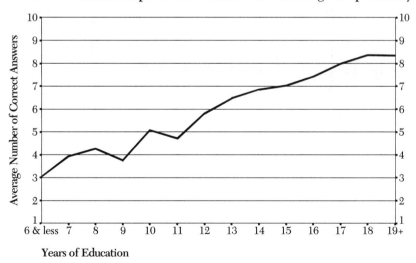

Years of Education

Figure 3.2 displays the strong positive relationship between educational attainment and this measure of verbal cognitive proficiency. The average number of correct answers on the vocabulary test is shown for each year of formal educational attainment. The relationship is strong, positive, and monotonic; verbal cognitive proficiency rises with each additional year of education. While those with a high school education or less can identify, on average, half or fewer of the words correctly, those with a college degree or above can identify eight or more correctly out of the total of 10. The correlation between years of education and the measure of verbal cognitive proficiency is a very substantial 0.55.

While educational attainment and verbal cognitive proficiency as measured by the vocabulary test are strongly associated with one another, they are nonetheless measures of distinct concepts and phenomena. We argue that verbal cognitive proficiency is among the more important outcomes of formal education and that the vocabulary test is a good measure of the cognitive capabilities that are relevant to politics. In addition, we assume that neither the measure of verbal cognitive proficiency nor formal educational attainment are proxies for "general intelligence."[12] Greater understanding of words and concepts is a direct consequence of additional years of formal education. As such, we argue for the causal placement of verbal cognitive proficiency after formal educational attainment.[13]

THE POSITIONAL PATHWAY: EDUCATION AND SOCIAL NETWORK CENTRALITY

In addition to creating greater verbal cognitive proficiency, formal education takes a second pathway to characteristics of democratic citizenship in the way it affects the placement of individuals in society. Politics and public affairs take place at the center of society. While societies maintain diverse types of social networks organized around geography, occupations, industries, commerce, hobbies, beliefs, entertainment, and many

---

12. See, for example, Gould, 1981; and Herrnstein and Murray, 1994, for two competing views on the measurement and meaning of intelligence. See also Jensen, 1969; and Herrnstein, 1971. We can contribute little to the debate over the extent to which general intelligence is measurable. All we assume here is that individuals differ in their ability to comprehend ideas and process information. All else being equal, these abilities would then translate into higher levels of the cognitive attributes linked to the characteristics of democratic enlightenment. However, the conversion of inherent potential into actual capabilities is a complex process—one more complex than the data here can address.

other areas, networks also overlap and accumulate, most frequently, into the political realm. Because binding decisions that affect the lives and fortunes of all members of the political community emanate from the arena of politics and government, political networks are among the most dense nodes in society. As such, we know *a priori* what constitutes the center of politically relevant networks. Centrality in politics is defined by proximity to governmental incumbents and political actors who make public policy and to those in the mass media who disseminate and interpret the issues, events, and activities of people in politics.[14]

We argue that educational attainment has a profound effect on the positions of individuals by placing them in more- or less-central network positions. Those with higher levels of formal education are substantially more likely to be found closer to the central nodes of politically important social networks, while those with less education are much more likely to be found at the periphery. Citizens who are at the center of society also end up at the center of political networks. Proximity to those who make policy decisions, along with accessibility to sources of relevant political information, is easier and consequently less

---

13. While we take the position that verbal cognitive proficiency, as measured by the vocabulary test, is a consequence of formal educational attainment, it is important to acknowledge a competing hypothesis regarding the relationship between the two. This perspective argues for a reverse causal direction, positing a relationship from cognitive proficiency to educational attainment. This approach has most often been termed a model of an "IQ meritocracy." Contrary to our hypothesis that those who receive more formal education become more cognitively proficient, this competing hypothesis argues that the most cognitively proficient students are those who excel in grammar school, graduate from high school, and continue to college and beyond. As such, formal schooling separates individuals with a high degree of "native intelligence" from those with lesser levels. Such a causal configuration, positing the primacy of cognitive proficiency, assumes that such capability is innate rather than learned. However, the measure of verbal cognitive proficiency, such as the vocabulary test used here, is an indicator of the degree to which individuals can understand and are facile with words in the English language. We do not use it as a measure of innate ability but, instead, as a measure of reasoning ability acquired through schooling. In addition, various scholars have demonstrated the lack of empirical support for the IQ meritocracy hypothesis. See, for example, Jencks et al., 1972; Olneck and Crouse, 1979; and Krausz and Slomczynski, 1985. We would like to thank Kent Jennings for so clearly elucidating this alternative hypothesis.

14. While we argue that the centrality of politically important social networks is defined by the actors and reporters of government and politics, conceptualizing centrality for other types of networks is contested. See Friedkin, 1991, for a review of the theoretical foundations of network centrality measures. See also Freeman, 1979, for a discussion of network centrality as sociometric status; Coleman, 1973, for a description of network centrality as power; and Burt, 1982, for centrality as prestige. For a review of the application of a network approach to structural analysis, see the essays in Wellman and Berkowitz (eds.), 1988. See also Marsden and Friedkin, 1993; and Scott, 1991.

costly for those closer to the center of social and political networks.[15] Citizens closer to the center also have an easier time being heard. Conversely, to be socially invisible and out of the loop is to be at the periphery of the social network. Thus, the opinions and preferences of those sitting farther away are much more difficult for government to hear.[16]

The question then becomes how to measure the position of individuals in such social networks. Sociologists have traditionally measured network location by examining the communication patterns among those in a particular occupation, community, or industry.[17] By considering the frequency and direction of communications, analysts can then reconstruct a picture of the entire network, along with the location of a particular individual. This method, however, is virtually impossible to implement within the context of a survey of a national sample representative of the adult U.S. population, intentionally spread over hundreds of sampling units across the country.[18] The critical issue is to locate and measure the position of a citizen in the social network by assessing his or her proximity to those who make political decisions and to those who report on political events at various levels of government.

15. We emphasize the importance of network centrality for access to, and information about, politics. Most analyses of the importance of social networks to political behavior and attitudes, however, have focused on the role of communication within such networks in persuading individuals how to vote. Some of the earliest empirical studies accounting for the persuasive impact of ego-centered networks on political behavior and attitudes are Lazarsfeld, Berelson, and Gaudet, 1944; and Berelson, Lazarsfeld, and McPhee, 1954. See also Huckfeldt and Sprague, 1991, on the effect of discussions on vote choice; Huckfeldt, 1983; Huckfeldt and Sprague, 1987, 1992; and Huckfeldt, Beck, Dalton, and Levine, 1995.

16. We argue that education allocates access to social networks that in turn make political engagement much easier. In their 1993 book, Rosenstone and Hansen make a similar argument about the importance of social and political networks but, instead, highlight their importance in providing places for leaders *external* to the network to mobilize people into political engagement. In addition, we do not discuss political party membership or strength of affiliation because there is no significant relationship between educational attainment and either membership or strength of affiliation.

17. The classic Hawthorne studies of factory workers' networks in the Western Electric Company in Chicago and the Yankee City study are the most important early examples of social network analysis of small communities. See Roethlisberger and Dickson, 1939, on Hawthorne; and Warner and Lunt, 1941, 1942, on Yankee City. See also Laumann's 1966 study of occupational networks in Boston, and his 1973 study of networks of urban males in Detroit.

18. There are at least two examples of attempts to measure communication in social networks in mass surveys. In 1987, the General Social Survey included a series of questions on the people the respondent talked with about important matters. See Knoke, 1990a, for a discussion of some of the findings from these data. See Huckfeldt, Beck, Dalton, and Levine, 1995, for a report of some of the findings from a 1992 survey of the population of the United States that included social network measures.

In order to estimate the network position of each individual, the following series of questions was asked of respondents in the 1990 Citizen Participation Study: "We are interested in whether you are personally acquainted with various kinds of people—that is, if you met or called the person, would he or she recognize you or your name?"[19] Respondents were asked whether they were personally acquainted with, or would be recognized by, a current member of the U. S. Congress (House or Senate), a current member of the state legislature (either house), a member of the local elected council in their community, a member of some other local official board (for example, a school board or zoning board), someone who works for the local media (such as a local newspaper or television station), and someone working for one of the national media. This is a powerful measurement of both who is known and who is in the know *vis a vis* the center of the social and political network. The proximity of citizens to the center is measured by the number of those actors the citizen is acquainted with or who would at least recognize the citizen by name.

Figure 3.3 shows the distribution of the social network centrality measure, which is a simple additive scale of the number of political leaders and members of the media with whom the respondent is acquainted. Almost half of all respondents in the 1990 Citizen Participation Study are very far away from the center of the social and political network, with 48% reporting that not a single one of the six types of political actors would recognize them. At the same time, almost 1 in 10 are acquainted with, or would be recognized by, four or more of those elected officials and media personnel who define the center of the social and political network. Where cognitive verbal proficiency displays a more or less normally distributed curve, the distribution of social network centrality shows a pattern of steeply declining proportions of the population who claim to be known by more than one person at the center of the political stage.

---

19. See Appendix A for the exact wording of the question, along with the marginal distributions.

FIGURE 3.3 Distribution of social network centrality measure

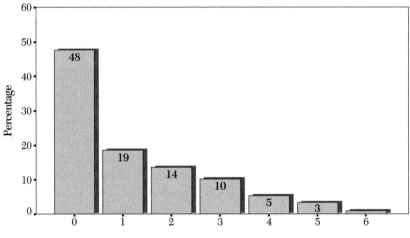

Number Acquainted with or Recognized by Political Players

FIGURE 3.4 Relationship between education and social network centrality

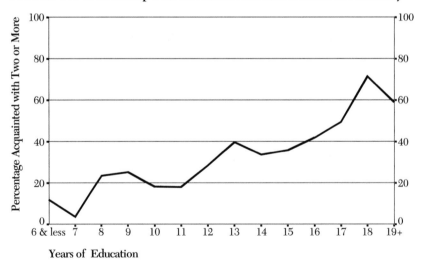

Years of Education

This measure of social network centrality is strongly related to formal educational attainment. Figure 3.4 displays the relationship between the two variables, showing the proportion within each category of educational attainment who say they are acquainted with, or would be recognized by, two or more of those political actors. On average, fewer than one-fifth of those with a high school education or less are known to, or would be recognized by, two or more of those actors who define the center of the social network. However, among those with some college education, between one-third and almost one-half are acquainted with at least two political figures. For those respondents with some graduate education, between one-half and three-quarters indicated that they would be acquainted with, or recognized by, two or more political figures. Years of educational attainment is substantially correlated with the measure of social network centrality at 0.26. While this is a strong relationship, it is not as strong as the relationship between education and verbal cognitive proficiency.

EDUCATION, SOCIAL NETWORK CENTRALITY, AND THE INTERVENING POSITIONAL OUTCOMES

Unlike the direct and unmediated relationship between education and verbal cognitive proficiency, there are several intervening outcomes of education that link education to social network centrality. We argue that there are three important positional outcomes that intervene between education and social network centrality: occupational prominence, family wealth, and membership in voluntary associations.

In post-industrial societies such as the contemporary United States, neither land nor monetary inheritance plays a substantial role in transmitting wealth and social position. Rather, social science research has demonstrated that it is formal education that functions as the primary engine of status attainment. Regardless of whether a functional, conflict, socialization, or allocation theory of stratification is adopted, the empirical findings in status attainment research show that formal educational attainment is the most important selection filter in the allocation of occupational prominence, which, in turn, is a critical determinant of family wealth.[20] Moreover, the impact of education on social position and wealth is further reinforced by "assortative mating"—marriage matching on similar levels of educational achieve-

20. See Sewell, Hauser, and Featherman (eds.), 1976; Meyer, 1977; and Collins, 1979.

ment.[21] A high degree of educational attainment thus creates a similar degree of ascendancy in social and economic position.

Those with a high degree of occupational prominence hold jobs that typically entail leadership, managerial, and supervisory responsibility. Making decisions and leading groups in the workplace are defining aspects of occupations with a high degree of prominence. Those with relatively high occupational prominence have greater frequency and intensity of communication and interaction with a wide variety of people, both within and outside of the workplace. Such leadership and supervisory roles pull people toward the center of social networks, in large part because of the connections they make.

The measure of occupational prominence we use in the 1990 Citizen Participation Study data is based on an innovative set of questions.[22] Respondents were asked a series of questions about their occupations regarding the kinds of activities they perform on the job—in particular, whether their work requires writing letters, attending meetings, planning meetings, and making presentations. They were also asked whether they supervise others on the job, and at what level that supervision is. Combined leadership, management, and supervisory level create a powerful description of overall occupational prominence. Respondents were assigned a score from 0 to 6, representing the sum of the number of leadership activities and the supervisory responsibilities required by his or her job.[23] The occupational prominence measure is strongly related to education, with its scores rising with each additional year of educational attainment. As an intervening variable, occupational prominence not only has a strong backward linkage to educational attainment, but is also significantly related in a forward direction to social network centrality. Appendix A presents the distribution of the measure of occupational prominence, along

21. See, for example, South, 1991; and Mascie-Taylor and Boyce (eds.), 1988.

22. See Verba, Schlozman, and Brady, 1995, Chapter 11, for an analysis of a set of similar questions in settings other than the workplace, such as churches.

23. See Appendix A for the exact wording of the question and the frequency distributions for the individual questions. The total number of the following six measures of occupational prominence were summed for the overall scale: supervise employees directly, supervise indirectly, write a letter, attend a meeting, plan a meeting, make a speech on the job. Those respondents who have never worked for at least one year were given a score of 0. Those respondents who were retired or temporarily out of the labor force were not asked four of the questions that make up the occupational prominence measure in the 1990 questionnaire but were asked the questions on supervision. These respondents were assigned the average score on the occupational prominence measure for those people who do work similar to that which they once did.

with a correlation matrix summarizing the relationships among all of the variables in the model.

Closely linked to occupational prominence is family income, which plays a parallel and reinforcing role in increasing social network centrality. The more highly educated are those with more prominent occupations, who supervise others, and perform other leadership roles on the job. Likewise, those with occupations that entail managerial and leadership activities are rewarded with higher salaries than those with lower occupational prominence. While weaker than the relationship between education and occupational prominence, the zero-order correlation between education and family income is nevertheless substantial, as is the forward linkage between family wealth and social network centrality. Appendix A details the distribution of the family wealth measure from the 1990 Citizen Participation Study, along with its relationship to other variables in the model.[24]

Social scientists have also long noted the critical role that voluntary organizations play in the maintenance of stable democracy.[25] Organized around the concerns, activities, interests, and hobbies of citizens, they constitute independent bases of extra-governmental power and influence. When combined with competitive elections, voluntary associations act as a major check on governmental power and its abuses.[26] These organizations form the basis of associational life, occupying a unique position, along with the workplace and religious institutions, in linking the individual to society and to the state.[27] Voluntary associations are the place, beyond the family, where citizens with similar interests interact with one another on a regular basis. Those who are members of voluntary associations are more likely to be exposed to the demands and regulations of government at all levels.[28]

---

24. For those respondents who were missing on the income measure, data from the income question in the screening portion of the Citizen Participation Study were substituted.

25. See, for example, Almond and Verba, 1963; and Eckstein, 1961.

26. This is precisely why no authoritarian or totalitarian state can tolerate a truly independent system of voluntary associations. In nondemocratic polities, such institutions are either banned outright, are made part of the state bureaucracy (where they can be controlled), or are coopted as in the corporatist model. See, for example, Bianchi, 1989; and Schmitter, 1986.

27. While we identify the importance of the workplace and occupational prominence in linking education and social network centrality, we do not consider involvement in religious institutions because it is unrelated to the level of educational attainment. See Verba, Schlozman, and Brady, 1995, chapters 11 and 13, for an interesting analysis of the relationship between activity and skills learned in churches and political participation.

28. See Hansen, 1985; Knoke, 1990b; and Walker, 1991.

Being a member of a seemingly nonpolitical organization, such as a gardening club, nevertheless substantially increases the likelihood that citizens will come into direct contact with government. Governments control what kinds of fertilizers and insecticides can be used, what kinds of plants can be grown, and how close gardens may be to streams or septic tanks. At the extreme, the government may even appropriate the land for its own use or simply zone the garden out of existence. To associate with fellow citizens organized around any interest therefore increases the probability of contact with regulatory elements of the state. And each associational affiliation is also likely to entangle the member with those in other organizations. Thus, voluntary associations are interrelated and form the networks that act to create further engagement with others in society.

The United States has among the most well-developed and vigorous voluntary associations in the world, covering almost every conceivable aspect of our lives, from hobby clubs to professional organizations.[29] Cross-national studies suggest that while other postindustrial western societies have almost as many nominal members of voluntary associations as are found in America, citizens of no other nation are anywhere near as engaged in the daily activities and governance of their voluntary organizations.[30] In short, membership in voluntary organizations is one of the defining features of American society.

The measure of organizational affiliation comes from a series of questions on voluntary group membership in the 1990 Citizen Participation Study. Respondents were asked whether they were members of 20 different types of organizations, from business and professional organizations to youth groups, neighborhood associations, and cultural organizations.[31] We created a measure of membership in only explicitly *nonpolitical* organizations in order to eliminate the possibility of contaminating this measure with our measure of political participation, one of the attributes of democratic citizenship. Thus, out of the range of 20 types of organizations, we counted only those organizations where the majority of the survey population who were members stated

---

29. See Verba, Schlozman, and Brady, 1995, Chapter 3; Baumgartner and Walker, 1988; Knoke, 1986; and Putnam, 1995a, 1995b. See the essays in Wuthnow (ed.), 1991, especially chapters 1 and 10, for a discussion of the extent to which the voluntary sector and organizations are necessary for democracy in advanced postindustrial societies.

30. See, for example, Powell, 1986; and Abramson and Inglehart, 1995.

31. See Appendix A for the exact wording of the question and marginal distribution of the individual organization measures.

that this type of organization did not take political stands. Membership in the following types of organizations was counted: service clubs or fraternal organizations; groups affiliated with one's religion; youth groups; literary or art discussion and study groups; hobby or sports clubs; neighborhood, home owner, or condominium associations or block clubs; health service organizations or organizations for service to the needy; educational organizations, and cultural organizations. In addition, if the respondent reported membership in one of these types of organizations and reported that his or her specific organization took political stands, we did not count this affiliation in the overall scale of the number of memberships in nonpolitical voluntary associations. Thus, while attempting to preserve a robust measure of voluntary associational memberships, every effort was made not to inadvertently confound nonpolitical organizational membership with the dependent variable—political engagement.

The relatively well-educated are much more likely to be members of voluntary organizations. As with occupational prominence and family wealth, organizational membership is also strongly associated with social network centrality. Appendix A displays the distribution of the measure of nonpolitical voluntary associational membership, along with its correlation to educational attainment and the other variables in the model.

To summarize, we argue that the three intervening positional outcomes of education—occupational prominence, family income, and nonpolitical organizational membership—strongly influence the placement of citizens in the social network. Thus far, we have only hypothesized about these relationships, and it has been our assertion that the path of education to verbal cognitive proficiency is more direct; essentially unmediated by the intervening positional outcomes. We now proceed to test the model, estimating the effect of formal education on verbal cognitive proficiency and social network centrality using data from the 1990 Citizen Participation Study.

ESTIMATING THE EFFECT OF EDUCATION ON VERBAL PROFICIENCY AND NETWORK CENTRALITY

Figure 3.5 is a path diagram showing how formal educational attainment influences verbal cognitive proficiency and social network centrality. We utilize path diagrams throughout the analysis of the cross-sectional data in Part I of the book. Recursive path analysis is a powerful tool for sorting out the complicated relationships emanating from a previously occurring independent variable through a series of intervening variables, and on to a causally subsequent dependent variable.[32] Path models are an obvious choice, as well as an excellent metaphor, for the type of causal argument we make here. The path diagrams can be best thought of as volumes of water passing through interconnected streams. The total amount of water moving from left to right is the total sum of all of the paths linking the independent variable to the dependent variable. Indirect paths are the products of the series of coefficients linking the independent variable to the dependent variable. The sum of the direct and indirect paths from beginning to end of the causal chain is equal to the zero-order correlation between the independent and dependent variables. To calculate the total flow of variance through any indirect pathway, the coefficients for each segment are multiplied. The larger the coefficient in any direct or indirect path, the more important that path is in explaining how the variation in the independent variable affects the dependent variable.[33] But it is in the indirect pathways where the real explanation lies.

The coefficients presented in Figure 3.5 are standardized coefficients, estimated with a maximum likelihood procedure.[34] We present the standardized coefficients in order to facilitate comparison among measures with different scales. The size of the relationship is reported above the line and is also indicated by the thickness of the line. The unstandardized coefficients, along with the standard error in brackets, are shown in the table below Figure 3.5.[35]

32. Of primary concern in estimating path models is that one is relatively certain about the causal order of the variables. We return to this in detail at the end of Chapter 5. See, for example, Heise, 1975; and Blalock, 1961.

33. The magnitude of the remaining direct path between the independent and dependent variables is identical to an ordinary least squares estimate of the standardized regression coefficient.

34. We use the linear structural relationship (LISREL) technique to estimate the coefficients. LISREL is often used to estimate structural equation models. However, the model specified in Figure 3.5 does not contain any structural or unmeasured components, and the coefficients reported here are virtually identical to those from estimates of a series of ordinary least squares (OLS) regression models. While it is not necessary to use a structural equation modeling program like LISREL in this portion of the analysis, it is useful for examining alternative nonrecursive specifications of the model. We will address this topic in Chapter 5.

35. Coefficients that were not statistically significant at the 0.05 level were removed from the model by fixing these paths to 0 and reestimating the model.

FIGURE 3.5 Estimation of pathways from educational attainment to verbal cognitive proficiency and social network centrality

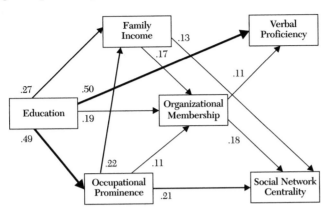

	Education	Occupational Prominence	Family Income	Organizational Membership
Occupational Prominence	.33 (.02)			
Family Income	.36 (.04)	.42 (.06)		
Organizational Membership	.07 (.01)	.06 (.02)	.05 (.01)	
Verbal Proficiency	.39 (.02)			.23 (.05)
Social Network Centrality		.17 (.02)	.05 (.01)	.28 (.04)

Standardized coefficients
Standard errors in parentheses below coefficients (unstandardized)

The relationship between formal education and verbal cognitive proficiency (0.50), is among the strongest in the model. Furthermore, the relationship between the two appears to be largely direct, with the overwhelming portion of the original zero-order relationship unmediated by the subsequent outcome variables in the model of occupational prominence, family income, and organizational membership. The data in Figure 3.5 show that membership in nonpolitical voluntary organizations is the only variable that plays any intervening role in the relationship between education and verbal cognitive proficiency. Being among the organizationally affiliated has a minor, but statistically significant, impact on the ability of respondents to correctly answer questions on the vocabulary test. The primary influence on the ability of citizens to understand words is simply the number of years spent in the classroom. In this sphere, at least, formal education does exactly what many hope and expect it to do.

In stark contrast to the direct path that educational attainment takes to cognitive verbal proficiency is the indirect journey education takes to social network centrality. The direct relationship between the two is mediated to the greatest extent by occupational prominence (0.21) and membership in nonpolitical voluntary organizations (0.18). Family wealth plays a somewhat smaller mediating role in assigning position in social networks (0.13). Together, these three variables completely account for the original bivariate relationship between educational attainment and social network centrality. The remaining coefficient is statistically indistinguishable from 0. Education is therefore connected to network centrality solely because educational attainment affects occupational prominence and associational membership and, to a slightly lesser degree, family income.

Perhaps the most striking finding is that, in the presence of the other variables in the model, the two outcomes of education—verbal cognitive proficiency and social network centrality—are completely uncorrelated. Recall that both variables are highly correlated with formal education. Table 3.1 shows the relationship between cognitive proficiency and network centrality with a series of zero-order and partial correlation coefficients, along with the level of statistical significance. The first line shows that the two have a zero-order correlation of 0.18. However, once the effect of formal educational attainment is accounted for, the relationship between verbal cognitive proficiency and social network centrality is reduced to 0.05. And, after controlling for the intervening positional outcomes of occupational prominence, nonpolitical organizational membership, and family wealth, the relationship is a statistically insignificant 0.03. In short, the two pathways are essentially uncorrelated with one another. Once the direct effect of education and its outcomes are accounted for, there is no remaining association between verbal cognitive proficiency and social network centrality.[36]

TABLE 3.1 Correlations between verbal cognitive proficiency and social network centrality

Zero-order correlation between verbal cognitive proficiency and social network centrality	.18 (p=.00)
Partial correlation controlling for educational attainment	.05 (p=.06)
Partial correlation controlling for educational attainment, occupational prominence, organizational membership, and family wealth	.03 (p=.30)

The cognitive pathway that education takes through verbal cognitive proficiency occurs in the minds of individual citizens. This process is influenced directly by the number of years that an individual sits in the classroom and is constrained only by the extent to which individuals limit their education. On the other hand, the positional pathways that formal education takes to social network centrality occurs within the context of social structures and relations. This proximity is never independent of social structures that are organized hierarchically and always characterized by scarcity and competition. The characteristics of political engagement that are embedded in the structure of these types of social relations, where education is linked through network centrality, are by definition limited, because not everyone can be at the center.

Thus, there are two independent outcomes of formal educational attainment. Verbal proficiency links education to attributes of democratic citizenship through a cognitive pathway, and social network centrality ties formal educational attainment to enlightened political engagement through a positional pathway. In this way, education can be thought of as the engine of two separate life trains that, we shall see, combine to shape the configuration of democratic citizenship.

36. All of the data presented here are for the entire sample. Separate parallel LISREL analyses were calculated for males and females, blacks and whites. No material differences were discovered for any of the subpopulations. The social mechanisms leading to the two uncorrelated outcomes of education are substantially the same, or apparently substantially the same, for all major segments of the population. Appendix C presents the estimation of the model for each of the four groups separately.

4

Integrating and Testing the Model

In Chapter 3, we traced the pathways from educational attainment to the two independent and uncorrelated outcomes of verbal cognitive proficiency and social network centrality. In this chapter, we argue that through these intervening variables, education takes a cognitive as well as a positional pathway to the two different dimensions of democratic citizenship. The model is quite straightforward—education is linked to the seven attributes of enlightened political engagement by one driving influence (education), three intermediate positional social outcomes (occupational prominence, nonpolitical organizational membership, and family income), and two uncorrelated intervening variables (verbal cognitive proficiency and social network centrality).

Through its influence on the positional outcomes of occupational prominence, family income, and voluntary associational membership, education influences the placement of who is at the center and who is at the periphery of the relevant social networks. The cost of political information, the price of staying tuned to politics, the difficulty of getting heard, and the ability to influence political outcomes vary dramatically depending upon where one is located in the social network. Because the components of engagement are more instrumental and essentially competitive in nature, what is most affected is the cost of that political engagement. In other words, through its influence on network position, education creates engaged citizens by cutting the cost of pursuing and protecting interests in politics. Perhaps the best analogy to social network centrality is the location of one's seat in a large amphitheater—those in the front rows have little trouble hearing or being heard, identifying the actors on stage, and being recognized by them. However, for those in the rows at the rear of the theater, it takes substantial effort to hear and identify the players and even greater effort to be heard by those on the political stage.

On the other hand, the components of democratic enlightenment are not, for the most part, limited and instrumental in nature. Rather, the enlightenment qualities of democratic citizenship are consensual and noncompetitive cognitions, values, and social norms, to which education takes an entirely different path. Individuals do not view enlightenment as a utility—as a commodity to be gained. Rather, education influences these characteristics of citizenship by increasing verbal cognitive proficiency, thereby creating a more sophisticated understanding of politics and governance, including an appreciation of the importance of tolerance for the expression of political views.

We begin this chapter by outlining our hypotheses about why verbal cognitive proficiency and social network location intervene as the main explanatory factors linking formal educational attainment to the components of enlightened political engagement. We next integrate the separate parts of the model and go on to test the model.

THE IMPACT OF COGNITIVE PROFICIENCY AND NETWORK LOCATION ON ENLIGHTENED POLITICAL ENGAGEMENT

We have identified verbal cognitive proficiency and social network centrality as the two major intervening variables through which educational attainment affects the characteristics of democratic citizenship. These intervening variables are also key to our ability to test the distinctions we have made among the components of democratic citizenship. Having examined the path from formal education to these intervening effects in the previous chapter, we can now test how verbal cognitive proficiency and social network centrality differentially link educational attainment to the seven separate attributes of enlightened political engagement—knowledge of political leaders, knowledge of the principles of democracy, knowledge of other current political facts, attentiveness to politics, participation in difficult political activities, voting, and tolerance.

The logic by which the two intervening variables relate to specific attributes of enlightened political engagement is detailed in Table 4.1 below. Here, we present our hypotheses of how verbal cognitive proficiency and social network centrality differentially link educational attainment to attributes of the two dimensions of citizenship.

TABLE 4.1 Hypotheses on relationships between education and attributes of citizenship

ATTRIBUTE OF CITIZENSHIP	DIMENSION OF CITIZENSHIP	EXPECTED PATHWAYS
Knowledge of democratic principles	enlightenment	verbal cognitive proficiency
Knowledge of other current political facts	both	verbal cognitive proficiency
Knowledge of leaders	political engagement	social network centrality
Political attentiveness	both	both
Participation in difficult political activities	political engagement	social network centrality
Voting	both	both
Tolerance	enlightenment	verbal cognitive proficiency

Politically engaged citizens, capable of defending and pursuing their self-interest, must be armed with certain types of political information, or else be forced to "fly blind" in the political world. In particular, citizens must be able to recognize political incumbents and elected officials. However, other types of political information, such as knowledge of the principles of democracy, are less important to the maintenance of interests and are, instead, attributes of the enlightenment dimension of democratic citizenship. Knowledge of the principles of democracy is critical to the maintenance of a democratic polity, because such an understanding signifies the recognition of what is to be defended. At the same time, knowledge of democratic principles is of only marginal importance in protecting private interests, compared with information about the current political leaders or knowledge of other current political facts. By the same token, concrete information about who must be petitioned, and about what, can do little to enhance the democratic character of the polity.

We hypothesize that varying levels of verbal cognitive proficiency will be the dominant explanation for why education is so strongly related to knowledge of the principles of democracy. This more abstract type of knowledge is most dependent upon the effect that education has on the general enhancement of conceptual reasoning. On the other hand, the ability to identify current political incumbents is short-lived and unlikely to have been learned in school. Verbal cognitive proficiency should influence knowledge of leaders to a lesser extent; instead, we predict that it is the influence of formal educational attainment on proximity to the center of social networks that constitutes the main explanatory pathway between education and the knowledge of political leaders. Those in the front rows are the most likely to recognize the political players, while those seated at the rear require both greater assistance and persistence to closely follow the players in the political game.

Knowledge of other current political facts lies somewhere in between. Knowing which party is in control of Congress or which agency spends more tax money (NASA or the Social Security administration) should certainly enhance political engagement, for without such facts, the citizen cannot know where his or her interests lie. In addition, the absence of this type of information makes it more difficult for the citizen to be alert to threats to democratic procedures. Therefore, this type of knowledge can be characterized as enhancing both political engagement and enlightenment. Consequently, knowledge of other current political facts requires both verbal cognitive proficiency and social network centrality.

Political attentiveness, we hypothesize, is also an attribute of both political engagement and enlightenment. Attentiveness is clearly a prerequisite for political engagement; without paying some attention to politics and governmental affairs, it is difficult for citizens to adequately pursue and defend their interests in politics. At the same time, citizens cannot be vigilant in the protection of democracy if they do not regularly monitor the affairs of the polity. Thus, higher levels of verbal cognitive proficiency are necessary to understand this connection between individual interests and political events. Most clearly, however, we expect those nearer the center of social networks to be more attentive to politics and public affairs. Being politically attentive is much easier and less costly for those near the center, for they have superior access to both the events and the people in politics.

And because they are in close proximity to the political game and its players, those at the center of social networks have more incentive to follow political events. In contrast, for those at the periphery, the actions of political players are seen as incomprehensible movements on a distant stage, and there is little incentive to become involved. For these reasons, we expect social network location to play a major mediating role between education and political attentiveness. Attentiveness is one of three components of democratic citizenship that we expect to be strongly affected by both of the intervening variables—verbal cognitive proficiency and social network centrality.

Participation in difficult political activities is perhaps the ultimate manifestation of citizen engagement. By taking part in political activity, citizens are in the act of pursuing and protecting their political interests. Because these activities entail a substantial commitment of time and energy, as well as the negotiation of significant social barriers, we expect closeness to the center of society to play the major explanatory role in linking education to participation in difficult political activities. Being acquainted with or recognized by governmental decision makers dramatically lowers both the psychological and behavioral costs of political activity. Because there are always more demands from individual citizens than even the most responsive government can process, let alone satisfy, making oneself heard is a highly competitive business. Those at the periphery are much more likely to be discouraged from participation. For these citizens, the costs of figuring out the issues and who to petition are not only greater, but the probability of actually being heard is also much smaller. Consider two individuals with the same policy objective—an executive in a large corporation and an assembly-line worker in the same business. How many calls would it take for the executive to reach his or her member of Congress? How many more calls would it take for the assembly-line worker? This is not a matter of verbal cognitive proficiency, for it is possible that the assembly-line worker is a crossword puzzle wizard or loquacious amateur actor. Thus, there is little reason to expect verbal cognitive proficiency to be an important factor distinguishing those who are more politically active from those who are relatively quiescent. Rather, we hypothesize that access to leaders is almost entirely a matter of social position.

A different type of political activity—voting—entails a mix of motivations and expectations. Voting is distinct from participation in the more purely instrumental difficult political activities discussed above. Voting is certainly a major part of citizen political engagement; however, because of its inability to convey specific information about the content of specific interests, it is primarily a retrospective and defensive tool.[1] Voting can be considered political engagement insofar as it enables citizens to express their general preference for one leader or party over another or, at occasional historical junctures, one set of policies over another. An equally important contribution of voting to democratic politics is in the long-term protection that elections with substantial turnout provide against the abuses and corruption of political power. Electoral accountability over time turns potential tyrants into replaceable, and therefore responsive, governors. Well-educated citizens are more likely to vote regularly, at least in part because they are more likely to understand the long-term relationship between the exercise of their franchise and the effect of the act of voting on the preservation of a democratic system. Therefore, we expect verbal cognitive proficiency to play a substantial part in the explanation of the connection between formal education and regularity of voting. We hypothesize that it is precisely this understanding that keeps the more educated citizen voting with greater frequency than the less educated, despite the fact that the well-educated are also more likely to understand the paradox of voting.[2] However, because voting is a characteristic of enlightenment as well as political engagement, we expect network centrality to influence frequency of voting and to help explain why education enhances the use of the ballot. Those who know and are known by contestants for political office and the members of the media who surround them should be substantially more motivated to vote than those spectators at the periphery who see only strangers in the distance.

Finally, support for the freedom of expression of unpopular views represents an understanding of the meaning of an open and democratic polity. To a substantial extent, tolerance is the cornerstone of a democratically enlightened citizenry. Thus, the main explanatory pathway

---

1. See, for example, Verba and Nie, 1972; and Verba, Schlozman, and Brady, 1995.

2. This paradox, as it is often cited by students of rational choice, is a function of the remoteness of the probability that the vote of any individual citizen will significantly affect the outcome of an election. See, for example, Downs, 1957.

from education to tolerance should prove to be through the impact of formal education on verbal cognitive proficiency. In this instance, proximity to the center of the social network should matter little, if at all.

A SUMMARY OF THE MAIN FINDINGS

Table 4.2 summarizes the central findings from our analysis across the seven individual attributes of democratic citizenship. The specification of these seven models includes formal educational attainment, the three positional results of education, and the two major uncorrelated educational outcomes. A detailed examination of each of the maximum likelihood path models follows in the second half of this chapter.[3] The results of the models presented in Table 4.2 provide strong support for our hypothesis that formal education influences the characteristics of democratic enlightenment almost exclusively through verbal cognitive proficiency. On the other hand, the data for all of the attributes of political engagement display the opposite pattern, showing a strong pathway from education *via* social network centrality.

The second column in Table 4.2 presents the zero-order correlations between education and the individual characteristic of democratic citizenship. The third column in the table presents the magnitude of the direct path between formal educational attainment and each dependent variable *after* controlling for all intervening variables in the models. The fourth and fifth columns summarize the magnitude of the effects of these two uncorrelated educational outcomes—verbal cognitive proficiency and social network centrality—on each of the seven attributes of citizenship.

What is most striking in the second column of Table 4.2 is the similarity in magnitude of the relationships of all seven measures of enlightened political engagement with formal educational attainment. With the exception of frequency of voting, which is slightly weaker, all of the dependent variables are correlated with educational attainment between 0.28 and 0.39. However, the rest of the data in the table show how this uniformity in magnitude obscures the substantial differences in the mechanisms that link education to the distinct components of enlightened engagement. The third column, labeled *Direct Path*, provides information on the extent to which the model explains the original bivariate relationship

3. See Chapter 3 for a discussion of path analysis and the method of estimation used for these models.

between education and each of the components of citizenship. The size of the standardized coefficient in this third column indicates how much the introduction of the controls for the positional variables plus verbal cognitive proficiency and social network centrality reduce the original relationship between education and each citizenship characteristic.

The fourth and fifth columns in Table 4.2 contain symbols representing the magnitude of the coefficients for verbal proficiency and network centrality, which are presented in the legend below the table. This presentation allows us to see clearly which measures of enlightenment and political engagement are most strongly influenced by these two intervening variables.

TABLE 4.2 Summary of the impact of education and the intervening variables on seven attributes of citizenship

ATTRIBUTE OF CITIZENSHIP	CORRELATION WITH EDUCATION	DIRECT PATH	VERBAL PROFICIENCY	SOCIAL NETWORK CENTRALITY
Knowledge of democratic principles	.39	.17	***	*
Knowledge of other current political facts	.37	.25	**	
Knowledge of leaders	.28	.09	**	***
Political attentiveness	.38	.20	*	**
Participation in difficult political activities	.29	.08		***
Voting	.24	.07	**	***
Tolerance	.35	.23	***	*

*** Major effect (standardized coefficient of .20 and above)

** Secondary effect (standardized coefficient between .10 and .19)

* Minor effect (standardized coefficient below .10)

(Blank) no effect

Intervening Effects: Verbal Cognitive Proficiency

The data clearly show that verbal cognitive proficiency has its strongest impact on the three enlightenment measures of democratic citizenship: knowledge of democratic principles, knowledge of other current facts, and tolerance, shown in the first, second, and last rows of Table 4.2. In all three instances, verbal proficiency is the most significant variable linking formal education to each. In contrast, and as expected, cognitive proficiency appears to play a smaller role in another of the measures of political knowledge—knowledge of political leaders. Though significant, the cognitive pathway for this type of contextual knowledge is only a fraction of the size of the path through network centrality. This pattern is consistent with the notion that knowledge of political leaders is more a characteristic of political engagement than of enlightenment. Finally, verbal cognitive proficiency also plays a role in linking formal education to political attentiveness, but its contribution is much smaller than the role played by the pathway of social network centrality. This is consistent with the notion that political attentiveness, while mainly a characteristic of political engagement, is also relevant to enlightenment. On the other hand, verbal cognitive proficiency has absolutely no independent effect on participation in difficult political activities, a characteristic of political engagement. When it comes to voting, however, the situation is different. Cognitive proficiency is an important mediating variable that helps explain why education increases the frequency with which citizens vote. This finding is consistent with the hypothesis concerning the dual character of voting as an attribute of both political engagement and democratic enlightenment. Moreover, social network centrality and verbal cognitive proficiency together almost fully account for the relationship between formal education and voting (the remaining direct path is 0.07).

Intervening Effects: Social Network Centrality

As predicted, the patterns revealed in the data in Table 4.2 for social network centrality are the mirror image of those for verbal cognitive proficiency. Network centrality has a dominant impact on the ability of citizens to identify political incumbents and on the number of difficult political acts performed—both central characteristics of political engagement. In these two instances, being known or recognized by those at the center of social networks is the main mediating variable. Moreover, in both of these instances, network centrality and the positional variables that link it to education account for at least two-thirds of the original zero-order relationship between education and these two core measures of political engagement. On the other hand, in the fully specified model, network location has little or no influence on knowledge of the principles of democratic government, knowledge of other current political facts, or level of political tolerance. These three characteristics are the central indicators of enlightenment. Evident once again is the double-barreled nature of voting as part instrumental and part symbolic behavior, with network location and cognitive proficiency both intervening to help explain why education is predictive of the regularity with which citizens turn out to vote. Finally, network centrality also plays a larger role than verbal cognitive proficiency in explaining why education so strongly and positively influences political attentiveness, and we expect that attentiveness is a characteristic of both political engagement and enlightenment.

Thus, a quick summary of the data reveals that while verbal cognitive proficiency has the dominant role in linking education to the qualities of democratic enlightenment, network centrality shows its greatest explanatory power in mediating the relationship between formal education and the attributes of political engagement.

INTERPRETING THE PATTERNS THROUGH PATH DIAGRAMS

The discussion of the overall findings presented in Table 4.2 concentrated on the columns in the table in order to highlight the relative importance of the intervening variables of cognitive proficiency and social network centrality on the seven characteristics of enlightened political engagement. In this section, we examine in detail the fully specified model for each of the characteristics of enlightened political engagement in order to demonstrate the contrasting ways in which formal educational attainment is linked to each.

Beginning with Figure 4.1, we present seven separate path diagrams with the results of the estimation of the model. Each of these figures displays only paths between education and the intervening variables with magnitudes greater than or equal to 0.10.[4] The coefficients presented are standardized coefficients; however, the tables below the figures document the unstandardized coefficients, t values, and standard errors for all variables in the model linked to the dependent variable. In addition to presenting the actual coefficients on the paths, Figure 4.1 to Figure 4.7 are drawn so that the thickness of the lines corresponds to the magnitude of the estimated relationship.

---

4. While only paths greater than or equal to 0.10 (standardized coefficients) are presented in the path diagrams, all paths statistically significant at the 0.05 level or above are presented in the table below the diagram.

Path Model: Knowledge of Principles of Democracy

We begin by examining the model estimated for the enlightenment characteristic of knowing the principles of democracy. These estimates are shown in Figure 4.1. Formal education increases this type of political knowledge primarily through its impact on verbal cognitive proficiency. Those with more years of formal schooling are more facile with language and are better able to think analytically; the more educated individual also learns to think abstractly. Approximately half of the original zero-order relationship between educational attainment and knowledge of the principles of democracy is explained by the measure of verbal cognitive proficiency, while the remaining half is unexplained by any other intervening variable in the model (a fact that we attribute more to the lack of comprehensiveness in our measure of verbal cognitive proficiency than to alternative explanations).[5] In fact, while there is a statistically significant path from social network centrality to knowledge of democratic principles, it is by itself far too small to constitute a meaningful cause of this type of knowledge. Moreover, its backward links to education are so fragmented that neither network centrality nor any of the positional variables that link it to education can be considered important intermediating variables in this instance.

5. It is important to acknowledge that formal education has cognitive effects beyond verbal proficiency. A measure of quantitative skills, for example, would provide another intervening variable that might account for some of the remaining direct path from educational attainment. In addition, there is the possibility that socialization and inculcation of democratic values within the educational environment are the reasons for the direct path. Such effects could be operating independently of the degree of cognitive proficiency that an individual attains. A good deal of support for such a hypothesis exists. For example, see Jennings and Niemi, 1974, 1981; Almond and Verba, 1963; Easton and Dennis, 1969; and Verba, Schlozman, and Brady, 1995. While the actual mechanism behind political socialization is not entirely clear, educational settings that emphasize ideas and the consideration of alternative points of view have the potential to expose people to democratic values. One might also argue that the settings of formal education provide a powerful socializing experience that teaches individuals socially desirable values. This hypothesis argues that because the environment that enhances verbal cognitive proficiency is the same environment that transmits the norms of social desirability, one cannot isolate the true effect of cognitive proficiency. The strong observed relationship between formal education and the attributes of democratic citizenship may thus reflect the effect of learned social desirability. Viewed from this perspective, a more highly educated individual only appears more tolerant because he or she is better able to give the socially desirable response to a survey researcher. While this hypothesis has merit with respect to political tolerance, it has little relevance to the effect of education on knowledge of the principles of democracy, where the correct answers are objective.

FIGURE 4.1 Education to knowledge of the principles of democracy: Standardized coefficients from maximum likelihood estimation

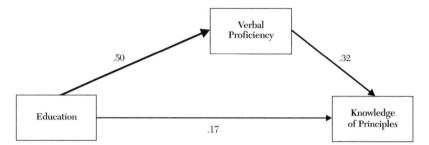

	Standardized Coefficient	Unstandardized Coefficient	Standard Error	t value
Education	.17	.05	.01	5.53
Occupational Prominence				
Family Income				
Organizational Membership				
Verbal Proficiency	.32	.13	.01	10.75
Social Network Centrality	.07	.04	.01	2.80

Path Model: Tolerance

The findings explaining why education is linked to tolerance are parallel to those described above for the knowledge of democratic principles. Recall that tolerance is at the heart of the definition of the enlightenment dimension of democratic citizenship. Figure 4.2 displays the estimates of the coefficients from the model for tolerance. Once again, verbal proficiency is the main mediating variable. No other pathway in the model accounts for a meaningful amount of the covariation between education and tolerance. As can be seen in the table below the figure, family wealth and social network centrality maintain statistically significant direct paths to tolerance, but neither their forward nor backward linkages are large enough to account for more than a very small portion of the covariation between the independent and dependent variables.[6]

FIGURE 4.2 Education to tolerance: Standardized coefficients from maximum likelihood estimation

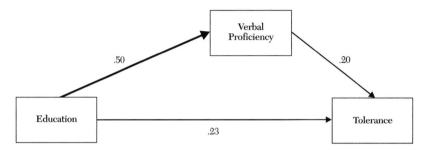

	Standardized Coefficient	Unstandardized Coefficient	Standard Error	t value
Education	.23	.12	.02	7.04
Occupational Prominence				
Family Income	.09	.03	.01	2.94
Organizational Membership				
Verbal Proficiency	.20	.13	.02	6.26
Social Network Centrality	−.09	−.09	.03	−3.43

Thus far, the data clearly indicate that the more educated citizen is much more likely to understand that he or she has a stake in protecting the right of all citizens to express their political views and are more tolerant of the expression of unpopular, and even extreme, political views than those with less education. The more highly educated can reason that the process that protects freedom of expression for those whose beliefs may seem marginal is the same process that, in the long run, also protects the rights of all. Freedom of expression costs open societies very little, yet the coercion required to prevent it is costly indeed, and the more educated the individual, the more likely he or she is to understand and believe this. Tolerance requires even greater conceptual

6. Part of the large remaining unexplained path between education and tolerance is due to the inability of our measure of verbal cognitive proficiency to account for all of the cognitive effects of education. However, as we will see in the second part of the book, a clue to the remaining unexplained path between education and tolerance lies in a complex set of dynamic relationships between education and generations. These relationships also help to explain the small negative path from social network centrality to tolerance.

understanding than simply recognizing either the guarantee of the fifth amendment or the most important difference between democracy and dictatorship. As such, it is at the center of our conceptualization of the enlightenment dimension of citizenship. Most importantly, it is the cognitive outcomes of education, rather than the positional outcomes, that are responsible for the connection between education and tolerance.

Path Model: Knowledge of Leaders

The linkage between education and knowledge of current political leaders is totally different from that connecting education to knowledge of the principles of democracy and tolerance. Figure 4.3 displays the paths that formal educational attainment takes to the ability to identify leaders. While verbal cognitive proficiency plays a mediating role between education and this type of political knowledge, most of the explanation of the role of education is in its impact on social network location and, in turn, the impact of network centrality on the citizen's ability to identify leaders. In short, this type of political knowledge varies most with distance from the center of the social-political world and less from the impact that education has on verbal cognitive proficiency.

The pattern in the data makes sense intuitively; the names of current political leaders would not have been learned in the classroom. For most in the sample, formal schooling was long ago and far away. Even an educated hermit living in the woods is likely to remember the principles of democracy, but the ability to name the current head of the local school district, state representatives, or U. S. senators depends primarily on how completely, and for how long, he or she has been socially isolated.

The data in Figure 4.3 make it clear that the role of education in imparting knowledge of leaders is quite different from its role in instilling the principles of democracy. The impact of education on the allocation of occupational prominence and family wealth, as well as its role in increasing membership in voluntary associations and, in turn, the effect of these on social network centrality result in the strong positive relationship between educational attainment and the ability of citizens to identify political leaders. Unlike the relationship between education and the two attributes of democratic enlightenment discussed above, the relationship between education and the ability to identify political leaders is almost fully mediated by the intervening variables in the model, and only a minor, if statistically significant, direct path remains from education to the dependent variable. In this instance, it is both what education makes a person and where education places citizens, and not what education teaches them directly, that determines the level of leadership knowledge.

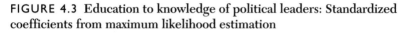

FIGURE 4.3 Education to knowledge of political leaders: Standardized coefficients from maximum likelihood estimation

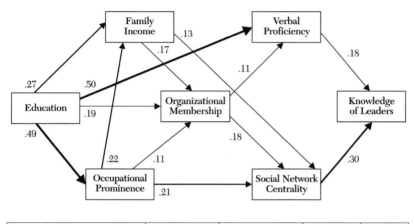

	Standardized Coefficient	Unstandardized Coefficient	Standard Error	t value
Education	.09	.05	.02	2.92
Occupational Prominence				
Family Income				
Organizational Membership	.08	.13	.04	2.99
Verbal Proficiency	.18	.13	.02	5.84
Social Network Centrality	.30	.30	.03	11.23

Path Model: Participation in Difficult Political Activities

A similar pattern of the importance of social network centrality is evident in the estimation of the model predicting participation in difficult political activities. Figure 4.4 displays these data. It is clear that it is network centrality that determines whether, and with what frequency, individuals will engage in time- and energy-consuming political activities, such as working on political campaigns, working with others in the local community, serving on local governmental boards, and contacting elected officials. The role of membership in voluntary associations also displays a substantial direct link to these acts of participation, highlighting the importance of organizational membership, as well as placement in social networks. The data clearly indicate that the most obviously instrumental component of political engagement—knowledge of who is to be petitioned and monitored, as well as activities clearly aimed at the pursuit of political goals—is linked to educational attainment through the role of formal education as an allocator of positions within the networks in society. Note that there is no link between education and participation in difficult political activities that runs through the cognitive outcomes of formal education and that there is only a minimal remaining direct path between education and participation. The intervening positional variables and their impact on social network centrality fully account for the relationship between education and citizen participation. The contrast between this path diagram and those in Figure 4.1 and Figure 4.2, which present the comparable analysis for knowledge of democratic principles and level of tolerance, are a clear and dramatic demonstration of the distinct pathways leading formal education to political engagement versus democratic enlightenment.

FIGURE 4.4 Education to participation in difficult political activities: Standardized coefficients from maximum likelihood estimation

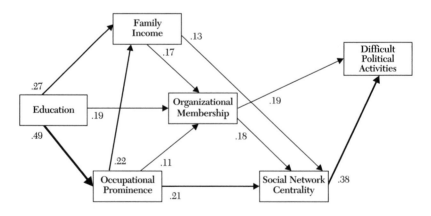

	Standardized Coefficient	Unstandardized Coefficient	Standard Error	t value
Education	.08	.03	.01	2.95
Occupational Prominence	.09	.05	.02	2.99
Family Income				
Organizational Membership	.19	.20	.03	7.39
Verbal Proficiency				
Social Network Centrality	.38	.26	.02	14.77

Path Model: Voting

The impact of education on the frequency of voting is, as predicted, explained by both social network location and verbal cognitive proficiency. The estimates of the model are displayed in Figure 4.5. Being at the center of society clearly increases the frequency of voting and, in this regard, voting appears to be another tool for the articulation of instrumental interest. But unlike performing more difficult political activities—where network centrality captures all of the explanation—cognitive proficiency shares almost equally with network position the causal connection between education and voting. In this instance, voluntary associational membership also has a smaller, but statistically significant, direct path to voting.

Most important here is the fact that little in the voluminous literature on voting suggests that the frequency of voting is significantly more dependent on cognitive proficiency than is the performance of other political activities. Rather, one would surmise just the opposite. This finding may lie at the heart of one of the great puzzles of voter turnout. The more educated and therefore more cognitively proficient the citizen, the more likely it is that he or she understands that one vote is extremely unlikely to have an impact on the outcome of any given election. Yet, micro-level data from the United States over the past half-century show that the more educated the citizen, the more likely he or she is to cast a ballot. One way to interpret this finding is that, for the well-educated, voting is more than simply an instrumental act. It is, as well, an expression of understanding that the maintenance of a system of electorally accountable leaders requires that citizens vote regularly, even though it is highly improbable that any individual citizen will cast the deciding ballot. Understanding the system-level implications of nonvoting may have more in common with knowing the principles of democracy or believing in tolerance than one might first expect. One of the benefits of voting that overwhelms the rationality of nonvoting is that it signals to others that voting is essential for the survival of democracy.[7] In this instance, social network centrality and verbal cognitive proficiency together almost fully explain the original bivariate relationship between education and frequency of voting.

FIGURE 4.5 Education to voting: Standardized coefficients from maximum likelihood estimation

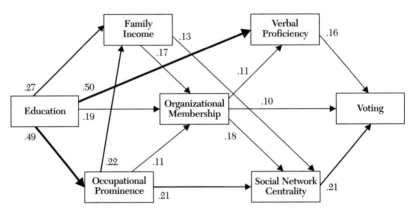

	Standardized Coefficient	Unstandardized Coefficient	Standard Error	*t* value
Education	.07	.02	.01	2.28
Occupational Prominence				
Family Income				
Organizational Membership	.10	.06	.02	3.46
Verbal Proficiency	.16	.05	.01	4.89
Social Network Centrality	.21	.09	.01	7.68

Path Model: Political Attentiveness

We earlier hypothesized that political attentiveness was a characteristic of both democratic enlightenment and political engagement. Only those continuously engaged in political surveillance could be sure to know

7. See, for example, Quattrone and Tversky, 1986.

enough to protect their own interests and recognize a threat to democratic governance. The data in Figure 4.6, although not conclusive, are consistent with this view. Network centrality and cognitive proficiency both have a large positive impact on political attentiveness, and both play a substantial role in explaining why education is related to political attentiveness. However, network centrality has a larger direct path to political attentiveness. But the path between education and network centrality is fragmented among occupation, family income, and voluntary group membership, each explaining some portion of network centrality. In addition, nonpolitical organizational membership also acts directly to increase political attentiveness, once more highlighting the importance of shared interests for attributes of political engagement. Finally, a substantial proportion of the relationship of education to attentiveness remains unmediated by any of the variables in the model.

FIGURE 4.6 Education to political attentiveness: Standardized coefficients from maximum likelihood estimation

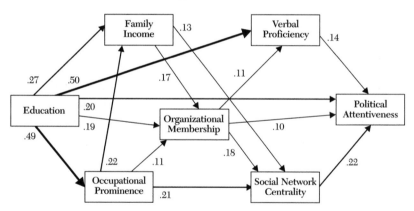

	Standardized Coefficient	Unstandardized Coefficient	Standard Error	t value
Education	.20	.09	.01	6.39
Occupational Prominence				
Family Income	.07	.02	.01	2.50
Organizational Membership	.10	.13	.03	3.65
Verbal Proficiency	.14	.08	.02	4.60
Social Network Centrality	.22	.18	.02	8.36

While verbal cognitive proficiency plays some role, those nearer to the center of society have more incentive to follow politics, because for those who know and are known by the players, attentiveness is both less costly and more gratifying. They are, after all, acquainted with those in the game. But those citizens at the periphery of the social and political world have to work much harder to see and understand what is going on in politics and, therefore, have fewer incentives to be attentive to politics, even when they are, on the basis of their cognitive proficiency, more likely to be politically attentive.

Path Model: Knowledge of Other Current Political Facts

The path model pertaining to knowledge of other current political facts presents us with the most puzzling findings thus far. In fact, this is one of the first instances in which the data are inconsistent with (but not necessarily contradictory to) the general argument. According to the argument, knowledge of other current political facts, such as the relative size of major governmental programs, which political party controls the U.S. Congress, who supported primary election reform, and how old one has to be to vote, should be important for the pursuit of individual interests as well as the preservation of a democratic polity. The point is simple: this kind of operational information is critical to understanding the lay of the political land and to acting in pursuit of political goals. Because verbal cognitive proficiency is the main explanatory link between education and knowledge of democratic principles, and network centrality is the most important intervening factor for the ability to identify incumbents, both intervening variables were expected to play major roles in explaining the relationship between education and this third type of knowledge.

FIGURE 4.7 Education to knowledge of other current political facts: Standardized coefficients from maximum likelihood estimation

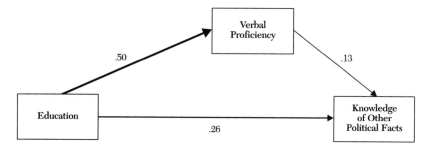

	Standardized Coefficient	Unstandardized Coefficient	Standard Error	*t* value
Education	.26	.10	.01	7.69
Occupational Prominence	.09	.05	.02	3.07
Family Income				
Organizational Membership				
Verbal Proficiency	.13	.06	.02	4.02
Social Network Centrality				

Surprisingly, the data in Figure 4.7 indicate that this is not the case. The impact of education on verbal cognitive proficiency plays the only substantial and significant role in explaining the relationship between education and knowledge of other current political facts. Social network centrality has no effect. The pathways from education to this type of knowledge are closely parallel to those for knowledge of the principles of democracy, rather than those for leadership knowledge. Most of the relationship between education and other current political facts is unaccounted for by any of the mediating variables in the model. The meaning of these anomalies will become clearer in Chapter 5, in which we examine the internal validity of our concepts of citizen political engagement and democratic enlightenment by analyzing the pattern of relationships among the seven dependent variables themselves.

5

Confirming the Enlightenment and Political Engagement Dimensions

The analyses in the previous chapter revealed similar patterns in the way in which education influences the characteristics of enlightenment, including tolerance, knowledge of democratic principles, and knowledge of other political facts through the *cognitive* pathway of verbal proficiency. On the other hand, the path models demonstrated a *positional* pattern of the influence of education on characteristics of political engagement, including participation in difficult political activities, knowledge of political leaders, voting, and political attentiveness. The analyses raise the question of the extent to which the two dimensions—democratic enlightenment and political engagement—are observable in the 1990 Citizen Participation data. In this chapter, we analyze how the seven individual measures of democratic citizenship are interrelated and determine whether they form the dimensions recognizable as democratic enlightenment and political engagement. We then test the extent to which the patterns of the influence of education on the individual measures of citizenship are replicated with the overall measures. Finally, we assess the degree of certainty we have regarding the specification of the causal order in the models.

Table 5.1 presents the rotated pattern matrix of principal components analysis of the seven individual citizenship measures.[1] Principal components analysis is a technique for identifying underlying factors that represent the relationship among a set of variables. It identifies

---

1. An oblique, as opposed to orthogonal, rotation method was employed because the attributes of political engagement and democratic enlightenment are correlated. As an additional check, Appendix D documents additional dimensional analyses.

the best linear combinations among the variables and provides a measure, comparable to a correlation coefficient, that describes how each individual item relates to each dimension. There are two components underlying the seven measures, and they together account for more than half of the total variance among the seven citizenship attributes.[2] The larger the loading, the more important a variable is to the definition of the underlying dimension and, in turn, the greater the ability of the dimension to account for variation in the variable itself.[3] Loadings of less than 0.50 are usually considered of little or no importance in identifying a dimension.

TABLE 5.1 Pattern matrix from principal components analysis of citizenship measures

	Component 1: Political Engagement	Component 2: Democratic Enlightenment
Voting	.80	−.14
Political attentiveness	.71	.15
Knowledge of political leaders	.65	.07
Participation in difficult political activities	.66	.01
Tolerance	−.21	.85
Knowledge of principles of democracy	.22	.61
Knowledge of other current political facts	.20	.58

Solution rotated with direct oblimin

Much of our previous analysis has shown that all seven of the measures of democratic citizenship will, to some degree, be correlated with each other. That is, citizens who are enlightened are also likely to be politically

2. The two factors have eigenvalues greater than or equal to 1.0. The first component has an eigenvalue of 2.60, and the second, 1.08. A third component has an eigenvalue of 0.76, well below the 1.0 standard. Component 1 (political engagement) accounts for 37.1% of the variance. Component 2 (democratic enlightenment) accounts for 15.5% of the variance.

3. The loadings from the factor pattern matrix reported in Table 5.1 are the same as the beta coefficients obtained from a regression in which the original items are the dependent variables and the predictors are the enlightenment and political engagement dimensions constructed from the factor analysis. In this sense, the loadings are the partial correlations between the original seven measures and each of the underlying dimensions, while controlling for the other. When the underlying components are correlated, as they are here, the loadings from the pattern matrix provide the appropriate information to evaluate how each variable relates to the components extracted.

engaged. The opposite is also true: those scoring low on any of the seven measures are more likely to score low on all of the others. This is true because a substantial portion of the variance in each of the measures can be traced back to educational attainment and the consequences that follow from it. At the same time, our expectation was that those measures indexing primarily levels of political engagement, on the one hand, and measures of enlightenment, on the other, would be most highly intercorrelated within each of the two dimensions, rather than across dimensions.

The general conclusion of the principal components analysis clearly confirms the existence of two identifiable and separate underlying dimensions. Moreover, the pattern of the loadings leaves little doubt about the identification or interpretation of these components. The first underlying component is centered around four measures—participation in difficult political activities, voting, attentiveness to politics and public affairs, and knowledge of political leaders. We argue that these measures are at the heart of the definition of citizen political engagement. The second component in the table is defined by tolerance for the expression of unpopular political views, followed by knowledge of the principles of democracy and knowledge of other current political facts. There is little doubt that this is the enlightenment dimension. The pattern of the loadings unambiguously identifies and confirms the two expected dimensions. However, it is important to keep in mind that while the two underlying components are identifiable and distinct latent variables, they are not unrelated. Rather, the two are substantially and positively correlated at 0.31, providing empirical verification that the more politically engaged also tend to be more enlightened, and vice versa. At the same time, a correlation of this magnitude also indicates a substantial degree of uniqueness, with political engagement and democratic enlightenment sharing less than 10% of their variance.

While the overall picture is unmistakable, a few of the details are not as we expected. First, and most troublesome for the argument detailed in previous chapters, is the fact that frequency of voting loads only on the political engagement component and fails to show any meaningful relationship to enlightenment. Second, although political attentiveness is theoretically requisite for protecting democracy, according to this analysis it functions only as a by-product of the surveillance maintained by citizens in the pursuit and protection of their political interests. Those with high scores on the political engagement component tend to be particularly vigilant, while those low on engagement report that they are relatively uninterested in things political. This pattern does not hold true for enlightenment, where there appears to be no special tendency for the more enlightened to be particularly attentive. However, this point can be easily over-interpreted, since political engagement and enlightenment are, as we have just observed, intercorrelated. Thus, while there is no direct path to the enlightenment dimension from voting and attentiveness, there is an indirect link by virtue of the association between the two overall dimensions. The failure of voting and attentiveness to actually load on both dimensions does not invalidate the previous analyses; it simply highlights that these two measures are more empirically bound to the other measures of political engagement than our earlier empirical analyses would have led us to expect.

We use a method of oblique rotation of the principal components solution to compute scores for the two underlying overall dimensions. One corresponds to the level of political engagement and the other, to the degree of enlightenment.[4] Table 5.2 shows the correlations between the enlightenment and political engagement components, the individual measures of citizenship, and educational attainment.

TABLE 5.2 Correlations between education, political engagement, and democratic enlightenment

	EDUCATION	POLITICAL ENGAGEMENT	DEMOCRATIC ENLIGHTENMENT
Engagement	.41**		.31**
Enlightenment	.50**	.31**	
Tolerance	.35**	.05*	.78**
Knowledge of democratic principles	.38**	.41**	.67**
Knowledge of other political facts	.29**	.39**	.65**
Knowledge of leaders	.38**	.67**	.27**
Political attentiveness	.39**	.76**	.37**
Participation in difficult political activities	.29**	.66**	.22**
Voting	.25**	.75**	.11**

** Statistically significant at .01
* Statistically significant at .05

4. The regression method of calculating factor scores was used to create these overall measures.

Educational attainment is strongly related to both of the overall measures of political engagement and enlightenment. While the existence of these relationships is hardly news, the correlation between formal education and these multi-item components is considerably stronger than the parallel correlations for any of the seven individual measures from which the two scales are derived. This is an important finding, and it is indicative of the true underlying magnitude of the relationship between educational attainment and the two aspects of democratic citizenship. Dimensional analysis of the sort used to build the summary variables often strengthens and clarifies the relationships among variables by providing a better measurement of the full range of variation in the underlying continuum and minimizing random measurement error. The principal components scales mute the idiosyncratic and capture only what the measures have in common, thereby reducing the forces that act to attenuate relationships.[5] As a result, the dual nature of the individual characteristics of voting and political attentiveness seen in the path models in Chapter 4 does not appear in the principal components analysis.

FROM EDUCATION TO POLITICAL ENGAGEMENT AND DEMOCRATIC ENLIGHTENMENT

Now that we have demonstrated the existence of the two underlying dimensions of political engagement and democratic enlightenment and have built overall scales, we will test the extent to which our model of the two effects of education is supported by the data. We will repeat the analysis from Chapter 4 and estimate the effect of education and the intervening variables on the overall scales of enlightenment and political engagement. Figure 5.1 and Figure 5.2 contrast the results of the path models between education and the two summary dependent variables.[6] The contrast in patterns is striking. How education leads to the overall

5. There are several sources of noise in survey data, including the interview setting, the difficulty of operationalizing and measuring concepts lacking universally accepted definitions, interviewer error, question placement within the instrument, and sampling error, all of which act to lower the signal-to-noise ratio in survey data. It is quite likely that if the sources of error could be eliminated, the true relationship between formal educational attainment and political engagement and enlightenment would prove even stronger than what we now observe.

6. As in the path analyses discussed in previous chapters, the models were estimated with a maximum likelihood method, and only coefficients statistically significant at or above the 0.05 level were estimated. The path models in Figure 5.1 and Figure 5.2 show the standardized coefficients, while the tables below the figures present the unstandardized coefficients and their standard errors for all statistically significant paths.

measure of enlightenment shown in Figure 5.1 is simple to the point of elegance. A significant portion of the original 0.50 relationship between education and democratic enlightenment is explained by the impact of education on cognitive proficiency and, in turn, the impact of this variable on enlightenment. The more educated citizen is more tolerant of the freedom of expression of unpopular political views, more knowledgeable of the fundamental principals of democracy, and maintains more information on other current political facts because of the substantial impact that the number of years of formal schooling has on overall verbal cognitive proficiency. Further, it is the impact of formal educational attainment on increased verbal cognitive proficiency that is the primary linkage between education and democratic enlightenment. However, a strong direct and unexplained path between education and enlightenment remains. The table below Figure 5.1 also indicates that there are two statistically significant, but minor, paths to democratic enlightenment—one of 0.09 from occupational prominence and a smaller one of 0.06 from family income.

FIGURE 5.1 Education to democratic enlightenment summary scale: Standardized coefficients from maximum likelihood estimation

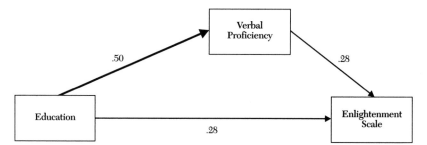

	Standardized Coefficient	Unstandardized Coefficient	Standard Error	t value
Education	.28	.10	.01	8.85
Occupational Prominence	.09	.05	.02	3.07
Family Income	.06	.02	.01	2.35
Organizational Membership				
Verbal Proficiency	.28	.13	.01	10.08
Social Network Centrality				

FIGURE 5.2 Education to political engagement summary scale: Standardized coefficients from maximum likelihood estimation

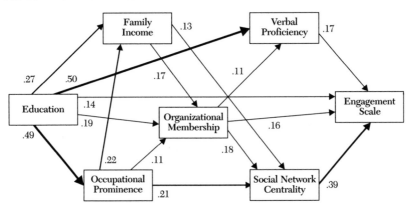

	Standardized Coefficient	Unstandardized Coefficient	Standard Error	t value
Education	.14	.05	.01	5.10
Occupational Prominence				
Family Income	.06	.02	.01	2.59
Organizational Membership	.16	.16	.02	6.36
Verbal Proficiency	.17	.08	.01	6.36
Social Network Centrality	.39	.26	.02	16.29

The paths that lead education to political engagement are fundamentally different. Figure 5.2 presents the estimates for the model predicting overall political engagement. The only path appearing in both models is from education through verbal cognitive proficiency, which plays the main role in enlightenment and a supporting role in linking formal educational attainment to political engagement. However, for political engagement, it is the nexus of the relationships surrounding education and social network centrality that constitute the major explanation for the link between educational attainment and increased political engagement. The role of education as an allocator of occupational prominence, family wealth, and voluntary nonpolitical organizational membership—and the effect of these variables, in turn, through social network centrality—explain a substantial proportion of the original relationship between education and political engagement. It is those citizens with more education who are found at the center of social networks, and it is those at the center who pay more attention to public affairs, know whom to petition, and more frequently act to further their interests.

CONFIRMING THE CAUSAL ORDER OF THE MODELS

The models for each of the seven components of enlightenment and political engagement, as well as the models for their summary scales, describe a process in which education and its cognitive and positional outcomes account for the observed levels of the dependent measures. In presenting the pathways from education to the characteristics of democratic citizenship, the causal order of the outcomes of education relative to these seven components was justified on theoretical grounds. At the same time, however, we acknowledged the possibility of alternative causal orderings. Two of the most vexing of the rival causal sequences involve network centrality and two central measures of political engagement—participation in difficult political activities and knowledge of political leaders. These relationships are examined here, both conceptually and, to the degree feasible, by estimating models with competing specifications of causal order.

For the remaining five of the attributes of democratic citizenship, the direction of the causal arrow from the principal predictor—either verbal cognitive proficiency or social network centrality—is not in question. For the three measures that link education by its cognitive outcome—knowledge of democratic principles, knowledge of other current political facts, and tolerance—there is no feasible potential for these variables to increase verbal proficiency. Furthermore, in the case of political attentiveness, which is partially a function of verbal proficiency, the likelihood of ambiguity in terms of the causal ordering is also very small. Paying attention to politics in the media may potentially increase one's vocabulary, but it is far more plausible that those who pay attention to politics have more extensive vocabularies because they tend to read more—a tendency likely owing to higher levels of formal education.

Similarly, in the case of two of the four components of political engagement that are driven primarily by social network centrality, the direction of causality is also unambiguous. Neither attention to politics nor voting can reasonably be thought of as activities that can increase the number of political and media figures who know or recognize individual citizens. However, for the other two components of political engagement—participation in difficult activities and knowledge of political leaders—there is potential ambiguity regarding the causal order between these two dependent variables and the intervening variable of being known or recognized by political leaders and media figures, which serves as our measure of social network centrality. In the case of these two components, it is plausible that the causal direction of the relationships could be reversed, or at least reciprocal. In order to justify and confirm the causal order of social network centrality preceding both participation in difficult political activities and knowledge of political leaders, we will examine some additional issues and evaluate an alternative specification.

Causal Order: Social Network Centrality and Participation in Difficult Political Activities

Participation in difficult political activities is at the heart of our measurement of political engagement and includes contacting public officials, working in political campaigns, attending meetings of local boards and councils, and taking part in informal political activity in the community. Participating in any of these activities might result in a political leader coming to know someone or at least recognizing his or her name. Therefore, the way in which social network centrality is measured in the 1990 Citizen Participation Study creates the potential for overlap with the measure of participation. In addition, it is also possible that engaging in political activity may lead to an enhanced position within the social network. The implication of both of these observations is that there may be a reciprocal, rather than recursive, relationship between social network position and participation.

Because the data used to estimate the models are cross-sectional, it is not possible to determine whether social network position at a given point in time leads to a certain level of political activity that, in turn, enhances social network centrality. Observing such a process at work would require repeated interviewing of respondents over time or the pooling of numerous repeated cross-sectional surveys. While not completely conclusive, alternative model specifications can be examined and their relative efficacy assessed. The resulting patterns can help lend support to one model specification over competing ones. In estimating all of the models presented thus far, each characteristic of citizenship was treated as a dependent variable with respect to everything that was considered causally prior, and as an independent variable with respect to everything that followed. This left-to-right causal sequence, shown in the path diagrams, means that no causal arrows point backward. Models of this type are described as recursive. To estimate the extent to which there is a simultaneous relationship between social network centrality and the performance of difficult political acts, a causal pathway must be added that represents the backward path from political participation to social network centrality. This specification is a nonrecursive model. The two models can then be compared by evaluating the magnitude of the coefficients and the overall fit of the model to the data for each specification.

More specifically, we examine an alternative model in which a reciprocal path between network centrality and political activity is included. If this added path were significant, it would suggest that there is a reciprocal relationship between these two elements and that they enhance each other. Were the coefficient for the backward path to actually prove greater than the path in the original recursive model, there would be strong grounds for reversing the order of social network centrality and political activity. Table 5.3 reports the coefficients and the fit statistics for just such an alternative specification.[7] The data show that the coefficient for the original path from social network centrality to participation in difficult political activities is not reduced at all when the reciprocal path is added to the model. The t value is smaller due to the increase in the standard error, but the forward path is still quite significant.[8] More important, the path from political activity back to network centrality is 0 (and not statistically significant), and there is no improvement in the overall fit of the model due to the addition of this parameter.[9]

7. Appendix E presents the full results of the maximum likelihood estimation, including the unstandardized coefficients and the standard errors of the estimates.

8. In reciprocal models such as those estimated here, the standard error is large for the coefficients associated with the bidirectional path. This is due to the inherent collinearity in models estimating a coefficient in both directions between a pair of variables.

9. The value of the chi-square statistic for the reciprocal model must be at least 3.84 less than the chi-square for the recursive model in order for there to be a significant improvement in the overall fit associated with the addition of the reciprocal path.

TABLE 5.3 Recursive and reciprocal models of social network centrality and political activity: Standardized coefficients from maximum likelihood estimation

	RECURSIVE MODEL	RECIPROCAL MODEL
Forward path: network centrality to political activity	.38 (14.8)	.40 (2.2)
Backward path: political activity to network centrality		−.02 (−.1)
Chi-square	9.27	9.22
Degrees of freedom	6	5

t values in parentheses below coefficients

Establishing the true causal relationship between sets of theoretical constructs and verifying that it holds for the measures used as indicators for those constructs is an essential part of model building. Accomplishing this task is always dependent on the strength of the logical arguments that are advanced in support of the underlying theory. Examining alternative model specifications that follow from a different view of how the process functions can provide some useful evidence in support of either the original specification or competing ones. In this case, the weight of both the theoretical explanation of the relationships and the empirical evidence is in favor of the recursive model as originally specified.

Causal Order: Social Network Centrality and Knowledge of Political Leaders

The situation with regard to leadership knowledge and network centrality is not as clear as that for participation in difficult political activities. Given the way in which social network centrality is conceptualized in the theoretical discussion, it must be causally prior to the acquisition of specific political information, such as knowing the names of current political leaders. The potential ambiguity with respect to the causal sequence of concern here, however, stems not from a lack of clarity within the theory underlying the models presented, but from the manner in which these two measures were operationalized in the 1990 Citizen Participation Study. Social network position represents here the relative location of an individual as either closer to or farther from the center of the political stage. Ideally, network position would be measured by studying the flow of communications to see who knows what and how they came to possess that information. Clearly, some individuals are more central to the process of communication than others and therefore know more and know it sooner. They are also able to influence the subsequent flow of information and, to a degree, modify the content.

As we argued in Chapter 3, measuring a characteristic such as social network position by actually tracking the flow of messages is not feasible when working with national survey data. Our best approximation is based on a set of survey questions asking respondents to report whether people in various elite positions within government and the media would recognize them or their names. This measure serves to differentiate people in terms of their location with respect to the center of the social network. Because of the way in which network centrality is measured, there may be some overlap between it and the measure of knowledge of political leaders, because the latter is based upon correctly identifying the names of some of the same political leaders used in the construction of the network position measure. Therefore, it is reasonable to argue that if a political leader recognized you or knew your name, you would be more likely to know his or her name. This leads to the potential for reciprocal or reverse causation.

We repeat the same process used in the previous nonrecursive analysis for network centrality and political participation. If the reciprocal model here is more appropriate than the recursive model, the added path should have a significant coefficient associated with it, and the overall fit of the model should improve significantly. If this revised model is a better representation of the data, one would also expect that the chi-square measure of model fit would be significantly reduced.[10] The results of the model comparison are shown in Table 5.4.[11] A comparison of the path coefficients shows that the original coefficient between network centrality and knowledge of political leaders drops from 0.30 to 0.18 when the reciprocal path is added to the model. Nevertheless, this forward coefficient remains significant. The pathway from knowledge of political leaders back to network centrality does not attain statistical significance even though it is only slightly smaller in size (0.14). In terms of the overall fit of the two

10. By estimating an additional path, one additional degree of freedom is utilized.
11. See Appendix E for the unstandardized coefficients and the standard errors of the estimates for this model.

models, adding the reciprocal path between network position and knowledge of leaders does not result in an improved model. The decrease in the chi-square is not large enough to be a significant improvement, given the change in degrees of freedom. Given this outcome, we conclude that the original recursive model is a better fit to the data. At the same time, the similarity in the size of the two pathways in the reciprocal and recursive models suggests that there is some overlap in the two measures used to operationalize network centrality and leadership knowledge.

TABLE 5.4 Recursive and reciprocal models of social network centrality and knowledge of political leaders: Standardized coefficients from maximum likelihood estimation

	RECURSIVE MODEL	RECIPROCAL MODEL
Forward path: network centrality to knowledge of political leaders	.30 (11.2)	.18 (2.1)
Backward path: knowledge of political leaders to network centrality		.14 (1.7)
Chi-square	10.62	8.42
Degrees of freedom	6	5

t values in parentheses below coefficients

The analysis demonstrates that there is no backward arrow from participation in difficult political activities to social network centrality but that there may be a backward path from knowledge of leaders to social network centrality. While there may be some reciprocal causation, it does not diminish the main argument that education influences the characteristics of political engagement through positional outcomes rather than the cognitive outcome of verbal proficiency.

CONCLUSION

We began in Chapter 2 by introducing the concept of enlightened political engagement and detailed our expectations about how each of the seven specific measures of democratic citizenship relates to the ability to pursue and protect political interests (political engagement). We also discussed how each measure relates to the belief that the long-term well-being of the individual, as well as the community, is best served by the promotion and preservation of a democratic polity (democratic enlightenment). We then demonstrated that education is substantially correlated with all of these measures at surprisingly similar magnitudes, given the diversity of their content and the distinctiveness of the measurements. In Chapter 3, we examined the two major prepolitical outcomes of educational attainment—verbal cognitive proficiency and social network centrality—and hypothesized about how each of these differentially links education to political engagement and democratic enlightenment. We traced the paths from formal educational attainment through occupational prominence, family income, and nonpolitical voluntary associational memberships to verbal proficiency and social network centrality. We then demonstrated that these two major outcomes of education are independent and uncorrelated. In Chapter 4, we used path analyses to confirm that the pathway from education to the individual measures of political engagement operates primarily through social network centrality, while verbal cognitive proficiency is the fundamental link between education and the attributes of democratic enlightenment. In this final chapter of Part I, we confirmed the enlightenment and political engagement dimensions in the data and tested the extent to which education influences the overall measure of political engagement through social network centrality and the extent to which it influences the overall measure of enlightenment through verbal proficiency. While the 1990 data have taken us a long way indeed, they—like any cross-sectional data—can take us no further in our analysis of how educational attainment influences democratic citizenship.

Part Two

Education and Citizenship in the
United States, 1972–1994

6

Reconceptualizing
Educational Effects

In Part I, we provided both a theoretical model and empirical evidence to answer the question of how education affects democratic citizenship. We now draw upon what we learned from the cross-sectional analysis and ask the following questions: What happens to the average levels of citizenship behaviors, attitudes, and cognitions in the population when levels of education change over time? What would the two distinct models that we developed from the cross-sectional analysis predict about levels of enlightenment and political engagement over time when aggregate levels of educational attainment change?

In political science, the prevailing model holds that formal educational attainment has an overwhelmingly positive influence on what individuals do in politics, how they think about politics, and what citizens know about political life.[1] Education is the most important explanatory variable in analyses of individual-level political behavior. Philip Converse's characterization of the effect of formal education as the "universal solvent" in what he terms a "simple education-driven model," is in essence the dominant, and in fact the only, causal model, which we term the "absolute education model" (AEM).[2] According to the AEM, formal education works as an additive mechanism. The higher the level of education, the greater the amount of political behavior or cognition.

---

1. See, for example, Lazarsfeld et al., 1944; Berelson et al., 1954; Lane, 1959; Campbell et al., 1960; Verba and Nie, 1972; Wolfinger and Rosenstone, 1980; Rosenstone and Hansen, 1993; and Verba, Schlozman, and Brady, 1995.

2. Converse, 1972.

According to this prevailing view, not only is education highly correlated with a wide range of citizenship characteristics in individual cross-section surveys, but the relationship remains strong and invariant over time. Taken together, the findings imply that we should expect these political attributes to rise at a level commensurate with the increase in levels of formal education among individuals in the population, holding other variables constant.[3] As formal education increases, so should citizen participation in political activities, interest in politics, political knowledge, and tolerance. Extending the argument of the AEM over time implies that increases in education in the population should drive a similar increase in levels of democratic citizenship. Likewise, if educational levels decline over time, the absolute education model predicts a decrease in average rates of political engagement and enlightenment.

However, the evidence from the very same surveys that show dramatic increases in formal education also documents the decline or stagnation over time in many of the citizenship characteristics for which education has such a positive, strong, and consistent relationship. The empirical inadequacy of the AEM in explaining change over time for a whole range of characteristics of democratic citizenship appears obvious; for certain of the characteristics, the absolute education model applied to data predicts change in the dependent variable in the wrong direction.

How can it be that in cross-sections, formal education is so strongly related to the citizenship characteristics of political engagement, but that over time, the rates at which citizens participate and know their leaders, and so on, are stagnant or decreasing at the aggregate level? This apparent incongruity is far from a novel observation; some 20 years ago, Converse puzzled over the opposite directions in which formal education and political efficacy were going.[4] This puzzle is also at the core of Richard Brody's 1978 classic research on political participation, in which he begins by identifying formal education as the critical explanatory variable for citizen participation: "Under the rigors of mul-

---

3. While Verba, Schlozman, and Brady (1995) conceptualize and estimate their explanatory model of participatory behavior with an absolute measure of education, they argue that the resource model does not also imply that participation will grow along with educational attainment. "We should make clear that, in placing education at the center of the understanding of participation and in specifying its multiple effects of activity, we are not arguing that aggregate changes in the level of education of the population will be associated with commensurate changes in the aggregate level of participation." Verba, Schlozman, and Brady, 1995, p. 436.

tivariate analysis only education appears to be related to rates of participation across the full range of its variation."[5] Brody goes on to show
that while levels of education in the population are increasing, voter
turnout is decreasing.

> "[O]ver the past quarter-century, the proportion of the population
> continuing on to post-secondary education has doubled. In light of this
> development and the manifest relationship between education and
> participation, the steady decline in turnout since the 1960s is all the
> more remarkable."[6]

The standard analytic response to the puzzle has been to search for
other factors—not directly related to or caused by formal education—
to explain the decline or stagnation. The task is to identify those factors
that are powerful enough to overwhelm the positive effects of increasing educational attainment and result in the decline or stasis in political engagement over time. This is a difficult task indeed because
education is typically the single most powerful explanatory variable in
the model. Political scientists have used over time survey data to make
compelling arguments that despite increasing levels of education,
voter turnout has been declining steadily as a result of declining partisan affiliation, lower political efficacy, higher alienation, the decline of
local communities, and demographic changes in the population, such
as generational effects.[7] In addition, Rosenstone and Hansen, in an
exhaustive analysis of electoral and governmental participation since
the mid-twentieth century, identify the heretofore underutilized concept of political mobilization to help to explain the decline in political
activity over the time period. It is clear that other factors, in addition to

---

4. See Converse, 1972. Interestingly, while he identifies the incongruity of the two
trends over time and suggests the possibility that efficacy is influenced, *not* by what he calls
an "education-driven" model but by a "relative pecking order" model, he nevertheless con-
cludes that subsequent increases in education will also produce increases in efficacy (the
"education-driven" model). "All that is known with certainty is that the educational level of
the electorate has been increasing rapidly and must continue to do so for decades into the
future. Less certain, but highly probable, is that this increase will keep upward pressure on at
least the personal-competence component of political efficacy, along with manifestations of
political attentiveness and citizen participation" (Converse, 1972, p. 336).

5. Brody, 1978, p. 295.

6. Brody, 1978, p. 296.

7. See Cassel and Luskin, 1988; Abramson and Aldrich, 1982; Shaffer, 1981; and Teixeira, 1987, 1992. See Miller, 1992, for an important analysis of generational effects in
explaining the puzzle.

education, are relevant in a causal model explaining changes in political engagement over time.[8]

Despite the differences in conceptual approaches, data sources, and statistical analyses among many of these studies, a single model of the impact of education remains. Education is always treated theoretically in absolute terms and operationalized by years of educational attainment.[9] No one challenges the basic premise that more years of formal educational attainment necessarily imply more regular voting, more knowledge, or more attentiveness. The absolute education model continues to predominate among explanations of the effect of education on attributes of political behavior despite the continuing over time evidence to the contrary. Our findings in Part I lead us to question the AEM. Social network centrality, the critical intervening variable linking education to political engagement, is a positional outcome of education. Aggregate levels of education can change, but the number and rank of seats in the political theater are fixed, suggesting some type of sorting model rather than a simple additive model such as the AEM.

Our criticism of the AEM actually begins with the set of assumptions about the nature of the *dependent* variable. The absolute education model has its origins in a popular conception of democracy and citizenship. It is often argued that a higher incidence of the practice of democratic citizenship among individual citizens—whether it means taking part in the democratic process by participating in political activities, demonstrating an interest in political phenomena, or adhering to democratic values—is a good thing for democracy. More participation, more knowledge, and more tolerance are frequently invoked as normative goals for democracy. While there is much disagreement regarding the minimum qualifications for those who are allowed to engage in self-rule, most would agree that a substantial amount of citizen engagement is a necessary condition for a viable democracy.

---

8. In modeling the importance of education to democratic citizenship in the statistical analyses that follow, we account for as many of these factors as the data permit. These structural and contextual factors are important in helping to explain why political engagement has stagnated or decreased over time. However, the central concern of this second part of the book is to sort out the impact of changes in educational attainment on political engagement and democratic enlightenment. As important as these additional factors may be, they cannot overwhelm the strong and direct influence of education.

9. Instead of an interval-level measure of educational attainment of actual years of formal education completed, most analyses include a categorical measure of educational attainment, differentiating between those with some high school education, high school graduates, and college graduates, for example.

But what are the upper boundaries of the characteristics of citizen political engagement? What is the maximum proportion of the polity who can write letters to their elected officials or express interest in politics and public affairs? What are the practical limits on the percentage of the citizenry who will give campaign contributions or be knowledgeable of the names of their elected officials? Interestingly, these questions are rarely raised in contemporary empirical and quantitative scholarship in American political behavior, despite its objective to both measure exactly those proportions and explain why so many (or so few) citizens are active, interested, and knowledgeable. Even though the question of the practical limits of the proportion who demonstrate qualities of political engagement is rarely addressed as either a prediction or an explicit assumption, much of the work in the field assumes implicitly that the upper boundary on citizen engagement is 100% participation or knowledge, for example.[10] The argument that belies this assumption is a familiar one. It is commonly argued that, all else being equal, individual-level resources, such as income, or motivational factors, such as interest in politics, will always be positively influenced by that one independent variable positioned causally and temporally prior to all of these intervening characteristics—formal education. More education, so the argument goes, will cause the dependent variable to increase. Pushed to its logical extreme, then, this model would predict no variation in the dependent variable if there were no inequities in income or other resources and if everyone had a lot of education. In cross-sectional data, then, everyone who had a lot of education would be politically active. But what constitutes "a lot of education"?

This observation takes us to the heart of our objection to the singular conceptualization of education in strictly absolute terms and, therefore, to our rejection of the assumption of the essentially unbounded nature of all aspects of citizenship. We argue that certain aspects of democratic citizenship are in fact bounded, or limited, by their essentially competitive nature. The instrumental behaviors and cognitions of political engagement can be seen as more of a zero-sum game, bounded by finite resources and conflict, where one's gain will necessarily be another's loss. Elected representatives can vote only one way

10. This assumption about the upper bound for the dependent variable as 100% should not be confused with the normative position that full participation is the best possible situation for democracy. For example, it is not inconsistent for one to argue from an elitist democratic theory position and still maintain the upper boundary for characteristics of citizen engagement to be 100%.

on a proposed piece of legislation, and bureaucrats cannot regulate to everyone's satisfaction.[11] This competitive nature of democratic institutions—and therefore of political engagement—is based on the notion that conflict and the acceptance and encouragement of contestation are necessary conditions of democracy.[12]

Governmental responsiveness amidst competing claims is a scarce and limited good. Because the pursuit of political engagement entails interaction with representative democratic government, the attainment of interests—the payoff to individual citizens—is constrained by that system. The most obvious constraint occurs within the context of a crowding effect and results from the inability of the system to respond to all competing claims. While congressional offices may today have more staff and resources to listen to constituent requests as compared with 50 years ago, there are nonetheless still 435 representatives and 100 senators. Despite a dramatic increase in the numbers of citizen voices in the population, the number of national legislative offices that can listen is fixed. Likewise, the numbers of federal employees has also remained virtually constant since 1950.[13] When all take part in some form of activity or engagement, the effect on the intended target (government or representatives) is diminished. Similar to the argument made by economist Fred Hirsch,[14] we argue that the value added to the payoff of political engagement in many political activities diminishes as more individuals join in. Just as lounging on the beach becomes less valuable as more sunbathers stake out a portion of the sand, the payoff of communicating preferences to elected officials diminishes when one's letter is one among thousands rather than one among only a handful.

For political engagement, then, the boundaries are limited by an interaction of the maximum capacity of the institutions of government to respond to individual (or group) demands, mediated by the calculation of individual citizens of the costs incurred and benefits gained by such engagement. When the payoffs are clearly limited and the costs in time

11. Of course, if there were complete consensus on a particular policy, there would be no losers.

12. Przeworski (1991) writes: "There is competition, organized by rules. And there are periodic winners and losers....Yet beneath all the institutional diversity, one elementary feature—contestation open to participation (Dahl, 1971)—is sufficient to identify a political system as democratic."

13. Heclo, 1977.

14. Hirsch, 1976.

and energy are substantial, the incentives to become politically engaged—to pursue and protect political interests—are likely to be quite small.

The prediction of the distribution of political engagement under these assumptions, then, would be the equilibrium point of system responsiveness and individual expectations about costs and rewards. Individual action is constrained by the structure of representative democracy itself. The simple illustration in Figure 6.1 helps to demonstrate the point. Along the vertical axis is the expected attention per message, and along the horizontal axis is the number of messages sent. The two curves represent an aggregation of average citizens and an aggregation of governments (levels of government or various institutions and agencies of government). The slope of the citizen curve is positive, representing the relationship between the two axes. As the expected attention per message increases, so too will the number of messages sent; citizens will send more messages if the government pays attention to them. On the other hand, the slope of the government curve is negative. As more messages are received, the less efficient representative democratic government is at processing and responding to those messages. Thus, as the number of messages sent by citizens increases, the less responsive government can be per message.

FIGURE 6.1 Political engagement as bounded

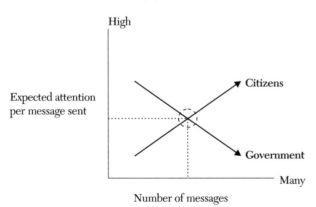

While the exact shape of the curves is unknown, the slopes and the fact that they intersect below full engagement are really the critical issues. The purpose of this illustration is to provide an understanding of how political engagement is constrained by the very nature of the representative democratic process. It is clear that the point at which the two curves intersect—the "equilibrium point"—is far less than the total number of messages that would be possible if all citizens were politically engaged.[15] The structure of the representative democratic system of government and the negative crowding effect on the payoffs from activity make full engagement by all citizens impossible to achieve.

In addition, historical studies of the practice of democracy in both the United States and elsewhere provide evidence to support the fact that citizen political engagement has never approached 100%. Herman Hansen discusses participation among citizens of the Athenian democracy and documents that only a small proportion of those eligible actually took part.

> "Experience seems to show that an assembly of 10,000 or more is too large for genuine debate, and the Athenians could not live up to the ideal that everybody should know everybody else; so Athens was not, in fact, a face-to-face society, and the political community of the citizens could only function *because* out of the 30,000 full citizens not more than 6,000 as a rule, turned up for the Assembly and the People's Courts."[16]

In American examples, Mansbridge, Lockridge, and Kotler found political engagement in local town meetings to never reach full participation.[17]

It is important to emphasize that we are not arguing that formal education creates the bounded and essentially competitive nature of political engagement. More or less education among citizens in a democratic polity will not alter the fundamental structure of competition for social, political, and economic rewards. Instead, we argue that formal education is the main contemporary mechanism by which individual citizens are allocated their standing in the competitive environment.[18] Therefore, while formal education neither constitutes nor creates the competitive situation characterizing certain aspects of democratic citizenship, it is nevertheless critical because education is

15. We draw the equilibrium analogy from microeconomic theory, where the equilibrium point for the price of a particular good is defined at the intersection of supply and demand curves. This equilibrium point is understood to be the "optimal" price. However, we do not argue that the "equilibrium point" for political engagement is the optimal or best place from a normative perspective.

16. Hansen, 1991, p. 60, *emphasis original*.

17. See Mansbridge, 1980, Chapter 9; Lockridge, 1970; and Kotler, 1974.

18. See Meyer, 1977.

the fundamental mechanism by which individuals are sorted into the positional competition characterizing political engagement. And it is this position, or standing, that determines the amount of time and energy that must be expended to both hear and be heard. In short, the cost and benefits of pursuing political interests depends, to a great extent, on one's standing in the social network.

The impact of formal education on qualities of citizenship characterized by competition must therefore be estimated by a *relative* measure of educational attainment that takes into account the context of educational competition.[19] The value of an absolute level of education to political engagement must be assessed in relation to the degree of educational attainment among others in the population. This approach acknowledges the central role that education plays in seating individual citizens either closer to, or farther from, the political stage, relative to those who are already seated and to those entering in the same cohort. The position of one's seat influences the calculus of the costs and benefits of political engagement in a world where the concerns and interests of all cannot be heard and processed. Thus, we hypothesize that education is of *relative* importance as a positional mechanism, where increasingly well educated citizens are forced to compete with each other for access to a fixed number of positions. Economist Lester Thurow makes a similar argument.

> As the supply of educated labor increases, individuals find that they must improve their educational level simply to defend their current income positions....*In effect, education becomes a defensive expenditure necessary to protect one's 'market share.'* The larger the class of educated labor and the more rapidly it grows, the more such defensive expenditures become imperative.[20]

---

19. Conceptualizing education—or other important explanatory variables—in relative terms is not unprecedented; however, the insight is limited. Tom W. Smith (1995) suggests drawing over time comparisons with a measure of relative educational positioning. Likewise, in their study of political socialization, Jennings and Niemi (1981, Chapter 8) separate generations into equal educational attainment strata specific to each generation and emphasize the importance of relative position rather than absolute attainment. In *Equality in America*, Verba and Orren (1985, Chapter 10) distinguish between political and economic equality and argue that it is relative position that counts in the zero-sum game of politics. And while addressing relative position with respect to income, Filer, Kenny, and Morton (1993) provide evidence that a measure of relative, rather than absolute, income is a superior predictor of voting turnout.

20. Thurow, 1972, p. 78, *emphasis original.*

More education does not change the nature of the hierarchy; rather, it simply shifts the baseline upward. As Hirsch argues, "To the extent that education conveys information about the innate or acculturated relative capacity of the individual who has undergone it, more education for all leaves everyone in the same place."[21] Thus, formal educational attainment contributes to political engagement in a relative fashion by sorting citizens with higher levels of formal education into a higher rank than their competitors.

At the same time, however, there are other characteristics of democratic citizenship to which we believe the assumption of unboundedness (and, therefore, the AEM) does in fact apply. Unlike political engagement, characteristics of democratic enlightenment are noncompetitive in nature and are characterized by a positive-sum situation. Citizens are not in competition with each other to understand democratic principles or to embrace values of tolerance. An increase in one citizen's understanding of democratic principles or degree of tolerance does not diminish the amount of these qualities available to other citizens. Thus, for aspects of citizenship that are not competitive, the boundaries are not necessarily limited, and the upper limit for the distribution of characteristics of enlightenment, such as tolerance and knowledge of democratic principles, is not constrained by the structure of the representative democratic system. In Part I, we found that verbal cognitive proficiency was the main intervening variable linking education to characteristics of democratic enlightenment. Unlike social network position, such intellectual skills are unbounded educational outcomes in that there is no inherent competition or limitation constraining their amounts. As a result, we expect increases in education to lead in a positive-sum fashion to increased democratic enlightenment in society. For these qualities of democratic citizenship, the impact of education can be estimated by an absolute measure of educational attainment.

Instead of identifying a single causal process from education to the entire range of citizenship behaviors, attitudes, and cognitions, we argue that there are at least two ways in which education influences democratic citizenship—absolute and relative. The key to solving the puzzle of stagnant or declining political engagement amidst a period of increasing educational attainment lies not only in identifying particularly important independent variables with negative coefficients but

21. Hirsch, 1976, p. 49.

also in reconceptualizing the effects of education. Because there are two independent effects of formal education, there must also be two corresponding models of the effect of formal education on characteristics of democratic citizenship. We term them the *sorting* model for political engagement and the *additive* or *cumulative* model for democratic enlightenment.

At the crux of our argument about both the sorting model and the additive or cumulative model is the notion that the individual-level characteristic of educational attainment must be considered within the context of the educational environment in which the individual citizen operates.[22] For characteristics of enlightenment, the educational environment represents the cognitive sophistication of those with whom one has contact and by whom one is influenced. In the cumulative model, a more educated environment works in a positive direction in its influence on certain characteristics of enlightenment, such as tolerance. For the sorting model, however, the educational environment represents something altogether different and is a measure of the amount of competition for political engagement. As the people with whom one is surrounded become more educated, it takes more and more education to obtain the same relative network position and, thus, the same amount of political engagement. A more educated environment therefore works in a negative direction in its influence on the characteristics of political engagement. What is relevant about the educational environment is not the average level of education of those with whom one is surrounded, as in the absolute model. Rather, the important factor in a competitive system is one's relative standing in the educational hierarchy.

Two predictions necessarily follow from a theory of education as having both absolute and relative effects on democratic citizenship. First, if formal education affects characteristics of political engagement in a relative fashion, then increases in education over time should not result in a commensurate rise in the level at which citizens

22. While we make the argument here for the educational environment in particular, one can extend the assertion about incorporating context more generally and argue that other measures of context—such as Rosenstone and Hansen's elite mobilization measures—are vital to such models using *individual-level* data. As Rosenstone and Hansen (1993, p. 3) argue, "The reigning theories of participation in American politics, amazing as it may seem, do not have much to say about politics. Instead, they trace activism to the characteristics of individual American citizens, to their educations, their incomes, and their efficacy. They assume that attitudes determine behavior. When asked to account for the changes in citizen involvement over the last half-century, these explanations largely fail."

participate in politics, know their political leaders, or are attentive to politics. Rather, as educational attainment rises in the population over time, it should take more education for individuals to reach the same relative network position to support parallel levels of political engagement. For example, in the early 1950's, being a college graduate (an educational standing shared by only 4% of the population at that time) earned one a position near the center of the social network. But having the identical educational achievement in the mid-1990's is worth less because one-quarter of the population now has a college degree. Those with college degrees obtained in the later time period are sorted into a lower network position relative to those with the same educational achievement in the 1950's. This is so because they now compete with a substantially more educated population. Just as a dollar today does not buy what it did 20 years ago, neither does a college degree facilitate the same level of citizen engagement. Thus, individual educational attainment in the sorting model must be adjusted to reflect the level of education of others, given the present competitive value of that level of attainment. The sorting model predicts that a rise in average educational attainment within the population will *not* increase the incidence of political engagement. Second, because we hypothesize that education has an absolute impact on democratic enlightenment, increases in education should have a positive effect on qualities of enlightenment. In its real function, the accumulation of formal education should drive similar increases in verbal cognitive proficiency and, therefore, in enlightenment characteristics. The additive and cumulative models would thus predict that as formal educational attainment rises in the population, so should average levels of enlightenment.

CONCLUSION

Because of the presence of a rich set of intervening variables, the data from the 1990 Citizen Participation Study analyzed in Part I provide a unique opportunity to build two models of the distinct influences of formal education on democratic citizenship. Measures of verbal cognitive proficiency and social network centrality were critical to the development of the theoretical linkage between education as an additive mechanism for the qualities of democratic enlightenment and education as a sorting mechanism for the qualities of political engagement.[23] But this rich collection of variables that enabled us to detect and isolate the alternative pathways between education and the dimensions of democratic citizenship cannot adequately test the validity of the two propositions stated above. Instead, the additive or cumulative model versus the sorting model can only be inferred from the relationships in the cross-sectional data.

Regardless of the care with which models are specified, the validity of the argument can never be fully confirmed when one relies exclusively on measurements at a single point in time. Rather, the models can be tested only when there is observed variation over time in the critical independent variable, formal educational attainment. Thus, the only way to demonstrate convincingly the extent to which education works as a sorting mechanism for the qualities of political engagement and the degree to which it is an additive or cumulative mechanism for the characteristics of democratic enlightenment is through the analysis of data over time. That is, when levels of educational attainment change, does political engagement change in the way predicted by the sorting model? And does this same change in educational attainment influence enlightenment in the way predicted by the additive or cumulative model? While the cross-sectional data from the 1990 Citizen Participation Study made it possible to generate the models, they can take us only so far. Instead, the true test of the theory of education as a *sorting* mechanism for the qualities of political engagement versus education as an *additive* mechanism for the qualities of enlightenment must be made by testing the models with additional and independent data over time.

Thus, we extend the empirical test of the argument about the two distinctive pathways that formal education takes in the development of democratic citizenship by examining the relationship over time using data from several sources. In Chapter 7, we describe and analyze the over time data on education, political engagement, and enlightenment that we will use as evidence of the relative versus absolute effect of formal education. In Chapter 8, we specify and estimate the two models with data from two widely used data collections from the United States: the National Election Study and the General Social Survey. In that chapter, we also test the extent to which the predictions from the

23. In addition, without the numerous individual measures of political engagement and enlightenment (which gave each of the summary measures in the cross-sectional study both high face validity and analytic distinctiveness), it is doubtful that we would have even arrived at the point of exploring the cumulative and sorting models over time.

sorting model and the additive model reflect observed change over time. If a relative measure of education does a better job of both explaining and predicting political engagement over time than an absolute measure, and if the opposite is true for democratic enlightenment, then there is good evidence indeed for our argument about the dual effects of formal educational attainment on democratic citizenship.

7

Education and Democratic Citizenship from the 1970's to the 1990's

Defining and Operationalizing the Measures

In Chapter 6, we argued that formal education has two theoretically distinct effects on democratic citizenship. Education is of *relative,* rather than absolute, importance for qualities of political engagement and works as a sorting mechanism, allocating more central positions in the social network to citizens who have higher educational standing than those with whom they compete for political engagement. Formal education orders the distribution of political engagement among citizens on the basis of a shifting average of educational achievement in the adult population as a whole. On the other hand, education is of *absolute,* rather than relative, importance for characteristics of democratic enlightenment, adding to enlightenment as years of education increase.

The over time consequences of the argument are dramatic. If, indeed, education is of relative importance to political engagement, then changes in the aggregate levels of education over time should have no effect on political engagement, all else being equal. If educational attainment in the population increases over time, more and more education is required to reach the same place in the social network because rising levels of education in the population make the environment more competitive. At the same time, the theory of the dual effects of education predicts an entirely different outcome for enlightenment, where education is of absolute, rather than relative, importance. As educational levels in the population rise, so too does the extent to which citizens demonstrate characteristics of democratic enlightenment. Aggregate increases in educational attainment have an additive effect on democratic enlightenment.

In this chapter, we lay the groundwork for the empirical test of these arguments and introduce the sources of data that we use in the over time analysis. We document the dramatic rise in educational attainment among the American citizenry during the last several decades, as well as over the last century, and then describe in detail how absolute and relative education are measured. Next, we describe the measures of enlightenment and political engagement in the over time data and document changes in them during the period between the mid-1970's and the mid-1990's. In so doing, we show the degree to which democratic enlightenment and political engagement have increased, decreased, or stayed the same over the last two decades.

THE GSS AND NES SURVEY SERIES

To our considerable good fortune, there is an over time data source for each of our dependent variables. In addition, both of these sources contain the information on educational attainment necessary to test the competing models of the sorting versus the additive or cumulative effect of education. Since the early 1970's, the National Science Foundation has sponsored an almost annual data collection at the National Opinion Research Center of the University of Chicago, which has come to be known as the General Social Survey (GSS).[1] This series of surveys is the only continuous monitoring of a comprehensive set of noneconomic attitudes, orientations, and behavior in the United States today. Most important for our purposes, the GSS contains a comprehensive set of questions on political tolerance of the free expression of views by unpopular groups that has been asked consistently during the period between 1976 and 1994. As we argued in Part I, tolerance is a central component of what we have defined as the enlightenment dimension of democratic citizenship. There is a core of 15 tolerance questions in the GSS covering five nonconformist groups and their freedom to express political views in three different social forums. These questions have remained unchanged between 1976 and 1994 and will be discussed in detail later in this chapter. In terms of measures of political engagement, however, the GSS data include only voting in the last presidential election.

Good measures of political engagement do exist, however, in the National Election Studies (NES), administered by the Survey Research Center and the Center for Political Studies at the Institute for Social

---

1. The GSS is conducted under the direction of James A. Davis and Tom W. Smith as principal investigators.

Research at the University of Michigan.[2] With a ragged start-up beginning in 1952, these studies of the voting behavior of individual citizens in national elections have become regularized over the years, and since the early 1970's, NES has asked a reasonably stable set of questions measuring aspects of political engagement. These measures enable us to construct an overall scale of political engagement for all national election years between 1972 and 1994. Included among these items are questions on voter turnout, campaign participation, political attentiveness, and leadership knowledge, which parallel the measures of political engagement in the cross-sectional analysis of the 1990 Citizen Participation Study data employed in Part I. In stark contrast to the GSS, the NES surveys contain no questions on democratic enlightenment as we have defined it.

Both the GSS and NES contain nearly identical questions on the highest level of formal education completed, and each has the appropriate components to construct measures of both absolute and relative educational attainment. In addition, both surveys include a sufficient battery of measures to correctly specify explanatory models of both political engagement and enlightenment. Neither the GSS nor the NES contains the intervening variables available in the 1990 Citizen Participation Study that allowed us to trace the pathways between formal education and dimensions of citizenship.[3] Nevertheless, the measures available in the GSS and the NES data do enable us to test whether education has both relative and absolute effects on citizenship. While the broad range of intervening variables available in the 1990 Citizen Participation Study enabled us to generate hypotheses to test their validity, our study now requires only that the most central independent variable (formal education) and dependent variables (political engagement and enlightenment) be observed and measured regularly over a considerable period of time.[4] Thus, our analytic task has shifted from defining and tracing the separate pathways between education and the dimensions of citizenship to testing how well the theory of the two pathways is supported by the pooled cross-sectional data.

2. The NES is currently conducted under the direction of Warren E. Miller, Donald Kinder, and Steven J. Rosenstone.

3. The analysis in Part I is, however, limited by the uncertainty inherent in drawing causal inferences with cross-sectional data from a single point in time.

4. In addition to the main measures of political engagement and enlightenment and formal educational attainment, it is also necessary to include in the model additional variables that explain changes over time. Many of these are measured in the GSS and NES data. We discuss the specification of the models in detail in Chapter 8.

CHANGES IN EDUCATIONAL ATTAINMENT: 1972–1994 AND A LONGER RETROSPECTIVE

The period between 1972 and 1994 appears, at least at first glance, to be one in which educational attainment is rapidly increasing. Figure 7.1 presents three independent estimates of the proportion of the adult population with at least a high school education across the 22-year period.[5] The solid line represents data collected by the U.S. Bureau of the Census.[6] The data for the other two lines come from the General Social Survey and the National Election Study and are displayed as the dashed and dotted lines, respectively. With some minor variation, the two surveys and the census data all tell the same story: the proportion of the population 25 years and older with at least a high school education increases from around 60% in 1972 to over 80% in 1994. Parallel findings of increasing educational attainment beyond high school also show impressive growth over the same time period. In 1972, for example, 13% of the adult population had obtained a college degree. Twenty-two years later, that proportion had doubled to 26%. Table 7.1 presents the more detailed data from the GSS and the NES.

FIGURE 7.1 Percentage completing high school and beyond: 1972–1994

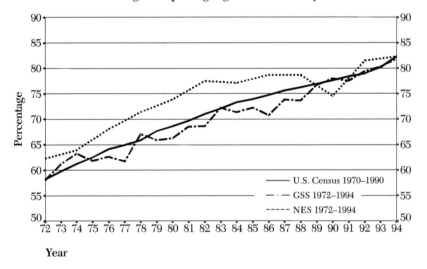

5. As with our analysis of the 1990 Citizen Participation Study data, we include only those respondents who are 25 years and older.
6. *Statistical Abstract of the United States*, 1972–1994.

TABLE 7.1 Percentage completing high school and college: 1972–1994

	GSS % COMPLETING HIGH SCHOOL	NES % COMPLETING HIGH SCHOOL	GSS % COMPLETING COLLEGE	NES % COMPLETING COLLEGE
1972	58.0	62.3	12.7	13.1
1973	61.2	—	14.7	—
1974	63.2	63.9	15.7	14.4
1975	61.8	—	14.4	—
1976	62.6	68.1	16.0	15.6
1977	61.7	—	15.7	—
1978	67.1	71.4	15.5	16.4
1979	—	—	—	—
1980	66.3	73.9	18.0	17.0
1981	—	—	—	—
1982	68.6	77.5	15.8	19.8
1983	72.2	—	18.9	—
1984	71.4	77.1	18.8	17.6
1985	72.3	—	19.0	—
1986	70.8	78.7	20.1	20.2
1987	73.8	—	21.5	—
1988	73.6	78.8	21.0	19.8
1989	76.7	—	21.0	—
1990	78.0	74.6	23.3	19.6
1991	77.5	—	23.6	—
1992	—	81.5	—	23.1
1993	80.3	—	25.8	—
1994	81.9	82.3	26.7	25.1

Source: GSS, 1972–1994; NES, 1972–1994

While average levels of formal educational attainment in the adult population 25 years and older appear to be increasing monotonically, the rise in aggregate levels of educational attainment between 1972 and 1994 is somewhat illusory. Instead of reflecting increasingly well educated newer cohorts, the steady rise in average education in the general population is actually more a function of the departure of older, less educated cohorts. Figure 7.2 displays the average number of years of education over time for those 25 to 29 years old compared to the rest of the population 30 years and older.[7] The data show that there has been little or no change in the levels of educational attainment among the youngest cohort. There is only a modest increase of just over a half-year of education for those 25 to 29 years old over the 20-year period.[8] In the early 1970's, the average young adult had completed just over one year of college, and by the early 1990's, Americans 25 to 29 years old reported completing 13.8 years of education.

FIGURE 7.2 Mean years of education for those under 30 and over 30

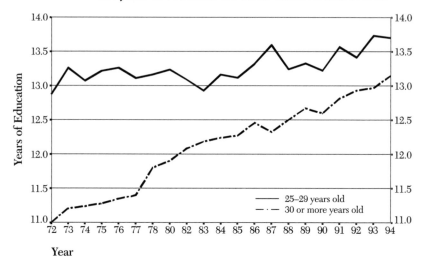

In contrast, while there has been little growth in educational attainment among the youngest cohorts in the population, mean levels of educational attainment for those 30 years and older have increased dramatically. In 1972, those 30 years and older had completed, on average, 11 years of formal education. By 1994, however, the average amount of education among this group had grown almost two full years —to 13 years of formal education. Moreover, the difference in years of

7. The average number of years of education are computed for each year by taking the average of the NES data and the GSS data.

8. While it is too early to tell definitively, educational attainment for this cohort appears to begin to increase again after 1990.

educational attainment between the youngest cohort and those 30 years and older is decreasing. That difference—more than two years in 1972—was reduced to approximately a half-year of education separating the newest entering cohorts from those already in the population. These data by cohort demonstrate that the substantial increase in educational attainment between 1972 and 1994 (documented in Figure 7.1) is not due to more highly educated entering cohorts but, instead, to the replacement of older, less educated cohorts with those who obtained more education in the following decades. With the exception of the small proportion of citizens returning to school later in life, increases in levels of educational attainment have been achieved mainly through generational replacement.

The pattern of a slowed rate of increase in educational attainment among younger cohorts is documented in Figure 7.3,[9] which shows the average years of education for each cohort at the year of educational maturity.[10] For example, citizens born in 1900 reached educational maturity in 1925, and those born in 1950 reached educational maturity in 1975. Average educational attainment has increased for each successive cohort throughout the twentieth century, with those reaching educational maturity after the mid-1970's showing the least growth. In fact, for those who reached educational maturity after 1975, there was virtually no increase in level of educational attainment, while those reaching educational maturity after 1990 show only modest gains. The important point for the pending analysis is that educational attainment among the newest cohorts of citizens entering the population has grown only very modest amounts over the last 20 years. Thus, for the first time since

9. The data in this figure are the average of the GSS and NES data.

10. We assume that citizens reach educational maturity at age 25, when formal educational attainment is complete for the vast majority of citizens. While we do not have information on the precise point of educational completion for each individual, we follow the convention of the U.S. Bureau of the Census in using 25 years as the age by which formal education is assumed to have been completed. Graduate students pursuing Ph.D.'s notwithstanding, a relatively small proportion of the population over the age of 25 is still in school. While the vast majority of American *under* the age of 25 are enrolled in school (96% of those 7–15, 91% of those 16–17, 66% of those 18–19, and 35% of those 20–24), only 12% of people between the ages of 25 and 34 and 6% of those between the ages of 35 and 54 were enrolled in school. (See *We the Americans: Our Education*, U.S. Department of Commerce, Economics and Statistics Administration, Bureau of the Census, September 1993, p. 2). The age at which education is complete is likely increasing over time, as more individuals go on to graduate and professional school. However, this approximation at the age of 25 remains the best estimate for the period between 1972 and 1994.

the turn of the century, these newest entering cohorts have little or no educational advantage over previous cohorts.

FIGURE 7.3 Mean years of education by year of educational maturity

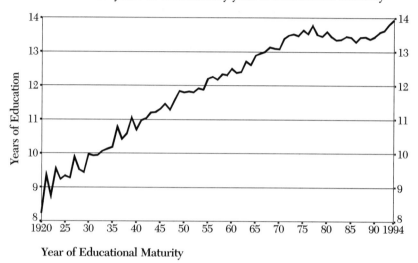

MEASURING EDUCATIONAL ENVIRONMENT AND RELATIVE EDUCATIONAL ATTAINMENT

The patterns of growth in formal education are relevant to both absolute and relative educational attainment. The absolute version of education is simply the number of years of individual educational attainment. While the operationalization of a quantitative measure of absolute education is straightforward, the conceptualization and measurement of relative education depend entirely upon the answer to the question *relative to what*? Recall that education in the sorting model is important because of the role that education plays in placing individuals in relative positions in the social network. It is not the absolute level of educational attainment that matters, but rather the citizen's position relative to others with whom one competes for political engagement. One might consider, therefore, that *relative education* means education relative to all others surveyed in a particular year. However, such a measure of relative education ignores the fundamental issue that the absolute amount of education earned at one point in time may place an individual in a very different rank than it would have at some other point in time. For example, the social network position predicted for two individuals, both with college degrees and interviewed in the same survey, is very different if one of those degrees was conferred in 1950 and the other, in 1990. In 1950, fewer than 5% of the population had obtained a college degree, while in 1990, almost one-quarter of the population was college educated. The occupational prominence, organizational involvement, income, and thus the social network position resulting from a bachelor's degree are entirely different in 1990 than they were 40 years earlier. When many people have a college degree, that degree buys a far lower network rank than when few people are college educated.

A relative measure of education should, therefore, be the ratio between the absolute level of individual educational achievement and the average level of education among those with whom one must compete. For political engagement, the educational environment represents the degree of competition for standing and access to political leaders. Because a citizen's placement in social and political networks occurs at educational maturity, we define the educational environment (the denominator of the relative education measure) as the mean education of those who are the same age as, and up to 25 years older than, the citizen when he or she reaches educational maturity.[11] The relative effect of education on characteristics of political engagement can therefore be measured either by including both absolute educational attainment and educational environment as separate terms in a causal model, or as the ratio between the two. Our analyses in Chapter 8 will employ both of these strategies for estimating the effect of relative education. However, while the educational environment has clear implications for the effect of education in relative terms for political engagement, it should also be pertinent to democratic enlightenment, but for a very different reason. For enlightenment characteristics, such as tolerance, the educational environment reflects the baseline level of tolerant attitudes in the surrounding environment rather than the degree of educational competition.

11. See Appendix F for a description of the educational environment and relative education measures created with the GSS and NES data.

ENLIGHTENMENT OVER TIME: GSS DATA

In Part I, we defined democratic enlightenment as citizen beliefs and cognitions signifying an understanding of and commitment to democratic principles. Recall that the measures of enlightenment in the 1990 cross-sectional analysis presented in Part I encompass both knowledge of democratic principles and questions on tolerance for the freedom of expression by members of unpopular groups. The over time measure of enlightenment from the General Social Survey includes 15 questions gauging political tolerance.[12] While it would have been ideal to have measures of both tolerance and knowledge of democratic principles over time, we do not. One might argue that our over time measure of enlightenment from the GSS is weaker than that in the 1990 Citizen Participation Study, since tolerance is but half of what we theorize constitutes democratic enlightenment. At the same time, however, the over time indicators of tolerance in the GSS are stronger in that there are more questions covering a wider variety of groups, issues, and settings.[13] The 15 tolerance items in the GSS between 1976 and 1994 ask about the rights of members of five groups to make a speech in public, teach at a college, and keep a book expressing their beliefs in the local library. Three of the reference groups for these activities represent perceived ideological dangers from the left of the political spectrum: communists, atheists, and homosexuals. The other two reference groups represent perceived ideological threats from the right: militarists and racists.

Tolerance is perhaps the more important component of democratic enlightenment because it signifies the adherence to a basic norm of democratic life allowing the free expression of ideas. Tolerance represents the voluntary tempering of the pursuit of immediate and short-term self-interest to silence groups whose ideas one disagrees with or finds repugnant. Agreeing to support the expression of these ideas indicates an understanding that one must put aside this short-term interest in order to protect the long-term benefit of protecting his or her own right of expression. At the same time, support for the freedom

12. The tolerance items in the GSS are variations of the civil liberties questions used by Samuel Stouffer in his classic 1955 study.

13. Recall that in the Citizen Participation Study, only 4 of these 15 GSS tolerance questions were asked. In the 1990 study, respondents were asked whether they would allow homosexuals and racists to keep a book representative of their beliefs in the local library and whether they would allow atheists and militarists to make a speech in the community.

of expression and the principle of democratic discussion may also come from a deeply held belief in the intrinsic value of deliberation that reaches beyond calculations of individual rationality. Adherence to the right, and social value, of the free expression of political ideas has been considered a necessary, if not sufficient, condition for democratic deliberation. Tolerance in the mass public has frequently been identified as one of the most important prerequisites for the health, viability, and survivability of democracy.[14]

Table 7.2 presents the proportion of the population in the first and last years of the GSS time series giving a tolerant response for each of the three activities across the five groups. Without exception, the proportion of Americans giving tolerant responses to all of the 15 questions increases between 1976 and 1994. This is true for each of the three venues, as well as for all five groups on both the right and the left of the political spectrum. These findings are not the accident of the two years chosen for comparison (shown in Table 7.3). An examination of the distributions for each of the measures of political tolerance across every year in the GSS time series shows a general pattern of increasing tolerance in successive years.[15] However, while there is an overall trend of increasing tolerance in the mass public across every one of the items, the magnitude of that increase is not uniform across groups. In particular, tolerance for leftist groups has grown considerably faster than tolerance for groups on the right.

14. See, for example, Sunstein, 1993; and Hanson, 1993. The strong principle of free speech, a fundamental aspect of what Robert Dahl calls "the democratic creed," is embodied in the individual and social toleration of the expression of unpopular political beliefs. In discussing the importance of such freedom of expression, Walter Lippmann (1927, p. 401) wrote, "...if we truly wish to understand why freedom is necessary in a civilized society, we must begin by realizing that, because freedom of discussion improves our own opinions, the liberties of other men are our own vital necessity." For the most part, political theorists have assumed that deliberation is good for American democracy and, therefore, that freedom of *all kinds* of speech is desirable. However, there have been significant challenges to the inclusiveness of all speech—in particular, by those who question the context and language of the deliberative dialogue. See, for example, MacKinnon (1993) on pornography as free speech and Matsuda (ed., 1993) on hate speech.

15. Appendix G presents the distribution for each of the 15 tolerance questions for each of the survey years.

TABLE 7.2 Percentage of tolerant responses in 1976 and 1994

TYPE OF INDIVIDUAL	ACTION	% GIVING TOLERANT RESPONSE		
		1976	1994	Difference
Communist	Allow to speak in respondent's community	53	68	+15
	Allow to teach in a college or university	40	57	+17
	Remove book from local library (% saying no)	55	68	+13
Atheist	Allow to speak in respondent's community	62	73	+11
	Allow to teach in a college or university	39	54	+15
	Remove book from local library (% saying no)	58	71	+13
Homosexual	Allow to speak in respondent's community	62	81	+19
	Allow to teach in a college or university	52	72	+20
	Remove book from local library (% saying no)	56	70	+14
Militarist	Allow to speak in respondent's community	53	64	+11
	Allow to teach in a college or university	35	47	+12
	Remove book from local library (% saying no)	55	65	+10
Racist	Allow to speak in respondent's community	60	62	+ 2
	Allow to teach in a college or university	41	44	+ 3
	Remove book from local library (% saying no)	60	68	+ 8

Source: GSS, 1976, 1994

While there is some controversy about whether tolerance has actually increased in the United States since Samuel Stouffer examined the degree of support for civil liberties in the 1950's, most studies confirm that support for the free expression of ideas has been steadily rising in the mass public over time.[16] Closely related to the issues of trends in tolerance over time is the question of its dimensionality. There is a general consensus that a single underlying predisposition for tolerance exists.[17] Our analysis of the 15 political tolerance questions in the GSS data between 1976 and 1994 confirms the findings in the literature of this unidimensional structure. Most impressive in our analysis of the items over time is the constancy of relationships among all of the items from year to year; the structure is invariant throughout the time series.[18]

Because we are confident in both the unidimensionality of tolerance and the constant structure of tolerance over time, we use a simple additive index to measure political tolerance in the over time GSS data.[19] Such a scale is intuitively appealing; observing growth (or decline) in tolerance over time is straightforward. A one-unit increase means that, on average, citizens are willing to permit a member of one more of the five reference groups the right to speak in public, teach in a college, or keep a book expressing his or her political views in the community library.

---

16. Two replicates of Stouffer's original survey (Davis, 1975; and Nunn, Crockett, and Williams, 1978) found substantially higher levels of tolerance in the American public using exactly the same questions Stouffer employed 20 years earlier. However, Sullivan, Piereson, and Marcus (1982) took issue with the approach used by Nunn et al. and argued that attitudes toward groups change over time. They noted the groups used to measure tolerance in both the original Stouffer study and its replicates were all on the political left and argued that this lack of balance led to an overestimation of the tolerance levels of those with a liberal political ideology. To address this problem, Sullivan et al. introduced the idea of content-controlled measures that used each person's least-liked group as the reference for gauging their tolerance. Using this approach they found that there had been very little increase in tolerance levels since 1954. McClosky and Brill (1983) took issue with the approach used by Sullivan et al. of assessing tolerance solely on the response to groups that the individual finds especially distasteful. They argue that this methodology does not take into account that an individual may be willing to tolerate many groups that he or she finds objectionable but still withhold that same toleration from one or two groups that he or she finds particularly offensive or dangerous. Chong (1993) makes the point that when using the content-controlled approach, someone who is not willing to tolerate one particular group— but is tolerant of many other groups—is considered less tolerant than an individual who is only minimally tolerant of any group. Using the same analysis technique as Sullivan et al. (a measurement model approach), Sniderman, Tetlock, Glaser, Green and Hout (1989) found that by eliminating socialists and including homosexuals, racists, and militarists in the pool of reference groups, the relationship of each group to a particular activity (for example, giving a speech) was virtually identical and eliminated many of the measurement concerns raised by Sullivan et al.

Figure 7.4 presents the mean number of tolerant responses to all 15 items in the GSS data for each of the survey years between 1976 and 1994. While there is minor variation and some small perturbations from year to year, the growth in tolerance in the mass public over time is unmistakable. Between the mid-1970's and the mid-1990's, the average number of tolerant responses among Americans 25 years and older has grown by almost two full responses—from a bit more than 7.5 responses to 9.5 responses. While there has been a substantial increase of one tolerant response out of 15 per decade, the rate of increase has slowed in the early 1990's.

Not only has tolerance been increasing over time but its rise has been basically monotonic between 1976 and 1994, and virtually all of the increase in tolerance over time is linear.[20] Documented in the GSS data, this trend over time is shown in Figure 7.4. It is consistent with what would be predicted by a model hypothesizing an absolute effect of formal educational attainment.

17. While McClosky and Brill identify several distinct components of tolerance, they conclude that there is a general underlying predisposition toward tolerance that runs through the individual components. Gibson and Bingham (1982, 1985) emphasize the need to consider tolerance within a specific context to obtain an accurate assessment of a citizen's true level of tolerance. Still, when they examined the nine indices that they constructed, they concluded that there was strong evidence for the existence of a single underlying dimension of tolerance.

18. The analysis of the dimensionality of the tolerance questions with a variety of scaling techniques is detailed in Appendix G and shows that there is a single underlying dimension of the tolerance questions that accounts for approximately half of the total variance across the 15 items. Moreover, this pattern of the relationship among the items does not vary in any of the 13 individual surveys conducted in the years between 1976 and 1994. In addition, each of the 15 questions plays a similar role in defining the underlying dimension of tolerance. There are two additional dimensions of substantive significance. The first measures ideology, with a left-right split among the groups. A second relates to the specific type of activity or venue being asked about—what happens in schools and community libraries versus public speech more generally.

19. Appendix G also compares the relationship between the simple additive index of tolerance and the other scales produced by the various dimensional analyses.

20. In order to determine the linearity of the increase in political tolerance over time, we examined an analysis of variance test. This test yields a linear F value of 244 and an F value for the nonlinear deviations of 2. The analysis of variance test shows convincingly that the relationship is strongly linear. While the statistic for the nonlinear deviations just reaches statistical significance, it is of little substantive importance compared with the overwhelming significance of the test for linearity. In addition, the large number of cases (15,995) from the stacked pooled cross-sectional GSS surveys makes statistical significance relatively easy to obtain.

FIGURE 7.4 Mean number of tolerant responses by year

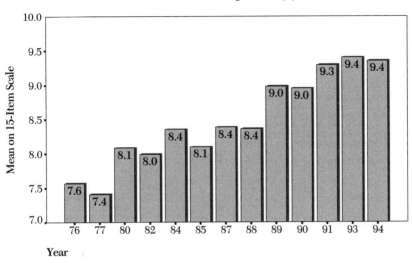

POLITICAL ENGAGEMENT OVER TIME: NES DATA

Our examination of the measures of political engagement over time in the National Election Study data spans a slightly different time period than our study of political tolerance in the General Social Survey data, with the time series beginning in 1972 rather than 1976.[21] NES data are collected every two years, in contrast to the basically annual data collection of the GSS. As a result, fewer time points are observed with the NES data, even though the observations extend across the same decades. In addition, we anticipate somewhat different patterns of political engagement during high-stimulus presidential election years versus the off-election years, when there is less intense media coverage of political events and actors and less strategic mobilization by parties and political organizations.

As with the GSS over time data, we face a similar problem in building an overall measure of political engagement that mirrors the measure that we developed in the cross-sectional analysis of the 1990 data in Part I. This difficulty arises because the NES data include a somewhat narrower range of measures of political engagement. The 1990 Citizen Participation Study includes measures of citizen participation

21. While it would have been most desirable to begin the GSS time series in 1972 rather than 1976, all 15 of the tolerance questions were not asked until 1976.

within and beyond the traditional electoral context, questions on political knowledge of leaders and current political events, and measures of attentiveness to politics. Recall that our conception of political engagement refers to those abilities and actions of individual citizens to pursue and protect their interests in government, reflecting the cognitive, psychological, and strategic enabling of citizens. There are four categories of political engagement measured in the NES data: voting in national elections; campaign activity, including working on a campaign, attending a campaign meeting or rally, and making a campaign contribution; knowledge of political leadership, measured by the ability of citizens to name congressional incumbents and candidates and to identify which political party currently controls the U.S. Congress; and, finally, self-reported political attentiveness.[22]

Table 7.3 presents the data from each of the NES survey years on the frequency with which citizens voted, took part in campaigns, knew about politics, and expressed interest in politics. Several patterns are immediately apparent in the data. Not one of the indicators of citizen engagement shows any meaningful increase across the period. The only exception in the data is the sharp increase in 1994 of voting, knowledge of House incumbents, and knowledge of the majority party in Congress. While the attention surrounding the Republican "contract with America" and the reversal of party control in Congress both mobilized voters and called attention to congressional leadership changes in Washington, D.C., neither campaign participation nor political attentiveness increased in 1994. In the other earlier off-election years, all of the components of political engagement show a pattern of steady decline or stagnation. Likewise, for high-stimulus presidential election years, political engagement has also fallen or remained constant across all components of political engagement, with the most precipitous decline between 1972 and 1992 occurring in political attentiveness. Even though Americans are much more educated, they are no more politically engaged. These trends present a major difficulty for the conventional wisdom of the absolute education model, which would predict an increase in political engagement commensurate with the rise in educational attainment.

22. Unfortunately, there are no measures of political participation outside of the electoral context, such as working with others in the local community. Similarly, there are no measures of political knowledge or political activity for levels of government other than at the national level in the NES.

TABLE 7.3 Changes in political engagement: Presidential election and off-election years

PRESIDENTIAL ELECTION YEARS	1972 %	1976 %	1980 %	1984 %	1988 %	1992 %
Vote in national election	75	74	75	77	73	77
Work for campaign	5	5	4	4	4	3
Attend campaign rally	7	5	7	7	6	7
Give money to campaign	11	17	9	9	10	8
Know House candidate	*	*	36	35	32	33
Know House majority party	66	63	73	58	62	61
Follow politics most of time	38	40	29	28	24	28
OFF-ELECTION YEARS	1974 %	1978 %	1982 %	1986 %	1990 %	1994 %
Vote in national election	57	60	65	57	50	61
Work for campaign	5	6	6	4	3	3
Attend campaign rally	6	10	9	7	7	6
Give money to campaign	9	14	10	11	7	8
Know House candidate	*	36	37	29	26	35
Know House majority party	**	63	33	35	52	76
Follow politics most of time	41	25	30	28	30	30

Source: NES, 1972–1994
* The data on knowledge of candidate for U.S. House of Representatives is unavailable in 1972, 1974, and 1976.
** The question on knowledge of which party is the majority in Congress was not asked in 1974.

An overall measure of political engagement should mirror the pattern and trends in the components of political engagement. Even though voting in national elections, campaign participation, knowledge of leaders, and political attentiveness constitute a somewhat disparate set of behaviors, cognitions, and orientations, they nonetheless form an overall dimension of political engagement. While we estimated several dimensional models of political engagement from the set of components, we settled on an ordinal method of principal components analysis.[23] This analysis reveals an underlying political engagement component that accounts for just under half of the common variance among all of the items. The overall political engagement measure is a standardized scale with a mean of 0 and a standard deviation of 1.0 and was rescaled to run from 0 to 100. Figure 7.5 displays the mean level of overall political engagement for each election year between 1972 and 1994.

FIGURE 7.5 Mean overall engagement score by year

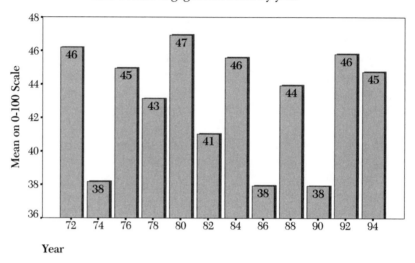

Year

The "sawtooth" pattern in the data between presidential election years and off-election years represents the fact that voting turnout is always higher during the higher stimulation of presidential election years. While political engagement is declining between 1972 and 1990, there is a bit of an upswing beginning in 1992. The introduction of third-party candidate Ross Perot in 1992 generated an unusual amount of interest and media coverage in electoral politics. In addition, overall political engagement also shows an increase in 1994 during the Republican resurgence in national elections. Whether this pattern of increase constitutes a major shift or realignment in the American electorate remains to be seen.[24]

23. We used the PRINCALS technique instead of a traditional principal components analysis to alleviate a problem created by missing data across the 1972–1994 NES data. Missing data are handled by minimizing a loss function that takes only the nonmissing observations into account. The results of the analysis are shown in Appendix G. Instead of including each of the individual items separately, we combined the measures of campaign participation and leadership knowledge into two scales, respectively.

CONCLUSION

The data on tolerance from the General Social Survey and the data on political engagement from the National Election Study show two divergent patterns over time. While tolerance has increased between the early 1970's and 1990's, political engagement during the same time period has for the most part decreased. These two dimensions of democratic citizenship are going in basically opposite directions in the midst of substantial growth in formal educational attainment. How can the trend in these two citizenship characteristics, for which formal educational attainment is the main causal factor, have such divergent trends over time? Clearly, there are important forces independent of educational attainment that push political engagement down over this time period—in particular, the decline in partisanship, loss of community, changing political generations, and elite demobilization of the electorate. However, despite their significance, they alone may not be responsible for the magnitude of the divergence as well as the direction in the changes over time in political engagement versus tolerance. In light of the strong positive relationship between education and both political engagement and tolerance, a single causal model of the effect of education in absolute terms can be feasible only if these other variables not only act to lower levels of political engagement but also have the power to overwhelm the large increases in political engagement predicted by the conventional wisdom of the absolute education model.

24. See Burnham, 1996.

8

Testing Educational Effects
Over Time

In Chapter 6 we identified the absolute education model (AEM) as the explanatory model of the conventional wisdom in political science. This model has become the conventional wisdom in large part because of the consistency with which the main finding is replicated in cross-sectional surveys wherever and whenever they have been conducted. Almost without exception, education is the most powerful explanation for all measures of political engagement. However, when invoked to forecast change over a time period in which formal educational attainment in the population has increased substantially, the AEM predicts change in the wrong direction. Instead of following the upward trend of educational attainment, the various components of political engagement have actually remained constant or decreased over recent decades. The expectation of a rise in rates of political engagement commensurate with increases in the main explanatory variable, compared to the observed reality of stagnation and decline in political engagement has resulted in the identification of a "paradox."

We argue that there is no paradox. Instead, it is an illusion resulting from the combination of an undertheorized explanation of the causal effect of formal education and an erroneous expectation concerning the upper boundary for political engagement. If, as we hypothesize, the effect of education on political engagement is *relative* rather than absolute, aggregate increases in educational attainment should not alter the amount of political engagement in the population. When education works as a sorting mechanism by placing those with higher levels of education in positions closer to the center of social and political networks, more education among citizens only raises the baseline level of education for all positions. As the population becomes more and more educated, an ever-increasing amount of education is required to arrive at the same relative position in the networks that, in turn, act to facilitate political engagement. As the educational environment becomes more competitive, the increasing aggregate level of formal education acts as a *deflator*. In other words, when everyone receives more education, there is educational inflation, with more highly educated people seeking the same number of positions. Thus, the sorting model represents a zero-sum game; what actual years of educational attainment add to the ability and incentive to take part in politics, the competition of the educational environment discounts.

The relative effect of education generates an entirely different prediction from that of the absolute education model. The rate at which citizens engage in politics should not change over time as education increases, all else being equal, and our sorting model would predict a flat line over time, with no upward or downward trend. Any change in the rate at which citizens turn out to vote or take part in political election campaigns, for example, should be due to factors other than changes in formal educational attainment, such as variation in the political mobilization strategies of elites, decline in party attachment, and the disappearance of face-to-face community.

For democratic enlightenment, on the other hand, we argue that the effect of education is *absolute* rather than relative. For components of enlightenment that are cognitively based, such as knowledge of the principles of democracy, we expect a simple additive model of absolute education to predict change over time, and the increase should be proportionate to the rise in education. However, for components of enlightenment that are value based, such as tolerance, we expect a cumulative model to operate. As citizens become more educated—that is, as the educational environment increases—the baseline of tolerance shifts upward. The increasing aggregate level of formal education thus acts as a cumulator, layering the individual citizen's tolerance on top of that which exists in the aggregate. Unlike the sorting model for political engagement, the cumulative model represents a positive-sum game; tolerance is the sum of the impact of actual years of individual educational attainment and of the educational environment.[1] Because tolerance is unbounded by the constraints that limit political engagement, each entering cohort stands on the educational shoulders of those already there. Both a cumulative model and the AEM would predict a rise in tolerance over time as education increases, all else being equal. However, there is one important difference. Because the cumulative model also takes into account the positive impact of the educational environment, it would predict a sharper rise in tolerance than suggested by individual education alone. In other words, the familiar AEM underestimates the amount of change in tolerance over time because it fails to account for the compounding positive effects of an increasingly educated social environment. In this respect, the AEM suffers from the omission of a particularly important variable for understanding over time changes in both tolerance and political engagement.

How can we test whether education works in a *relative* fashion as a sorting mechanism for political engagement, while operating in an *absolute* fashion as a cumulative mechanism for tolerance? The data analysis is complicated by a high degree of correlation among the main explanatory variables in the analysis: individual educational attainment, educational environment, life cycle, and generations. It is theoretically sound to include in the model all of these predictors that are so strongly intercorrelated; indeed, excluding any that belong in the model would result in biased coefficients. At the same time, however, it is difficult to estimate their various effects in the presence of a high degree of collinearity among explanatory variables in the model.

There are two pairs of variables whose strong linear relationship creates this difficulty. Age and birth cohort—the most common surrogates of life cycles and of generations—are an identity in cross-sectional data from a single point in time. It is therefore impossible to identify life cycle versus generational effects, which both have unique influences on political engagement and tolerance. Until recently, this has not been considered problematic, because political engagement was thought to be mostly a function of life cycle phenomena, while tolerance was influenced by generational effects.[2] However, more recent research suggests strong generational influences, in addition to life-cycle effects, for political engagement.[3] Data from a single point in time—even data as rich as the 1990 Citizen Participation Study—are

1. An additive model is a positive-sum game only when educational attainment is increasing. However, if education were to drop dramatically and precipitously, then tolerance would actually decrease over time.

2. See, for example, Verba and Nie, 1972; and McClosky and Brill, 1983.

3. Miller (1992) shows that realignments and dealignments in young adulthood play a role in determining who is more, or less, politically engaged. See also Jennings and Markus, 1988.

inadequate to test the extent to which life cycle (age) versus generational effects (birth cohort) influences citizenship characteristics. Fortunately, pooling the data from the General Social Survey (GSS) and the National Election Study (NES) across multiple cross-sectional surveys conducted as much as 20 years apart assists in one fundamental way in addressing this problem. In the pooled data, age and birth cohort are no longer identical, and their separate effects on the dependent variables can to some degree be simultaneously determined.[4] For example, a respondent born in 1940 and interviewed in 1972 is 32 years old, but a respondent with the same birth year (1940) and interviewed in 1992 is 52 years old at the time of the interview.

While the pooling of 20 years of repeated cross-section studies aids substantially in identifying life cycle and generational effects, it does not eliminate a second major obstacle—the near-perfect correlation between year of birth and the educational environment variable. The year of birth and the mean educational environment are strongly correlated because both have increased monotonically between the turn of the century and the 1990's. However, this relationship is a historical accident, since there is no reason that these two variables need be so strongly associated. For example, if the Great Depression had not ended by World War II, but instead had lasted another decade, levels of educational attainment in the population might have remained flat or even declined in the period following, thereby reducing the correlation between the year of birth and the mean educational environment. In fact, some reduction in the parallel upward movement of these two variables has actually begun to occur among those born after World War II, because educational attainment has remained constant. The departure of older, less educated cohorts is now mainly responsible for the continuing increases in the educational environment. If this trend continues over the next decade, we will see a sharp reduction in the degree of correlation between the educational environment and year of birth. For the respondents in our pooled surveys, however, the two variables are correlated at a very high level.

---

4. Pooling cross-sectional data from surveys conducted over a span of years has proven to be a particularly powerful way to separate age, period, and cohort effects. APC models typically use pooled cross-sectional data to isolate life cycle (age), period, and cohort effects, and the identification problems they face are similar to those we encounter with the pooled GSS and NES cross-sectional data. See, for example, Mason and Fienberg (eds.), 1985.

In this chapter, we take several steps to test our theory that formal education has both relative and absolute effects, using pooled cross-sectional data from the National Election Study and the General Social Survey over the past two decades. A first step is to compare a set of ordinary least squares regression estimations predicting political engagement and tolerance with the absolute and relative measures of education introduced in Chapter 7. If we are right, the measure of relative educational attainment should be a stronger predictor of political engagement than the absolute measure, and the reverse should be true for tolerance. However, because it does not take into account factors exogenous to education that affect political engagement and tolerance, this first step is an incomplete test. Our next step is to estimate a set of fully specified models predicting the two dimensions of citizenship. In these models, measures of both individual educational attainment and the educational environment will be included to assess the extent to which the latter works as a *deflator* for political engagement and as a *cumulator* for tolerance. A third and final step is to examine the extent to which the fully specified sorting model of relative education for political engagement and the cumulative model of absolute education for tolerance approximate actual changes in these citizenship characteristics over time. By comparing observed change over time in political engagement and tolerance with the values predicted by our sorting and cumulative models versus the AEM, we can evaluate whether our effort to reconceptualize the causal effect of education has been worthwhile.

It is crucial to emphasize from the outset that while we analyze the over time GSS and NES data on tolerance and political engagement, it is *not* our objective to explain the observed changes over the last two decades. Unlike the various compelling explanations for why characteristics of political engagement, such as voting or political attentiveness, are either decreasing or remaining constant over time despite increases in educational attainment, our model is not intended to explain the trend itself.[5] The sorting model and the cumulative model do not address explicitly the important questions of how political events, the erosion of the strength of political parties, the evolution of the mass media, the decline of community, or other sociological trends that are exogenous to changes in education have pushed tolerance and political engagement up or down over the last two decades. Rather,

5. See, for example, Rosentone and Hansen, 1993; Miller, 1992; Putnam, 1995a; Teixeira, 1987, 1992; Cassell and Luskin, 1988; and Abramson and Aldrich, 1982.

our goal is to isolate and explain the *structural relationship* between formal education and the two dimensions of citizenship. Regardless of whether political engagement is going up, down, or remaining constant, the structural coefficients in the sorting model should apply. Exactly the same should be true for the coefficients on the education variables in the model predicting tolerance.

The issue of the trends in the dependent variables is relevant here because the expectation of the direction is derived from the implications of a theory of how education influences citizenship. Furthermore, we cannot definitively isolate the structural influence of education on either political engagement or tolerance without controlling for their trends over time. We accomplish this "de-trending" by adding dummy variables for the year of survey to the explanatory models.[6] We include these controls to account for the effects of other independent factors responsible for the changes over time in political engagement and tolerance that are exogenous to formal educational attainment and thus not picked up by other independent variables included in the model. If these exogenous factors are left unaccounted for, their omission might bias the estimated coefficients on the two education variables. For example, in dependent variables that trend upward over time (mirroring educational attainment), the coefficient for absolute education will be inflated without controls for the trend.

TESTING THE SIMPLE MODELS

We begin this chapter with a comparison among ordinary least squares (OLS) regression estimates predicting political engagement and tolerance alternately with the absolute and relative measures of education. In these regressions, we control for observed changes over time in the citizenship variables by including dummy variables for the years in which the surveys were conducted so that we can observe how absolute and relative educational attainment affect political engagement and tolerance independent of the over time trends. If our hypotheses are correct, then these regressions should show that the measure of relative educational attainment is a superior predictor of political engagement

---

6. For the 13 GSS cross-sectional surveys between 1976 and 1994, we include 12 dummy variables for all surveys conducted after the reference year of 1976. For the 12 NES surveys between 1972 and 1994, we include 11 dummy variables for surveys conducted after the reference year of 1972.

and that the absolute measure should prove the stronger predictor for tolerance, a characteristic of enlightenment. Absolute education is measured by the highest year of education attained. Relative education is the ratio between that variable and the educational environment measure, which is the mean years of educational attainment for the population in the year that the respondent reached 25 years of age.

Table 8.1 displays the results of these estimations.[7] The findings clearly support our central hypotheses. For the two models estimated for political engagement, the second model, which includes the relative education measure, has a larger coefficient (0.44 compared to 0.40). In addition, the data fit the model better, with an R^2 four percentage points higher than in the model that includes the absolute measure of formal educational attainment. The results are the opposite, and even stronger, for the tolerance equations. The absolute measure of education is a much stronger predictor of tolerance than the relative measure, and the model fit produces an R^2 ten percentage points higher than in the model that includes the relative education measure.

TABLE 8.1 **Impact of absolute and relative education on political engagement and tolerance: Standardized OLS regression coefficients**

	MODEL 1			MODEL 2		
	Absolute Education	t value	Adj. R^2	Relative Education	t value	Adj. R^2
Political engagement	.40	61.9	.17	.44	71.4	.21
Tolerance	.46	65.5	.22	.33	44.3	.12

Source: NES, 1972–1994; GSS, 1976–1994

While appealing in their simplicity and encouraging in the strength and clarity of the resultant findings, these models are only a starting point and are not definitive tests of our hypotheses. Even though the year-of-survey dummy variables account for the factors that have produced changes in political engagement and tolerance over time, the

7. In order to ease comparison across political engagement and tolerance, the overall measures were rescaled to have a range from 0 to 100 for the analysis shown in Table 8.1. In addition, because the two education measures have such different scales, the standardized coefficients are shown in this table. The unstandardized coefficients, along with the estimates for the year-of-survey dummy variables are documented in Appendix H.

simple models do not contain any of the factors that independently influence levels of tolerance or political engagement. The omission of these factors may therefore bias the coefficients on the education variables in the simple models. Some obvious examples of additional important independent variables are gender and strength of partisanship for political engagement, and religious fundamentalism and political conservatism for the tolerance measure.

Even more important for this analysis is the fact that the simple models do not acknowledge the potentially confounding effects of life cycle and generations, both of which have been documented as determinants of the two dimensions of citizenship and are also strongly correlated with the education variables. Scholars have long noted the importance of political generations for tolerance and the curvilinear relationship between political engagement and life cycle, or age. However, as we demonstrate next, much of the positive relationship between age (as life cycle) and political engagement is actually attributable to the impact that growing educational competition has on political engagement. On the other hand, political attitudes, such as tolerance, have been found to develop by early adulthood and undergo little change beyond that point.[8] However, much of the relationship between birth cohort and tolerance found in cross-sectional studies is actually attributable to an increasingly educated environment, which in turn has a substantial influence on tolerance.

ESTIMATING THE FULLY SPECIFIED MODELS

In this second set of estimations of the relative effect versus the absolute effect of education, we include separately both components of the relative education term—actual years of individual educational attainment and educational environment, which is the mean years of educational attainment among those in the population 25 to 50 years old in the year the citizen reached educational maturity (at age 25). For political engagement, the educational environment variable corresponds to the level of educational competition in the society. For the sorting model of the relative effect of education, this term should be negative for political engagement and all of its components. As the citizens who compete for standing in the social and political networks become more educated, an increasing amount of education is required to attain the

8. See, for example, Alwin and Krosnick, 1991; and McClosky and Brill, 1983.

same standing. Moreover, if education in relative terms explains political engagement, the product of the estimated coefficient for years of education and its increase over the 20-year period should be *discounted* by the product of the estimated coefficient on the measure of educational competition and its change over time. In the sorting model, the net change over time predicted by education should be 0.

However, for tolerance, this same educational environment variable should have just the opposite effect. Instead of signifying competition, the educational environment should have a cumulative influence on individual political tolerance. The average level of the educational environment represents the cumulative degree of cognitive sophistication and understanding of the importance of free expression and deliberation. Tolerance should increase in the aggregate as individual educational attainment is reinforced and augmented by the impact of a more educated environment. As such, increases in education over time should have a positive-sum impact on tolerance. The more education the individual citizen has and the higher the education of fellow citizens, the greater should be the overall level of tolerance.

To complete the specification of both the political engagement and tolerance models, we include a series of measures to account for both life cycle and generational effects, in addition to other potentially relevant demographic and attitudinal variables. Based on our review of the literature on the causes of political engagement and its components, as well as the causal factors others have found to influence tolerance, we include as many of these independent variables as possible, given the limitations in the contents of the databases. We begin with the findings for political engagement and then move to the analysis for tolerance.

Political Engagement

The findings for political engagement are presented in Table 8.2. The summary political engagement measure has been scaled to run between 0 to 100 and has a mean of 43 and a standard deviation of 23. Presented in the body of the table from left to right are the unstandardized coefficients, their corresponding standard errors, *t* values, and the collinearity diagnostic for statistical tolerance. Only variables statistically significant at the 0.05 level are reported in the table.[9] The most important finding of the estimation of the sorting model reported in Table 8.2 is the support that it lends to our central hypothesis concerning the relative effect of education on political engagement. As we hypothesized, actual years of educational attainment have an enormous overall effect on political engagement. At the same time, the effect of absolute education is discounted by the amount of competition in the educational environment. In the fully specified sorting model, each year of educational attainment increases political engagement by 3.10 units on the 100-point scale. On the other hand, the estimated coefficient for the mean educational environment—the measure of the competitiveness of the environment—is negative and reduces political engagement by 3.69 units.

TABLE 8.2 Sorting model for overall political engagement: Unstandardized OLS regression coefficients

YEAR OF SURVEY (1972 BASE)	β	STANDARD ERROR	t VALUE	STATISTICAL TOLERANCE
1974	−7.40	.61	−12.0	.51
1976	−0.98	.62	−1.6	.52
1978	−3.26	.64	−5.1	.52
1980	0.18	.73	0.2	.62
1982	−6.50	.73	−9.0	.60
1984	−0.82	.68	−1.2	.51
1986	−7.93	.67	−11.8	.47
1988	−1.75	.71	2.0	.50
1990	−5.96	.71	8.4	.46
1992	1.08	.71	1.5	.42
1994	−0.06	.75	−0.1	.44
AGE AND GENERATION				
Age 25–29	−1.31	.48	−2.7	.64
Age over 75	−4.63	.68	−6.8	.53
Pre-New Deal generation	−3.08	.67	−4.6	.44

9. In the estimates reported in Table 8.2, Table 8.3, and Table 8.4, we include only those independent variables with t values greater than or equal to 2. By retaining only the substantively and statistically significant variables, we keep the degree of multicollinearity in the equations to a minimum. The statistical tolerance for each of the variables in the model is presented in the final column of the table and is a measure of collinearity. When the statistical tolerance is small, it indicates that the variable is almost a perfect linear combination of the other independent variables in the model. Care must be taken in interpreting coefficients for variables with values of statistical tolerance below 0.10.

TABLE 8.2 Sorting model for overall political engagement:
Unstandardized OLS regression coefficients (Continued)

Year of Survey (1972 base)	β	Standard Error	t value	Statistical Tolerance
AGE AND GENERATION (Continued)				
New Deal consolidation	1.14	.34	3.4	.72
Vietnam war and after	−2.00	.49	−4.1	.44
EDUCATION				
Years of education	3.10	.05	68.1	.78
Educational environment (years)	−3.69	.22	−16.4	.21
DEMOGRAPHICS				
Female	−6.42	.28	−23.2	.94
African-American	−2.55	.45	−5.6	.89
Other nonwhite	−5.79	.93	−6.2	.99
FAMILY AND COMMUNITY				
Married	2.61	.31	8.5	.80
Retired	1.89	.48	3.9	.59
Home owner	3.83	.33	11.7	.80
Recently moved	−3.00	.36	−8.3	.89
Never attend church	−3.13	.37	−8.3	.85
Attend church weekly	2.28	.32	7.2	.87
Reside in rural area	−0.66	.29	−2.3	.95
PARTISANSHIP				
Independent of party affiliation	−3.70	.42	−8.9	.89
Strong party affiliation	9.20	.31	29.7	.89
Adjusted R^2	.33			
Total N	20749			

Source: NES, 1972–1994

If education has a relative impact on political engagement, then the net combined impact of these two education variables over the time period we analyze should approximate 0. The sorting model of the relative effect of education predicts no change in political engagement over time. Indeed, the sum of the product of the unstandardized coefficient on actual years of formal education and the change in the mean of this variable in the population between 1972 and 1994 (1.93 years) and the product of the coefficient for educational environment over time and its increase (1.53 years) yield the *net effect* of changes in education over time for political engagement. The change in political engagement due to the growth of educational attainment is 5.98 units (3.10×1.93), while the discount due to increasing educational competition is a virtually identical negative quantity of -5.65 (-3.69×1.53). The sum of these is close to 0, indicating that *changes* in education over time have neither a positive nor a negative impact on political engagement between 1972 and 1994. The sorting model of the relative effect of education on political engagement does indeed produce a zero-sum. While absolute educational attainment has an important impact on levels of political engagement, increases in education over time do not lead to commensurate increases in engagement. This is true because the educational environment is also becoming more competitive, thus requiring more and more education to yield the same amount of political engagement.

It is clear from this fully specified model that, holding all else equal, education influences political engagement in a relative fashion. It is the disparity between the educational attainment of individual citizens as they enter adulthood and the education of others with whom they compete that determines their position in the social network. This placement, in turn, profoundly affects the incentives and costs of hearing and being heard in the political arena. Thus, it is precisely this relative effect of education in the sorting model that belies the paradox of increasing aggregate levels of education amidst declining or stagnant political engagement over time. With the correct conception of the dependent variable, along with the proper theoretical specification of the causal linkage between education and political engagement, there is no paradox to explain away.

The sorting model of education and political engagement reported in Table 8.2 also includes a series of other explanatory variables to ensure that the estimated coefficients for the two education variables are unbiased. While one can never be completely certain that all factors have been included in the model, a walk through the results of the model for the remaining independent variables demonstrates the breadth of its contents and the high face validity of its findings, thereby adding considerable credence to the specification of the model. We include dummy variables for the year of survey to de-trend the data to eliminate a potential source of bias—that exogenous changes over time may be inadvertently assigned to the education variables. Next, we include the life cycle and generational controls that may account for additional sources of bias. This potential clearly exists because several of the dichotomous cohort variables are not only significant predictors of political engagement but are also highly correlated with the two education measures.[10] Increases in aggregate educational attainment are driven almost exclusively by generational replacement, and the educational environment has been increasing almost monotonically throughout much of the century. Even though birth cohort and educational environment are strongly related, the ordinary least squares estimation sensibly sorts out their various effects, and the patterns are consistent with findings reported in the literature. There are three significant birth cohorts: those who came of age prior to the New Deal (born before 1910), during the New Deal consolidation (born between 1921 and 1940), and in the Vietnam war era (born after 1950). All three correspond to periods of documented realignment or dealignment of American voters.[11] Accounting for these generational differences, as well as controlling for the effect of being very old or very young (stages of life that correspond to low levels of political engagement), eliminates yet another potential source of bias in the estimates for education and educational environment.

The sorting model also accounts for possible differences between women and men, and minority and white citizens, as well as differences based on family status, community factors, and political partisanship. As is the case with birth cohort, gender and race are correlated with both political engagement and the two education variables. The results of the estimation, shown in Table 8.2, reflect the familiar findings that women and minority citizens are less likely to be engaged in politics than men and whites. On the other hand, measures that index

10. Only those life-cycle and cohort variables that were both theoretically relevant and statistically significant at the 0.05 level were included in the model.

11. See Burnham, 1970; Nie, Verba, and Petrocik, 1976; and Miller, 1992.

the degree of attachment to family and community, such as marital status, type of community, and strength of partisanship, represent more of a mixture in their relationship to the education variables, although they are all highly correlated with political engagement. Other independent variables, such as home ownership, are positively related to educational attainment, but the remaining variables have only a weak relationship to the education variables. In fact, two of the most powerful predictors of political engagement—church attendance and strength of partisan affiliation—show almost no discernible relationship to either educational attainment or educational environment. Collectively, however, this group of independent variables has substantial power in explaining political engagement, and accounting for their effects allows us to be more certain that the estimates for the two education variables are unbiased.

Relative Education and the Components of Political Engagement

Unlike the over time measure of tolerance, which is an index made up of parallel questions, the overall measure of political engagement is composed of a more heterogeneous set of cognitions, attitudes, and behaviors. In Part I, we argued that these components constitute a good overall estimate of political engagement and demonstrated with dimensional analysis that there is a single underlying component binding these seemingly diverse elements. Nevertheless, the question remains as to whether the findings for education and educational environment are replicated for all of the individual components of political engagement—political activity in campaigns, leadership knowledge, political attentiveness, and voting in national elections. Demonstrating that all of these individual components are best understood as outcomes of relative educational attainment would add considerable weight to our theoretical claim that it is relative education that explains political engagement.

The results shown in Table 8.3 provide the evidence. The coefficients for the two education measures are estimated with the same sorting model for overall political engagement used in Table 8.2. Because of the volume of the findings, we present here only the estimates of the coefficients on the education variables, and the full results are detailed in Appendix H. As was the case for the overall measure, each of the individual components of political engagement was rescaled from 0 to 100 to facilitate comparison.

TABLE 8.3 Sorting model for components of political engagement: Unstandardized OLS regression coefficients

	YEARS OF EDUCATION	*t* VALUE	EDUCATIONAL ENVIRONMENT	*t* VALUE
Voting in national elections	3.99 (.10)	40.0	−5.90 (.49)	−12.0
Leadership knowledge	3.60 (.08)	46.0	−4.14 (.39)	−10.6
Political attentiveness	3.42 (.07)	47.4	−4.62 (.36)	−13.0
Campaign activity	1.31 (.04)	32.6	−.68 (.20)	−3.4

Standard errors in parentheses below coefficients
Source: NES, 1972–1994

The pattern across all four individual components of political engagement from the NES data is unmistakable. For voting, leadership knowledge, political attentiveness, and campaign activity, the coefficient for educational attainment is positive, and the estimated coefficient for the level of educational competition (educational environment) is negative. Moreover, each pair of coefficients is approximately balanced. An additional year of formal education predicts an increase in each of the four components, while at the same time, the growing degree of competitiveness in the educational environment deflates the four engagement measures by approximately the same amount.

These findings reflect exactly the pattern predicted by the sorting model and confirm that these political behaviors and cognitions all appear to be linked to education by the relative mechanism. This is even more impressive because these four measures of political engagement present different trend lines over the 20-year period. Voting and campaign activity remain basically unchanged, while both leadership knowledge and political attentiveness have declined rather substantially (with the exception of 1994). Thus, despite differences in the direction in which the components of political engagement are changing over time, the sorting model of the relative effect of education produces consistent results. If a major electoral realignment bringing millions of additional citizens into politics occurs in the near future, the underlying trend lines would be radically altered for the indicators of political engagement. Nevertheless, these alterations should not change the fact that it is the effect of relative, and not absolute, education that explains why some citizens are, and others are not, engaged in politics.

Tolerance

The situation for tolerance and for other measures of democratic enlightenment should prove to be very different. Unlike political engagement, which involves competition to hear and be heard in the political arena, citizens are not in competition with each other to hold tolerant attitudes. Democratic enlightenment comprises values, beliefs, and cognitions that support principles of democratic governance, of which tolerance for free expression of all ideas is a central component. Tolerance increases as citizens become more cognitively sophisticated and capable of understanding the consequences of intolerance, such as nondemocratic governance. Education increases the ability and regard individuals have for rational deliberative discourse as a fundamental mechanism of decision making.

While approximate, the number of years one spends in the classroom appears to be the single most important explanatory variable differentiating citizens as to their level of democratic enlightenment. In Part I, we demonstrated that neither wealth, occupational prominence, organizational affiliations, nor the resulting proximity to the center of the political arena plays a mediating role in the path that formal education takes to democratic enlightenment. Rather, we found that the sole meditating variable is the influence that education has on verbal cognitive proficiency and, in turn, the effect of verbal cognitive proficiency on enlightenment. Thus, unlike its role in political engagement, education should have an absolute impact on tolerance and should increase with each additional year of educational attainment. In addition, the educational environment should play an important role in the development of tolerant attitudes in a democratic society. For the tolerance measure, each new generation does not need to insert and sort itself into society anew, as it does for political engagement. Instead, citizens begin by adopting the tolerant values of those who surround them in their formative years, and tolerance is then augmented in accordance with their own educational attainment. Education thus has a cumulative impact on tolerance.

Table 8.4 provides the results of a first estimation of the cumulative model of the impact of education on tolerance. Tolerance is scored from 0 to 15, representing the total number of tolerant responses given to the battery of 15 questions concerning the venues, groups, and ways in which the expression of unpopular opinions would be permitted. Similar to the strategy used for political engagement, we de-trend the data over time between 1976 and 1994 by including dummy variables for the year of survey.[12] In addition, only the theoretically relevant and statistically significant cohort controls are included in the model. Other variables known to have an independent effect on levels of tolerance, in what has become a substantial empirical research literature, have also been included in the model, including region, size and place of both current residence and residence when the citizen was 16 years old, political and religious orientations, and parental education.

TABLE 8.4 Cumulative model for tolerance: Unstandardized OLS regression coefficients

YEAR OF SURVEY (1976 BASE)	β	STANDARD ERROR	t VALUE	STATISTICAL TOLERANCE
1977	−.28	.16	−1.7	.54
1980	.10	.17	0.6	.55
1982	−.17	.16	−1.1	.49
1984	−.11	.17	−0.7	.54
1985	−.52	.16	−3.2	.51
1987	−.35	.16	−2.2	.47
1988	−.42	.19	−2.3	.61
1989	−.00	.18	−0.0	.60
1990	−.02	.19	−0.1	.62
1991	.23	.19	1.2	.61
1993	.03	.18	0.2	.58
1994	−.23	.16	−1.5	.43
AGE AND GENERATION				
Educational maturity after 1979	−1.02	.11	−9.7	.65

12. As with the political engagement data from the NES, we use the first year in the GSS data, 1976, as the point of reference.

TABLE 8.4 Cumulative model for tolerance: Unstandardized OLS regression coefficients (Continued)

YEAR OF SURVEY (1976 BASE)	β	STANDARD ERROR	t VALUE	STATISTICAL TOLERANCE
EDUCATION				
Years of education	.44	.01	33.9	.63
Educational environment (years)	.92	.04	25.6	.55
Education of parents (years)	.13	.01	11.0	.61
DEMOGRAPHICS				
Female	−.37	.07	−5.5	.96
RELIGION AND IDEOLOGY				
Frequency of church attendance	−.22	.01	−16.8	.85
Religious liberal	.68	.08	8.1	.87
Protestant	−.62	.08	−8.2	.84
Conservative views	−.25	.03	−9.7	.95
TYPE AND LOCATION OF RESIDENCE				
In rural area at age 16	−.66	.08	−8.2	.81
In suburbs at age 16	.40	.12	3.4	.92
Now reside in rural area	−.84	.09	−9.0	.89
In South at age 16	−.64	.11	−5.6	.39
In foreign country at age 16	−1.25	.16	−7.8	.95
Now reside in South	−.58	.11	−5.4	.42
Adjusted R^2		.36		
Total N		14984		

Source: GSS, 1976–1994

The results shown in Table 8.4 demonstrate that both years of individual educational attainment and educational environment have a strong positive influence on tolerance. Simply put, the more educated each citizen is and the greater the educational attainment of those with whom he or she is surrounded, the more likely citizens are to support freedom of expression for many different types of groups under a range of circumstances. For each additional year of education, there is an average increase of just under one-half of a tolerant response. For each year of increase in the educational environment, the model predicts an even more substantial gain of almost one full tolerant response. Parental education acts in the same way, but to a much more modest degree.

The finding that educational environment plays such an important and positive role in determining tolerance is underscored by the impact of the other independent variables in the model. Measures with implications for formative socializing experiences include the type of community and the region of residence at 16 years of age. Here, being raised in the South or outside of the United States shows a negative relationship to tolerance, as does being raised in a rural community. However, being raised in the suburbs shows a positive influence. Current residence in a rural community or in the South also decreases tolerance. In addition, defining oneself as a religious liberal increases tolerance, while frequency of church attendance and being a Protestant decreases tolerance. The only significant cohort measure is for those who reached adulthood after the late 1970's, who appear to be substantially less tolerant, after controlling for all other factors.[13]

The overall findings from this estimation of the cumulative model of the absolute effect of education on tolerance strongly support our hypotheses. The stark differences between the findings from this model and the estimation of the sorting model for political engagement are unquestionable. At the same time, however, the sheer size of the educational environment coefficient—particularly compared to that for individual educational attainment—is somewhat troublesome. Adding to our suspicion is the fact that the only significant birth cohort references those who came of age in and after the late 1970's. Is it possible that some of the effect attributed to educational environment is actually due to the effects of other generational factors unrelated to education?

Recall that there are several fundamental issues that render the partitioning of variance among the independent variables in these education models particularly difficult. First, both education measures are positively and strongly correlated with tolerance. Second, the education measures are strongly correlated with each other. Third, both

---

13. None of the dummy variables of age indexing life cycle effects proved to be statistically significant.

education variables are strongly associated with birth cohort. Most critical for our problem here, however, is that birth cohort (which indexes generational effects) and the measure of educational environment are strongly correlated over the period that we analyze here. Both have increased monotonically every year since the 1890's, the earliest point for which we have data on both measures. As we argued before, this is purely a historical accident, for if the nation had experienced any extended period during this 100 years when educational levels decreased or remained flat, these two variables would be substantially less correlated, and it would be far easier to gain an estimate of the independent effect of each on tolerance.[14]

In the estimation of the model in Table 8.4, we attempted to isolate the separate effects of educational environment and birth cohort by introducing dummy variables for generations. This strategy worked very well for political engagement because the relationship between birth cohort and political engagement is not linear over the century, and we were able to isolate their separate contributions. This is unfortunately not the case for tolerance, where, with the exception of those citizens coming to educational maturity after the late 1970's, all three variables—birth cohort, educational environment, and tolerance—increase monotonically across the century. The task, therefore, is to decorrelate the two independent variables, birth cohort and educational environment, without distorting the underlying relationship of either to tolerance.[15] By including the decade of educational maturity, rather than the year of birth, and by rounding the measure of the educational environment to whole years, we are able to reduce the high degree of correlation between the two measures sufficiently to estimate their separate effects on tolerance, while at the same time preserving their original relationship to tolerance.

---

14. In fact, we have evidence that this may be starting to happen now, but unfortunately for our current analyses, the pattern will not show up clearly for years to come.

15. After experimenting with polynomial transformations without an adequate reduction in the degree of collinearity, we use the very simple technique of reducing the precision of each measure by rounding the educational environment measure to whole numbers and collapsing the birth cohort variable to decade of educational maturity. Decade of educational maturity is an integer ranging from 0 to 8, and educational environment, a whole number from 9 to 13. Despite the fact that we did not change the scales of these measures, these transformations introduce measurement error into the explanatory variables.

Table 8.5 presents the OLS regression estimates from the revised model for tolerance. The only differences between the equation in this table and that in Table 8.4 are that educational environment is now entered into the regression as a rounded integer, and decade of educational maturity has been added to the equation. The substantive findings for all other independent variables are virtually identical, including those most critically affected by the problem of a high degree of collinearity. The estimated coefficients for individual educational attainment, parental education, and the cohort that reached educational maturity after 1979 are all nearly identical in both equations. The degree of collinearity between the decade of educational maturity and the recoded educational environment variable is quite large, with the remaining statistical tolerance under 0.10 for both of the variables.[16]

TABLE 8.5 Revised cumulative model for tolerance: Unstandardized OLS regression coefficients

YEAR OF SURVEY (1976 BASE)	β	STANDARD ERROR	t VALUE	STATISTICAL TOLERANCE
1977	−.28	.16	−1.7	.54
1980	.10	.17	0.6	.55
1982	−.16	.16	−1.0	.49
1984	−.09	.17	−0.6	.54
1985	−.50	.16	−3.1	.52
1987	−.34	.16	−2.1	.47
1988	−.41	.19	−2.2	.61
1989	.00	.18	0.0	.60
1990	−.00	.19	−0.0	.62
1991	.23	.19	1.2	.61
1993	.04	.18	0.2	.58
1994	−.22	.16	−1.4	.43
AGE AND GENERATION				
Educational maturity after 1979	−.89	.11	−8.0	.59
Decade of educational maturity	.32	.07	4.7	.07

TABLE 8.5 Revised cumulative model for tolerance: Unstandardized OLS regression coefficients (Continued)

YEAR OF SURVEY (1976 BASE)	β	STANDARD ERROR	*t* VALUE	STATISTICAL TOLERANCE
EDUCATION				
Years of education	.44	.01	34.1	.63
Educational environment (rounded years)	.44	.09	4.9	.09
Education of parents (years)	.13	.01	11.2	.61
DEMOGRAPHICS				
Female	−.38	.07	−5.5	.96
RELIGION AND IDEOLOGY				
Frequency of church attendance	−.23	.01	−16.9	.85
Religious liberal	.67	.08	8.0	.87
Protestant	−.62	.08	−8.3	.84
Conservative views	−.25	.03	−9.8	.95
TYPE AND LOCATION OF RESIDENCE				
In rural area at age 16	−.66	.08	−8.2	.81
In suburbs at age 16	.41	.12	3.5	.92
Now reside in rural area	−.83	.09	−8.9	.89
In South at age 16	−.63	.11	−5.5	.39
In foreign country at age 16	−1.24	.16	−7.8	.95
Now reside in South	−.58	.11	−5.4	.42
Adjusted R^2	.36			
Total N	14984			

Source: GSS, 1976–1994

In this model, the impact of educational environment, while still sizable, is now less than half of what it was in the earlier equation—0.44 instead of 0.92. Every year of increase in the educational environment

16. This degree of collinearity presents a challenge to the stability of the equation; however, OLS does a reasonable job of partitioning the variance between educational environment and generational effects on tolerance.

now predicts a little less than one-half of an additional tolerant response. This is identical to what is predicted by a one-year increase in individual educational attainment. In addition, for every decade later that a citizen reached educational maturity, tolerance increases by just under one-third of a response. These data suggest that factors other than educational change over many successive cohorts and throughout much of this century have also contributed to a more tolerant political community. This appears true at least for those citizens reaching educational maturity prior to 1980. From that point forward, the situation reverses. Holding constant all other variables in the model, those reaching educational maturity after the late 1970's are less tolerant by almost nine-tenths of a response.

How is it that all of these various factors balance out in their overall contribution to political tolerance? We can see what this set of educational and generational variables predicts for tolerance over the past two decades and then compare it to actual observed change. As we demonstrated in Chapter 7, tolerance grew by approximately 1.8 responses between 1976 and 1994. Table 8.6 displays the effect of individual educational attainment, educational environment and parental education, decade of educational maturity, and whether the citizen reached educational maturity after 1979. The unstandardized coefficients for each of these variables is shown in the first column, and their mean change between 1976 and 1994 is shown in the next column. The net change predicted by each independent variable over the 18-year period is the product of the unstandardized coefficient and its change over time and is shown in the third column. Increases in aggregate individual educational attainment alone predict an increase of a little less than three-quarters of a tolerant response. Increases in the levels of the educational environment and parental education together predict an increase of four-fifths of a tolerant response. Within the context of a fully specified cumulative model, increases in these variables alone account for 1.5 out of the total observed 1.8-response increase in the number of tolerance responses. Thus, 80% of the observed increase in tolerance can be traced to the cumulative impact of the three education variables. Add to this the positive and the negative cohort effects while accounting for all other controls in the fully specified model, and the cumulative model predicts an increase of 1.77 responses, almost identical to the observed growth in tolerance. Although challenged by a high degree of collinearity between educational environment and decade of educational maturity, the cumulative education model provides strong evidence that educational environment as well as years of education have an absolute and positive effect on tolerance.

TABLE 8.6 Net change over time in tolerance: Predicted by education and cohort measures

	EFFECT (β)	MEAN CHANGE	NET CHANGE
Education of citizen in years	.44	1.57	+ .69
Educational environment in years	.44	1.30	+ .57
Education of parents in years	.13	1.94	+ .25
Decade of educational maturity	.32	1.89	+ .60
Reached educational maturity after 1979	− .89	.38	− .34
Net effect on tolerance 1976–1994			+ 1.77

Source: GSS, 1976–1994

USING THE FULLY SPECIFIED MODELS TO RETROSPECTIVELY PREDICT CHANGE OVER TIME

Throughout this chapter, we have argued that a comprehensive explanation for the decline in political engagement and growth in tolerance over the past two decades is beyond the scope of our present investigation. At the same time, however, we have maintained that the fundamental direction of change in these variables can never be completely divorced from the theory underlying the causal impact of formal education. With that understanding, we now investigate how much of the observed change in the two citizenship measures is explained by our sorting and cumulative models, and what role the education variables have played in these changes over time.

The operationalization of these questions is straightforward, yet extremely demanding of the data. If the predictions generated by the sorting model for political engagement and the cumulative model for tolerance track actual changes over time in a more satisfactory way than does the absolute education model, then the findings would lend powerful support to the argument that the causal effect of education must be reconceptualized. Using the independent variables from the fully specified models in Table 8.2 and Table 8.5 above, we build a parallel regression equation employing the first four surveys in the time series 1972, 1974, 1976, and 1978 for the NES data, and 1976, 1977, 1980, and 1982 for the GSS data. We then apply the results of these regression estimates to the data from the later surveys, building predictions for political engagement and tolerance into the 1980's and 1990's. This entails applying the coefficients for all of the independent variables from the early surveys to changes in the means of all of the independent variables over the years.

Figure 8.1 presents the comparisons between the observed changes in political engagement over time and the trend predicted by the sorting model. The equation was estimated using the pooled NES surveys from 1972 through 1978—the first two presidential and nonpresidential election years in our time series. Two of each are required to obtain a stable estimate of the extreme sawtooth pattern. The only differences between this equation and the model specified in Table 8.2 are the survey years on which the regression is based, the addition of an accounting variable tagging presidential and off-election years, and the deletion of the year-of-survey dummy variables. The full results of the model are documented in Appendix H.

FIGURE 8.1 Political engagement: Actual and predicted with sorting model

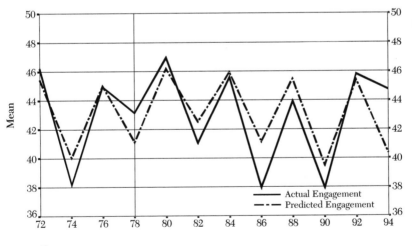

Year

1972–78 data used to predict 1980–94 scores
Source: NES, 1972–1994

The comparison between our projection, estimated with the sorting model of the relative effect of education, and the observed data is striking. While not accounting for all of the decline in political engagement across the 1980's and 1990's, the sorting model explains a very substantial portion of it. When both years of education and the deflator of educational competition are included in the equation along with other independent variables, political engagement, as predicted by the sorting model, shadows the downward trend of the observed measure.[17] The level of political engagement in 1994 is higher than in any off-election year in the entire time series, and it represents an important deviation in the general downward trend. Only time will tell whether this is an early herald of a realignment or the reflection of an unusual election.

As we know from the estimates of the sorting model presented in Table 8.2, the effects of the two education variables combined are responsible for neither an increase nor a decrease in political engagement. Rather, they cancel each other out, leaving everyone in the same place. The predictions help us see that other variables in the model are responsible for the downward trend over time in political engagement. In order for a variable to have a major impact on levels of political engagement over time, it must have an independent impact on the dependent variable, and it must increase or decrease over either cohort or survey years. A review of the coefficients in Table 8.2 and additional analysis of the change in their means illuminate some of the major factors pushing down levels of political engagement over time.[18] Factors contributing to the downward trend include the growing proportion of the population who are 75 years or older; the increase in the percentage of the population who are nonwhite; the substantial decline of partisanship over the generations (but not over the specific years of the surveys); and the decline of family and community (both by generation and for the

17. Given the tight range in which we have chosen to display the data, the predictions are even better than depicted, and in only one year are we more than 2 or 3 units off on an engagement index that has a standard deviation of 24 units.

18. We used a bivariate analysis to confirm that these independent variables are related to political engagement as well as to either age or year of birth. Two additional important factors that may have decreased engagement over time—efficacy and strategic mobilization—are not included in this list of measures. First, we do not have adequate measures of the latter, and while there are good measures of external efficacy in the NES data, we believe they are too close to the dependent variable of political engagement. Recall that our overall scale of political engagement includes a measure of attentiveness to politics. See Abramson and Aldrich, 1982, and Teixeira, 1987, 1992, for interesting analyses of the importance of political efficacy to voter turnout. See Rosenstone and Hansen, 1993, for an analysis of the importance of strategic mobilization to political activity.

years under investigation), indexed by the decline in the percentage of the population currently married as well as a parallel decline in home ownership and a generational decline in church attendance. In addition, the incremental replacement of generations—that is, the gradual demise of the more mobilized New Deal generation and the takeover of the apparently less engaged post-New Deal cohort—is also responsible for some of the decline. These generational effects are above and beyond those accounted for by the decline in strength of partisan identification.

FIGURE 8.2 Political engagement: Actual and predicted with absolute education model

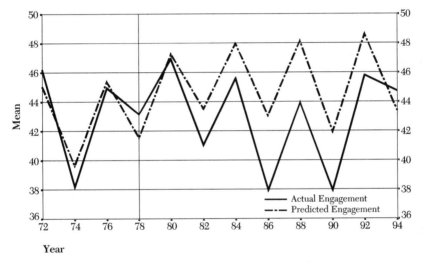

Year

1972–78 data used to predict 1980–94 scores
Source: NES, 1976–1994

How robust is the prediction from the sorting model compared to the AEM specification of the conventional wisdom? Without the correct understanding of the relative effect of education, even controlling for all of the other independent variables will result in a faulty prediction. Figure 8.2 displays the prediction generated with the model excluding the measure of educational competition. The contrast between this figure and Figure 8.1 is dramatic. Even when including the series of independent variables that help account for the downward trajectory in political engagement over time, the equation that excludes the educational deflator leads to a prediction of a slight increase, rather than a substantial decrease, in political engagement over the years. Thus, it is clear that a model of the absolute effect of education predicts change in the wrong direction, even holding constant the factors exogenous to education that drive political engagement down over time.

It is precisely this type of projection that led Richard Brody to identify the "paradox" of increasing educational attainment and declining voter turnout. However, if education is conceptualized as a competitive commodity in its relationship to political engagement, the amount of political engagement predicted by education depends not on the absolute amount of education but on the amount relative to the education of those with whom the citizen competes. Increasing aggregate levels of education over time do not imply a commensurate rise in political engagement. Thus, a more accurate model of the causal role that education plays in political engagement is seen in Figure 8.1, which presents the sorting model of relative education. While this model may still fall short of a complete explanation of the trend in political engagement over time, the sorting model provides a clear and convincing argument for how and why political engagement can decline in the face of rapidly rising educational attainment.

Predicting the Growth of Tolerance

While failure to include the impact of the educational environment leads to a mistaken prediction of growing political engagement, failure to take the educational environment into account leads to an underestimation of the growth of tolerance over time. As shown in Figure 8.3, we use the fully specified cumulative education model to track the observed growth in tolerance between 1982 and 1994. The process used to arrive at the prediction in the figure is parallel to that employed for political engagement. We use the first four surveys for which we have data on tolerance to predict the following years through 1994. The equation from which this prediction is made is the same as that estimated for Table 8.5, excluding only the year-of-survey dummy variables. Appendix H reports the coefficients for this model. The cumulative education model closely approximates the observed increases in tolerance. Moreover, on the basis of this analysis and the data presented in Table 8.6, it is clear that it is the combination of the three education variables that is responsible for the increase in tolerance. Thus, it is the cumulative effect of education that drives the growth in tolerance, and as long as education continues to increase, citizens should be increasingly supportive of the free expression of all political viewpoints.

FIGURE 8.3   Tolerance: Actual and predicted with cumulative model

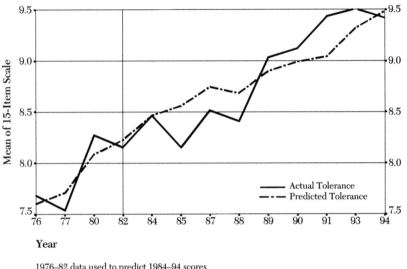

Year

1976–82 data used to predict 1984–94 scores
Source: GSS, 1976–1994

At the same time, social change leaves a distinctive mark on trends in tolerance. Other reasons for continuing growth in tolerance include waning religious intensity over the generations; dramatic decreases, again by cohort, in the percentage of the population who are of mainstream religions; the rise of cosmopolitan cities and the decline of homogeneous rural communities; and a modest decline in political conservatism across the century. However, even these factors do not fully explain the growth in tolerance by generations.[19] Tolerance has increased for every generation in our study except for those who reached educational maturity after the late 1970's, when this trend reverses. In addition to all else, tolerance is sensitive to political events and leadership and shows a decline during the Reagan years, while rebounding thereafter. It should be remembered, however, that while these additional contextual factors influence trends in tolerance, the vast proportion of its increase is attributable to the compounding effects of the continued growth in educational attainment throughout the twentieth century.

19. It should be noted that if these variables are omitted, the variables for education and decade of educational maturity increase to explain the growth by themselves. This, however, is a misspecified model.

ABSOLUTE AND RELATIVE EDUCATION, THE INTERVENING VARIABLES, AND OTHER SOCIAL OUTCOMES

The data we have presented thus far make a strong case indeed for the link between relative education and political engagement and for the cumulative impact of absolute education on tolerance. However, we can further strengthen these findings by demonstrating that it is relative education that influences the variables intervening between education and political engagement, and that it is absolute education that influences those variables intervening between education and enlightenment. Three social outcome variables are available in the GSS data: income, organizational memberships, and verbal cognitive proficiency. If we can demonstrate that the variables that intervene between education and political engagement (income and organizational membership) are in fact relative outcomes of education, while the variable that intervenes between education and tolerance (verbal cognitive proficiency) is an absolute outcome of education, we will have added an important piece of evidence in support of our overall argument. We intend to demonstrate that the relative and absolute education mechanisms apply to a range of social outcomes that have roots in educational attainment.

It would be ideal if these intervening variables could have been included in the specification of the sorting and cumulative models estimated in this chapter. Unfortunately, however, the GSS does not include a sufficient number of measures of political engagement and the NES contains none of these intervening variables.[20] Moreover, even within the GSS data, income, organizational membership, and verbal cognitive proficiency, as well as tolerance, are on different yearly rotation schedules—that is, they are not often measured together in the same year. And even when they do appear in the same year, they are often on separate segments of a split ballot and only a small proportion of the respondents are asked all of these questions. Therefore, we have an insufficient number of cases in which valid responses to all of these questions appear. Each of the social outcome variables thus will be treated separately as a dependent educational outcome: income and organizational memberships for political engagement, and verbal cognitive proficiency for tolerance.

For social outcomes that are competitive and for which education is a main causal variable, the sorting model of relative education should

---

20. The only variable available in the NES is the income measure, but it is only in four categories, based on income relative to others in the sample.

invariably apply. Wages and social leadership positions are but two examples of educational outcomes sharing the characteristics that should make them subject to the relative education mechanism. Each is scarce and to some degree competitive. As society becomes progressively more educated, such outcomes should conform, as does political engagement, to a zero-sum game, where it takes proportionately more education to achieve the same real wages and number of organizational memberships. With regard to outcomes such as wages and careers, this pattern appears to be commonly understood. One frequently hears tuition-paying parents remark that "a college degree today is worth no more than a high school degree when we grew up." The effect of the educational deflator is so obvious and pervasive that it is surprising that it is not routinely included in economic models predicting over time changes in earnings.

Certain other social outcomes of education are neither scarce nor competitive. For example, in the development of intellectual skills, the absolute education model would logically provide a better fit than the relative education model. Education is the main link to many types of cognitive skills, which are not inherently competitive because they do not need to be shared by members of society. Most types of political knowledge (other than knowledge of leaders) are not based on the positional outcomes of education, but are instead a direct result of formal education. For example, the more people who understand the concepts of, and connection between, inflation and unemployment, the more economically sophisticated the society. However, just as education does not affect cognitive outcomes in a relative fashion, neither does it have a cumulative effect. The educational environment should have little or no effect on these cognitive outcomes because contact with the social environment provides neither the protracted nor intense setting needed for complex learning.[21] The cognitive outcomes of education might be best described as the major social capital consequences of education.

Personal earnings and number of organizational memberships are clearly intermediate outcomes of education in the political engagement model. Verbal proficiency was found to be the only significant intervening variable linking education to democratic enlightenment. Earnings

---

21. Level of education of parents and spouse, however, may directly affect cognitive outcomes. The intensity and duration of these familial relationships present many opportunities for learning and cognitive skills.

would seem to be the quintessential relative outcome of education. Employers pay the highest wages to the most skilled labor they can find and afford. Once controlling for length of tenure in the labor force, educational attainment is almost universally used as a shorthand estimator of skill level. The highest-paying jobs generally go to those with the most education relative to those in the pool of competitors. Therefore, as the society becomes more and more educated, each individual will require proportionately more education to compete for the same dollars.

Although the grounds for competition are less clear than they are for wages, membership in voluntary associations is, we expect, the result of relative, rather than absolute, educational attainment. Members of associations obtain substantial psychic and social rewards for their organizational involvements. Moreover, voluntary membership requires time, energy, and often money, and those who are relatively near the center of the social network can better afford to pay the costs and are more likely to reap the benefits. Nevertheless, it is unlikely that individuals are in competition to see who can belong to more organizations but, instead, believe that they receive status and recognition for their activities. The greater the educational attainment relative to others, the more likely it is that the citizen will be pushed or pulled into joining.

As we have already indicated, there should be a very different pattern for verbal cognitive proficiency. We expect citizens to attain additional verbal skills for every year of school completed. If citizens become more educated over time, the aggregate verbal proficiency in the society should also rise. If there is a negative term on the educational environment measure, it should be much smaller than it would be for income and organizational memberships, and it should be the result of either the attempt to educate an increasingly larger segment of the population or a decline in the quality of education. A negative effect of the educational environment represents decreasing marginal returns for additional education rather than indicating increased competition.

Table 8.7 presents the findings of the impact of education and educational environment on personal earnings from all jobs in constant 1986 dollars, organizational membership, and verbal proficiency. Only the relevant coefficients for the two education variables are included in the table. The other predictors of the three dependent variables are included in the models, and the full results are presented in Appendix H. As with the fully specified political engagement and tolerance equations, dummy variables for the year of survey are included to de-trend the data.

TABLE 8.7 Net effect of educational change over time: Income, organizational membership, and verbal cognitive proficiency

	β PER YEAR OF EDUCATIONAL ATTAINMENT	INCREASE IN YEARS OF EDUCATIONAL ATTAINMENT[°]	PREDICTED INCREASE[†]	β EDUCATIONAL ENVIRONMENT	INCREASE IN YEARS OF EDUCATIONAL ENVIRONMENT[°]	PREDICTED DECLINE[‡]	NET EFFECT OF CHANGE
Income (1986 constant $)	1870	1.68	$3,142	–2541	1.38	$–3,507	$–365
Organizational memberships (0 to 16)	.20	1.68	.34	–.22	1.38	–.30	+.04
Verbal proficiency (0 to 10 words)	.32	1.68	.54	–.19	1.38	–.26	+.28

Source: GSS, 1974-1994

[°] Increase calculated from the combined GSS and NES samples

[†] Predicted increase due to effect of β x increase over time

[‡] Predicted decline due to effect of β x increase in educational environment

N for income: 15,252

N for organizational membership: 15,887

N for verbal proficiency: 13,197

The last column in Table 8.7 shows the net effect of change in each of the dependent variables due to the education variables. We begin with the results for earnings. In the pooled GSS surveys between 1974 and 1994, there is a $1,870 average increase in individual earnings (in 1986 constant dollars) for every additional year of educational attainment. There has been a 1.68-year increase in average educational attainment in the adult population over the same period.[22] Therefore, educational attainment, controlling for all other factors, predicts a $3,142 increase in real 1986 earnings over the time period. During the same period, however, the model estimates a $2,541 decline in real earnings for each year of increase in the educational competition. Educational competition has increased by 1.38 years over the 20-year period. Thus, the net effect of the increase in both education and educational competition over these 20 years is negative $365 (a 1.7% decrease), an amount very close to 0. Rising educational levels result in a zero-sum gain for earnings. Citizens will rationally continue to get as much education as possible in order to earn as much income as possible, but because everyone else behaves in kind, everyone stays in the same place. These estimates of the structural effects of education should remain constant regardless of whether wages increased, decreased, or stagnated (as they actually have) over the 20-year period between 1974 and 1994. If the model is correctly specified, the estimates for educational attainment and educational competition should prove to be approximately the same for the period between 1954 and 1974, when real earnings grew almost every year. If the theory is correct, the net effect of educational change for competitive outcomes of education should always approach 0, regardless of the direction or magnitude of the observed change in that outcome.

The results of a similar analysis predicting the number of memberships in voluntary associations are parallel.[23] Increases in educational attainment predict an increase of a little more than one-third of a membership over the 20-year period. However, the rise in educational competition predicts almost as much membership decline. The net effect of educational change is +0.04 of a membership. As with income, this is essentially 0.

---

22. This is the average increase in educational attainment between 1974 and 1994 for both the pooled NES data and the GSS data.

23. The corrected version of the organizational membership variable from the GSS was used in this analysis. See Helliwell and Putnam, 1996.

The results of the parallel analysis for verbal proficiency are quite different. Increased educational attainment predicts a rise in the correct identification of over one-half of a word out of 10 words in the vocabulary test. While the coefficient for the educational environment measure is negative, the net result of educational changes nevertheless predicts an increase of just under three-tenths of a word. More than half of the gain predicted by increased educational attainment remains. The meaning of the negative coefficient for educational environment is quite different. Unlike the competitive social outcomes, educational environment is not a proxy for the effects of competition in an increasingly educated society but, instead, is the result of the attempt to educate a larger and larger portion of the population. Over this 20-year period, the proportion of the United States population 25 years and older who have achieved at least a high school degree has increased by more than 20 percentage points. Assuming some distribution of innate abilities in a population, when a society moves from trying to educate 60% of its population through high school and beyond, to accomplishing the same levels of education for over 80% of its population, the marginal return will likely diminish as it reaches the tail of the normal distribution of intellectual ability. The model estimated for verbal cognitive proficiency is nevertheless still additive. The more educational attainment, the more vocabulary words will be identified correctly, with the rate of the increase flattening as we dig deeper into the pool of those who are more difficult to educate.

The sorting and cumulative models of the relative and absolute effects of education appear to be generalizable beyond the realm of political beliefs, behaviors, and cognitions. Other social outcomes also appear to be based on either relative or absolute education, depending upon the extent to which the outcome is competitive and bounded. Clearly, these are ideal types, and varieties of mixtures are possible. For political beliefs, such as tolerance, the effect of education is cumulative or compounding, rather than simply additive. And as we have just observed with verbal proficiency, there can sometimes be negative effects for the educational environment because of declining marginal rates of return from additional education.

The analysis of the pooled cross-sectional data from the General Social Survey and the National Election Study provide strong support for our theory that education has both absolute and relative effects for political engagement and tolerance. We are now left with one final empirical question. What are the implications of these findings for analyzing the effect of educational attainment on citizenship with cross-sectional data from a single point in time?

9

Absolute and Relative
Education in Synchronic Studies

Application to Cross-Sectional Surveys

The vast majority of empirical research on the political behavior and attitudes of Americans in the contemporary context has depended— and will likely continue to depend—upon survey data from a single point in time. Given the evidence presented thus far, it is clear that cross-sectional analyses employing the common absolute education model (AEM) specification have omitted a key variable. In this brief chapter, we consider the implications of our theory about the relative and cumulative effects of education for analysts of synchronic data. We suggest how scholars can incorporate the educational environment into their analyses of cross-sectional data from a single point in time. In addition, we demonstrate the consequences of omitting this crucial variable as a *deflator* for political engagement and as a *cumulator* for characteristics of democratic enlightenment.

Accounting for the educational environment while simultaneously controlling for life cycle and generational effects is a difficult task indeed. While it is theoretically correct to include a combination of these three factors in a model predicting political engagement or toler-ance, estimating models with this specification is impossible with cross-sectional data. Recall that age and year of birth are an identity in data from a single point in time, and that educational environment is almost perfectly correlated with these two variables because of the monotonic growth in educational attainment in the United States over the last 100 years. The analysis in Chapter 8 demonstrates the complexity of sorting out these effects, even when we can pool 20 years of cross-sectional data. However, in data from a single point in time, separating these effects is impossible. The question, then, is to decide which variables to include in the models. Because we have demonstrated that the effect of the educational environment is, for political engagement, substantially greater than the effects of life cycle and generations and that the same pattern is true to a lesser degree for tolerance, we include educational environment in the models estimated in this chapter.

At issue is the direction and extent of the bias in the estimates of models of political engagement that exclude the measure of educational competition. Because political engagement is competitive and bounded in its upper distribution, failure to include a measure of educational environment should result in an *underestimation* of the effect of years of educational attainment. Explaining political engagement with a measure of actual years of educational attainment, without accounting for the level of educational competition at the time when that education was attained, is a poorer predictor than when a measure of the degree of competition is included. In the misspecified model that excludes educational environment, the estimated coefficient for years of education is attenuated, because it is not simply the number of years of educational attainment that is relevant to political engagement, but rather the citizen's educational standing relative to the education of others. A simple example illustrates why this is the case. Those who were among the 5% of the population who attained a college degree in the 1950's appear to have the same educational standing as those who earned a bachelor's degree in the mid-1990's, when more than one-quarter of the population has become college educated. The college degree earned at a time when very few reached that level of educational attainment is worth more for political engagement than the college degree earned during a time when one in four reaches this level of education. Failure to account for the relative effect of education results in a biased coefficient that is underestimated in the absolute education model. Instead, either employing a measure of relative education or including educational environment yields the true estimate of the effect of education on political engagement.

The exact opposite should be true for unbounded dependent variables such as tolerance, where the educational environment constitutes a noncompetitive socializing agent that is augmented in a cumulative fashion by individual-level educational attainment. Omitting a measure of the educational environment here results in an *overestimation* of the causal impact of educational attainment on tolerance. This is the case because in the absence of the educational environment term, some of the effect of the degree of tolerance surrounding citizens is absorbed, or misappropriated, by the measure of years of educational attainment. After all, both education measures vary monotonically according to year of birth; in the absence of either, the other will garner some of the explanatory variance. Thus, estimating the AEM, rather than the cumulative model for tolerance, incorrectly inflates the causal impact of years of educational attainment. At the same time, however, there are some aspects of enlightenment for which the inclusion of the educational environment measure may have little or no impact on the overall explanatory power of the model and only a minimal impact on the estimate of the effect of years of educational attainment. We found such a situation in our analysis of the impact of years of education and the educational environment on verbal cognitive proficiency. For these types of intellectual skills, formal education appears to work as an additive rather than relative or cumulative process, and the absolute education model of the conventional wisdom is actually a good fit.

In Chapter 8, the comparisons of the over time predictions of both the AEM and the sorting and cumulative models to observed changes over time in political engagement and tolerance demonstrated clearly that theoretically correct specifications of the effect of education are critical for the prediction of trends over time. The following analysis, based on synchronic data, demonstrates the superiority of the sorting model for political engagement and the cumulative model for tolerance when this type of data is used. We analyze the individual years of the National Election Study data as independent cross-sections between 1972 and 1994—the same years included in our over time analysis in preceding chapters. For democratic enlightenment, we return to the General Social Survey and analyze cross-sectional data for the individual years between 1976 and 1994. The question now becomes how to weigh the gains of unbiased estimates of the effect of the critical independent variable along with a better model fit, versus the inevitable conflation of the effects of the three measures of life cycle, generation, and educational environment.

ESTIMATING THE MODELS WITH SYNCHRONIC DATA

For each year of the NES data, we estimated two OLS regression models. The first corresponds to the absolute education model and includes a measure of years of educational attainment along with the other control variables. The second model estimated was the sorting model, which also includes a measure of educational competition along with the other control variables included in the fully specified political engagement model presented in Table 8.2. Because both models are estimated with data from individual survey years in the NES, the year-of-survey dummy variables are no longer relevant and are therefore excluded. In addition, because of the high degree of collinearity among age, year of birth, and educational environment in a given cross-section, the dummy variables for life cycle and birth cohort effects are also excluded.

It is apparent from the pattern in the bar chart in Figure 9.1 and the accompanying table that the estimates for the impact of years of educational attainment on engagement is, for every year in the NES data, greater when educational environment is included in the equation. In Chapter 8, we demonstrated how failure to include the level of educational competition in the retrospective estimates of observed changes in political engagement leads to incorrect predictions about the direction and magnitude of change over time. It is evident that omitting educational environment in individual cross-sectional surveys leads to an *underestimation* of the effect of education on political engagement. Without accounting for the level of educational competition, the coefficient for years of education is attenuated because the AEM fails to correct for the actual worth of a given number of years of education, which varies according to the amount of educational competition in the environment at the time that the citizen reached educational maturity. At the same time, however, the findings demonstrate that the distortion of the effect of education is less severe for any given cross-section than in the analysis of data over time.

Failure to include educational environment as an explanatory variable leads to an approximate 10% underestimation of the true effect of education on engagement in politics. Moreover, the last column of the table accompanying Figure 9.1 shows that misspecifying the model sacrifices, on average, a little over two percentage points in overall explanatory power. Both the correction in the size of the coefficient on educational attainment and the improvement in explanatory power of the model are hardly earth-shaking differences, especially given the current level of precision in the social sciences. Nevertheless, these small empirical improvements add another piece of micro-level evidence to substantiate a large theoretical difference in our understanding of how education affects political engagement and other social outcomes.

FIGURE 9.1 Unstandardized coefficients for years of education predicting political engagement: Comparison of the AEM and sorting model

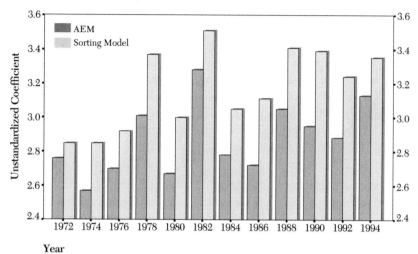

	Absolute Education Model		Sorting Model			Difference	
Year	Coefficient for years of education	Adj. R^2	Coefficient for years of education	Coefficient for educational environment	Adj. R^2	Amount under-estimated	R^2
1972	2.76	.26	2.85	−1.03	.26	.09	0
1974	2.57	.27	2.85	−2.81	.28	.28	.01
1976	2.70	.33	2.92	−2.24	.34	.22	.01
1978	3.01	.27	3.37	−3.97	.29	.36	.02
1980	2.67	.26	3.00	−3.96	.29	.33	.03
1982	3.28	.33	3.51	−2.67	.34	.23	.01
1984	2.78	.27	3.05	−3.00	.29	.27	.02
1986	2.72	.27	3.11	−5.69	.31	.39	.04
1988	3.05	.33	3.41	−4.84	.36	.36	.03
1990	2.95	.32	3.39	−5.75	.36	.44	.04
1992	2.88	.28	3.24	−4.89	.32	.36	.04
1994	3.13	.31	3.35	−3.97	.33	.22	.02

Source: NES, 1972–1994

On the basis of the evidence presented, absolute educational attainment does not itself determine levels of political engagement, nor do increases in education over time lead to proportional growth in political engagement. These findings call into question the implications of the absolute education model; the argument of more resources leading to more political engagement appears mistaken. Instead, in the sorting model of the relative effect of education, citizens are sorted into ranks representing distance from the social and political center of society. For the citizen, the distance from that center has a profound effect on the costs and potential benefits of varying levels of political engagement. The number of ranks are fixed, while the absolute amount of education seeking them continues to grow. Thus, whether examined from the perspective of a single year or across the decades, educational attainment *relative* to the competition determines variation in political engagement.

Does failure to include a term for educational environment also distort the educational coefficient when predicting tolerance in synchronic data?. The answer is yes, and even more so, but the mechanisms are totally different. The analysis presented in Figure 9.2 and its associated table are based on the fully specified cumulative education model for tolerance presented in Table 8.4. As in the case for political engagement, the year-of-survey dummy variables are now the bases upon which we stratify the regressions, and decade of birth has been omitted because of its nearly identical relationship with educational environment. All other independent variables from the model of tolerance presented in Table 8.4 are included.

As with political engagement, we estimate two regression equations: one corresponding to the AEM that excludes educational environment and one of the cumulative model that includes educational environment. As we expected, the absolute education model incorrectly *overestimates* the impact of educational attainment on tolerance. The paired bars in Figure 9.2 demonstrate that adding the educational environment variable reduces the impact of individual educational attainment on tolerance. Omitting the educational environment measure inflates the coefficient on years of education by about one-half of a tolerant response. In the correctly specified cumulative model, the estimate of the effect of years of education is reduced by about 15%. In addition, including educational environment not only redistributes the explanatory variance properly but also adds approximately three percentage points to the fit of the models to the data.

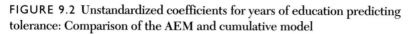

FIGURE 9.2 Unstandardized coefficients for years of education predicting tolerance: Comparison of the AEM and cumulative model

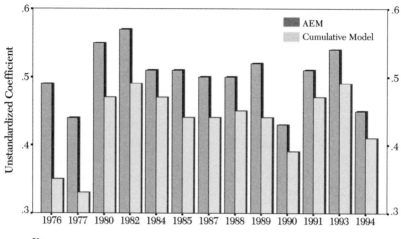

	Absolute Education Model		Cumulative Model			Difference	
Year	Coefficient for years of education	Adj. R^2	Coefficient for years of education	Coefficient for educational environment	Adj. R^2	Amount over-estimated	R^2
1976	.49	.31	.35	1.03	.35	.14	.04
1977	.44	.34	.33	.98	.38	.11	.04
1980	.55	.37	.47	.95	.41	.08	.04
1982	.57	.35	.49	.73	.37	.08	.02
1984	.51	.33	.47	.64	.35	.04	.03
1985	.51	.32	.44	.94	.36	.07	.04
1987	.50	.31	.44	.59	.32	.06	.01
1988	.50	.30	.45	.52	.31	.05	.01
1989	.52	.28	.44	.88	.32	.08	.04
1990	.43	.28	.39	.72	.31	.04	.03
1991	.51	.31	.47	.59	.33	.04	.02
1993	.54	.27	.49	.76	.29	.05	.02
1994	.45	.24	.41	.69	.26	.04	.02

Source: GSS, 1976–1994

Our review of the literature suggests that students of tolerance, unlike students of political engagement, have probably not systematically biased the estimates of the impact of formal educational attainment in their models. This is true because the effect of cohort has been incorporated into explanatory models of tolerance for some years now. At the same time, however, few, if any, have recognized that much of what has been interpreted as cohort effects is rather the result of a more educated society and, thus, more tolerant surroundings. Remember that the effect of cosmopolitan urbanization, regional origins, and the reduction in religiosity and conservative social philosophy are included in our tolerance model. We believe that shifts in the educational environment account for a major part of what is left unexplained in unspecified generational effects. Unfortunately, given the inseparability of year of birth and educational environment over the history of the last 100 years, we may have to wait a long time to substantiate this hypothesis with data.

Prevailing paradigms in science are often challenged by the very small increases in empirical fit provided by a new theory. However, the improvement in prediction often means very little in itself, even to those who advance the new paradigm. Rather, a change in the understanding of how and why A leads to B is often much more important. Whether future researchers choose to incorporate an empirical measure of educational environment into their cross-sectional studies is clearly much less important than understanding and conveying the correct model of the link between formal education and social outcomes, such as democratic citizenship.

Thus, while the explanatory power gained by including a measure of educational environment may in fact be small, the larger point is that the sorting model and the cumulative model are a more accurate reflection of the causal effect of education. For political engagement, it is important to specify the effect of formal educational attainment in relative terms within the context of an environment of competition. And since education has been increasing over the last 100 years, it is important to know not only how much education an individual has attained but also when it was obtained. When asked in the late 1950's whether the space program wanted the legendary pilot Chuck Yeager as an astronaut, NASA replied that they were taking only college graduates.[1] Today, those without a Ph.D. in astrophysics need not apply.

---

1. Wolfe, 1980.

While small improvements in the explanatory power of models are relevant when selecting between competing theories, most important are the divergent metaphors and expectations for the future that are generated by the models.

10

Education and Democratic Citizenship in Other Nations

An Exploratory Comparative Analysis

All of our analyses thus far have examined data on the cognition, behavior, and attitudes of Americans. To what extent are these patterns unique to American society, and to what degree do the same patterns of the effect of formal education on citizenship appear in other industrialized democracies? In short, what are the implications for cross-national analysis of the theory of the sorting versus cumulative or additive effects of formal education? Is political engagement best predicted and understood by relative education in other democratic societies, and is absolute educational attainment the central explanatory variable when it comes to democratic enlightenment? Further, is there evidence from other societies that tolerance is educationally cumulative, as we found it to be in the United States?

These are important questions that we hope future researchers will investigate. The brief analysis we present here is exploratory but nevertheless extremely revealing. The validity and generalizability of our theory of the two effects of formal education would be enhanced if we could demonstrate two things: first, that both absolute and relative education affect political engagement and tolerance in similar ways in other postindustrial democratic societies and, second, that growing levels of tolerance can be identified as a function of more education, even in *nondemocratic* societies. However, a thorough cross-national investigation would be a massive undertaking, and at minimum, an adequate study would require cross-sectional surveys in a number of countries containing independent and intervening variables parallel to those used in Part I, as well as over time data that could be pooled to facilitate analyses similar to those in Part II. Unfortunately, there are no such studies and no such data, and the greatest limitation of this comparative analysis is the absence of adequate data to test our models. Thus, the findings from this analysis must be interpreted with care, because the measures of education and democratic citizenship are from a single point in time. Data over time are necessary in order to create a denominator for the relative education measure, and the cross-sectional data that we utilize in this chapter do not include a sufficient number of cases to create this measure with a satisfactory degree of certainty, especially for the older cohorts. As a result, we are not able to estimate a fully specified model that takes into account the confounding effects of life cycle and birth cohort, as we did in the analysis of the over time data from the United States in Chapter 8. Despite these limitations, the analyses show patterns consistent with what our theory would predict.

There is one set of comparative surveys with sufficient data with which we can ask the question: Are the relationships between education, birth cohort and life cycle, on the one hand, and measures of the two aspects of democratic citizenship, on the other, uniformly consistent in direction and general magnitude with what our theory would predict? The surveys containing this information are from the 1990 International Social Survey Project (ISSP), an extension of the American version of the General Social Survey, which was conducted in 11 countries. We use data from only seven of these countries that are classifiable as political democracies. Four of these countries—Australia, Great Britain, Norway, and the United States—have been stable and continuous democracies during the entire life span of all citizens represented in the 1990 study. Three others have maintained democratic polities since the mid-twentieth century: the former West Germany, Ireland, and Israel. We treat these democracies separately because they obtained statehood or achieved democracy after many of the older respondents interviewed in the 1990 surveys had already entered adulthood, and certainly before even those in their middle years had completed their formal education.[1] In the final part of this analysis, we will consider data from one nondemocratic nation to test our hypothesis about the relationship between formal education and tolerance.

---

1. The remaining four countries that we do not use are the then Soviet eastern block countries of Hungary and East Germany, plus Northern Ireland. Italy, though fully qualified as a noncontinuous democracy, did not ask the questions on political tolerance.

In the 1990 ISSP surveys, there is a single measure of political engagement common in all seven nations: interest in politics and public affairs. Fortunately, it is exactly the type of measure we would want to find. Since political attentiveness is a mental state rather than a participatory activity, it is the component of political engagement least likely to be confounded by institutional constraints.[2] In addition, this question is very close in substance and format to the political attentiveness measures used in both the cross-sectional 1990 Citizen Participation Study data and the National Election Studies. For measures of democratic enlightenment, the ISSP surveys included an excellent series of eight questions on tolerance. These questions were specifically designed as cross-nationally applicable functional equivalents of the Stouffer tolerance items employed in the American version of the GSS.

Unfortunately, the 1990 ISSP data contain few comparable independent and intervening variables similar to those in either the cross-sectional or over time American data. In each of the seven democratic nations, there is a measure of formal educational attainment, but the measures are not identical. This is not an issue of survey mechanics alone; the educational systems in the countries are quite different.[3] In addition to measures of educational attainment, all seven surveys contain information on the age (and, therefore, birth cohort) of individuals. As discussed earlier, because these are cross-sectional data, age and year of birth are an identity. Therefore, the two measures of educational attainment—absolute and relative—in the presence of mea-

2. Our argument about the outcomes of educational attainment that relate to political engagement (occupational prominence, organizational membership, and family income), would not seem dependent on cultural settings specific to other postindustrial democratic societies. At the same time, however, nothing in the argument implies that any of the consequences of education are immune to variation in institutional settings and structures that do vary from nation to nation. Moreover, a good deal of research has demonstrated that many of the types of political activities that we characterize as political engagement are powerfully mediated by strong political parties and associated voluntary organizational structures. See, for example, Verba, Nie, and Kim, 1978; Powell, 1984; and Barnes, Kaase, et al., 1979. In societies with dominant political infrastructures, the sorting capacity of education might be overwhelmed, and where organizations of such political parties are dominant, the effect of individual-level educational attainment may not be as strong. Political institutions are much more likely to be successful at deterring or promoting participatory activities, rather than at affecting those aspects of democratic citizenship that have become internalized as values.

3. Because of this variation, we are able to provide little insight into whether a two-year degree course in Germany on power plant operation and administration, for example, has the same effect as two years of graduate education in the United States. More generally, it is not clear whether more vocational forms of education have a similar effect on either verbal cognitive proficiency or social network centrality.

sures of either age or year of birth are virtually equivalent in any society that has experienced more or less continuous increases in educational attainment since the turn of the century.

If our argument about the relative effect of education on political engagement is right, in the presence of historically increasing levels of educational attainment, the same absolute amount of education should everywhere purchase *less* engagement for more recent birth cohorts than it did for those born earlier, when levels of educational attainment in the population were lower. Therefore, while controlling for the life-cycle phenomenon of start-up and slow-down in relation to political attentiveness, our model would predict a negative coefficient for year of birth in all such countries, capturing, in part at least, the educational *deflator*. There is no other reason to expect or predict universally declining amounts of political attentiveness by year of birth.

In contrast, tolerance, which we argue is influenced principally by the impact of education on verbal cognitive proficiency, should be increasing by birth cohort everywhere that absolute levels of education have been rising. If we are correct, younger cohorts should be more tolerant everywhere, even after controlling for individual levels of educational attainment. Educational attainment, we assert, leads to tolerance because education increases cognitive verbal proficiency and sophistication, both of which lead citizens to understand and support the (democratic) principles of free deliberation.[4]

While there are various plausible hypotheses for why the young in most postindustrial democracies are becoming more politically tolerant, if the year-of-birth coefficients are positive in all seven nations, we can at least say that the findings are not inconsistent with our theoretical argument. Education should act to increase tolerance regardless of the nature of the political institutions and the political content of that education.

But first, has educational attainment been increasing at similar rates in all seven of the contemporary democracies? Table 10.1 presents the data on the zero-order correlations between education and the year of birth in the seven democracies. Unfortunately, we cannot directly compare the slopes for the year of birth on education, since not all of the educational measures are expressed in years attained. Instead, these

---

4. In a recent exhaustive study of the political attitudes and beliefs of citizens of industrialized democracies, Abramson and Inglehart (1995) document a strong relationship between formal educational attainment and values.

correlations are an estimate of the magnitude of educational change over the lives of representative samples of citizens in each of the seven countries. What is immediately apparent in Table 10.1 is that the coefficients are all positive and of approximately the same order of magnitude. In fact, with the exceptions of the United States and Great Britain, there is no statistically significant difference among the other five coefficients, which all range between 0.33 and 0.36.

TABLE 10.1 Correlation between formal education and year of birth in seven democratic nations

COUNTRY	CORRELATION
Australia	.35
Great Britain	.27
Ireland	.36
Israel	.33
Norway	.35
United States	.25
West Germany	.33

Source: ISSP, 1990

In terms of our argument about education and political engagement, the educational deflator should be operating in relation to the measure of political attentiveness in all seven of the nations. That is, the same amount of education should purchase less political attentiveness in successive birth cohorts. We therefore expect to observe a substantial positive relationship everywhere between education and political attentiveness, accompanied by a substantial negative relationship between the birth cohort and the measure of political engagement in the ISSP data. Table 10.2 reports the results of an Ordinary Least Squares (OLS) regression estimate predicting political attentiveness with formal educational attainment and year of birth.[5]

5. We include the gender of respondent in the model to account for the substantial differences in levels of education between men and women, as well as the discrepancies in life expectancy. In addition, two dummy variables for being very young (25-29 years old) and very old (70 years and older) are included in the model in order to account for the start-up and slow-down effects of the life cycle.

TABLE 10.2 Impact of education and year of birth on political attentiveness in seven democratic nations: Standardized regression coefficients

| | CONTINUOUS DEMOCRACIES | | | | NEW DEMOCRACIES | | |
	Australia	Great Britain	Norway	United States	Ireland	Israel	West Germany
Educational Attainment	.11 (4.9)	.19 (6.1)	.25 (8.4)	.27 (8.5)	.21 (6.0)	.22 (5.8)	.28 (13.2)
Year of Birth	−.18 (−6.0)	−.18 (−3.8)	−.17 (−4.2)	−.18 (−3.6)	−.14 (−2.7)	−.01 (−0.1)	−.14 (−4.4)
Female	−.16 (−7.5)	−.16 (−5.4)	−.12 (−4.2)	−.13 (−4.4)	−.19 (−5.8)	−.18 (−5.0)	−.21 (−10.7)
Youngest Respondents (25-29)	−.04 (−1.7)	−.01 (−.1)	.02 (0.6)	−.04 (−1.0)	.03 (0.7)	−.08 (−1.8)	−.01 (−0.6)
Oldest Respondents (70+)	−.03 (−1.1)	−.0 (−.1)	−.01 (−0.2)	−.10 (−2.2)	−.14 (−3.2)	.03 (0.6)	−.15 (−5.7)
N	2062	1022	1183	998	849	748	2203

Source: ISSP, 1990

t values in parentheses below coefficients

The data display a stunning consistency across the seven countries. Although there are some variations in the strength of the relationship between education and political attentiveness, this relationship is everywhere positive, substantial, and statistically significant. And just as the relative education model would predict, in every country except Israel there is also a substantial negative relationship between the year of birth and the measure of political attentiveness.[6] Throughout the democratic world, education in relative terms appears to play a central role in determining individual levels of political attentiveness. It appears that as a democratic society becomes more educated, it takes increasing amounts of education in successive generations to achieve the same amount of political engagement. This strongly suggests that the total amount of political attentiveness is at a more or less fixed equilibrium in all democratic societies and that a citizen's relative edu-

6. Israel has received numerous waves of very disparate populations of immigrants since World War I. Some have been rather well educated; others, uneducated. In addition, Israel has been in a state of almost continuous war since its establishment in 1947. In light of such factors, it is very difficult to assess the meaning of the absence of a relationship between year of birth and political attentiveness.

cational attainment acts as a sorting mechanism to assign a seat either near to or far from the political stage.

A parallel model was estimated with the data to predict tolerance in each of the seven democracies. The results of these estimations are reported in Table 10.3. The pattern for tolerance is also surprisingly parallel across all seven nations. Education is strongly associated with increased tolerance for the freedom of expression of unpopular views. At the same time, in all seven democracies, the year-of-birth measure is significant and positive. This pattern is consistent with our argument about the cumulative education model for political tolerance, where each new generation stands on the educational shoulders of the preceding, augmenting this baseline tolerance on the basis of its own educational attainment.

TABLE 10.3 Impact of education and year of birth on tolerance in seven democratic nations: Standardized regression coefficients

	CONTINUOUS DEMOCRACIES				NEW DEMOCRACIES		
	Australia	Great Britain	Norway	United States	Ireland	Israel	West Germany
Educational Attainment	.23 (10.0)	.14 (4.3)	.26 (8.1)	.31 (9.5)	.17 (4.5)	.17 (4.4)	.14 (6.1)
Year of Birth	.15 (6.4)	.23 (7.0)	.11 (3.5)	.15 (4.6)	.18 (4.9)	.11 (2.7)	.22 (9.4)
Female	−.10 (−4.6)	−.15 (−4.7)	−.08 (−2.5)	−.10 (−3.1)	−.19 (−5.4)	−.06 (−1.5)	−.08 (−3.7)
N	1933	906	950	831	738	674	1791

Source: ISSP, 1990
t values in parentheses below coefficients

One last cross-national finding is noteworthy. The tolerance items were asked in one country that could not be classified as a democracy in 1990—Hungary. If we are correct that the number of years of formal schooling acts to increase tolerance regardless of the manifest and subtle political content of that education, then educational attainment should act to increase tolerance even in regimes with contrary messages. We have consistently argued that education works this way with tolerance because education is fundamental in determining how people approach problems and the importance they place on open discourse. For example, one cannot expect engineering students engaged in analysis of problems of aerospace design through complex cooperative intellectual effort to discard these potent techniques when attempting to solve equally demanding social or economic problems. For these reasons, the communist regimes in Eastern Europe, with their emphasis for the last half-century on modernization through education, unintentionally created new generations of citizens who were prone to work for the toppling of the very regimes that saw to their education.

TABLE 10.4 Impact of education and year of birth on tolerance in Hungary and the average democracy: Standardized regression coefficients

	HUNGARY	AVERAGE DEMOCRACY
Educational Attainment	.27 (7.5)	.20
Year of Birth	.13 (3.6)	.16
Female	−.09 (−2.7)	−.11
N	797	

Source: ISSP, 1990
t values in parentheses below coefficients

The data in Table 10.4 lend some credence to this argument. Here, we compare the results for the regression model predicting tolerance for the average democratic nation in the ISSP 1990 surveys to results from data collected in Hungary.[7] The patterns are quite similar. In fact, educational attainment appears to have an even stronger impact on tolerance in Hungary than in the average democratic nation in the ISSP data. Only in the United States is the relationship between education and tolerance stronger than it is in Hungary. Moreover, the coefficient for birth cohort is also positive and close to the average for the democracies, suggesting here as well that the effect of education on tolerance is generationally cumulative.

7. The entries in Table 10.4 for the average democracy were computed as the mean parameter estimates of the seven democratic nations.

With the limited cross-national data available to us, there is no sure way to test the alternative hypotheses in the way we did with the data from the United States. However, nowhere is there a contradictory finding. And while only exploratory, these cross-national findings, when combined with the more detailed analyses from the preceding chapters, present compelling evidence indeed that our theory of the dual effects of education on democratic citizenship is relevant across time and geography.

11

The Future of Education and
Democratic Citizenship

Some Implications of Our Findings

Our findings about the relationship between education and democratic citizenship have several important theoretical and normative implications beyond the empirical predictions that political engagement will not increase with continued growth in educational attainment, while democratic enlightenment is likely to do so. If, as our sorting model holds, citizens do indeed vie for the best of a fixed number of social network positions, in large part according to their relative educational standing, then we have a good deal to say about the limits of equality of political voice and access. If one accepts our contention that the relative costs and benefits of hearing and being heard in the political process vary according to distance from the center of society, then equality of political access can never be fully achieved. Those seated close to the political stage can easily follow the actors and their actions and can readily gain the players' attention if they so desire. For those with seats at the periphery, the very opposite is true: following the action and identifying the actors requires much more careful attention, and making oneself heard by those onstage may be nearly impossible without creating a serious commotion. Whether expressed as "politics are too complicated for me," or "I wouldn't have any impact anyway," the implications of social distance are the same. Moreover, because education is primary among the factors used in assigning educational rank and seats, it certainly cannot be used to disassemble the very inequality it helps to delineate. Education may indeed be the "universal solvent," but because it is the central causal mechanism driving the maintenance of social stratification, we cannot

expect it to dismantle that hierarchy.[1] Sorted outcomes are by definition unequal, and more education will not change how many people sit
close to the center of the relevant social and political network. The
number of good seats is fixed. Rather, education can change only the
composition of the population that is at or near the top of the rank. In
the zero-sum game of political engagement, gains in proximity to the
social and political center of society by one individual or group means a
necessary loss of access to another.

Education, however, does not create the inequality. Inequality of
political access is inherent in the competition for what is invariably a
scarce resource. While not as obvious, the process is similar to that in
the competition for wages. The best-educated get the best-paying jobs,
and when everyone has more education, the baseline of competition for
the same jobs and wages increases. Two characteristics are critical. First,
the commodity sought after is scarce; that is, not everyone can have all
they want of it. Second, society values the claims of some individuals
more than others, and relative educational attainment is the primary
variable on which the value of competing claims is assessed. In previous
centuries, land, inherited wealth, and social rank at birth ordered claims
regarding the division of scarce social resources. However, bit by bit
over the last centuries, education has replaced these other factors as the
main sorting mechanism for positional social outcomes.[2]

An implicit assumption of what Philip Converse termed the "simple
education-driven model," and what we have referred to as the AEM, is
that more education means more political engagement. The mechanism is sometimes explicit—but more often implicit—that more education produces more social and political resources. A corollary of this
resource metaphor is that if everybody gets more resources, the playing field for political voice and access will be leveled.[3] Such a model
expects that a more educated citizenry is likely to create a society with
less participatory inequality. The relative education model envisions no
such leveling of the playing field. Sorted outcomes that chase scarce

1. See Bourdieu, 1987; and Lash and Urry, 1994.
2. Numerous factors seem to be driving the increasing importance of education over a
variety of types positional outcomes. The demise of nobility, growth in inheritance taxes,
increasing demands for formal occupational certification, more emphasis on intellectual
skills, and vastly increased demands for meritocratic performance have increased the reliance
on educational sorting.
3. Verba and Nie, 1972; Verba, Nie, and Kim, 1978; and Brody, 1978.

resources are by definition unequal. So long as the number of seats in the political theater remains fixed and education continues to play a strong role in determining social network position, the amount of inequality in the participatory hierarchy should be constant regardless of the degree of increase in educational attainment over time. Let us consider each of these claims in turn.

ARE THE NUMBER OF RANKS FIXED?

One of the immediate questions that follows from the sorting model of the relative effect of education on political engagement is whether levels of engagement might be raised and degrees of inequality of engagement reduced by expanding the number of citizen demands. We are, after all, in the midst of a great technological revolution in interactive communications, resulting in greater efficiency in sending and receiving messages. Anyone who is connected to the World Wide Web can contact any elected or administrative official from the president of the United States on down virtually instantaneously via electronic mail. Groups of citizens with similar interests can be easily organized and rapidly mobilized regardless of how physically dispersed they may be.

Are these changes likely to lead to improving the political access and voice of those in seats much further back in the theater? At first glance, this is an attractive hypothesis, but there remains one fundamental problem. Someone on the receiving end of these contacts has to read, deliberate upon, and answer each demand. The time and effort it takes to respond to political messages in a meaningful way is not at all diminished by this technological change. In fact, what is more likely to be created is an explosion of input with no appreciable increase in the ability of government to process the increased number of demands. The number of national elected officials in the United States has remained basically constant, as has the size of the federal bureaucracy.[4] This is true despite substantial population growth and the potential of increased demands based on the latest communications revolution.

4. Heclo, 1977.

EDUCATION-BASED SOCIAL SORTING AND EQUALITY OF ACCESS

A generation or two ago there appear to have been many more opportunities than at present for attaining rank and network centrality on the basis of factors other than educational standing. This is true, we believe, for a variety of reasons. First, more and more occupations have come to require specific as well as *de facto* educational credentials as jobs have become more complex and intellectually demanding. But it is also true because in a large-scale, highly mobile labor force, other types of traditional information on the unique talents and capacities of individuals are less available, less reliable, and less verifiable than educational attainment. These are simply system requisites in a large, postindustrial high-technology society. However, there is yet another reason why noneducational routes to social centrality are declining, and it is a reason that has to do with the tightening of any system as efficiency of competition improves over time. Paleobiologist Stephen Jay Gould has written about the importance of this tuning and tightening process in the evolution of biological systems, using the history of baseball as an analogy.[5] The .400 hitter or Joe DiMaggio's 56-game consecutive hitting streak could only happen when a system is relatively young and when competition is imperfect. Under these circumstances, room for extraordinary feats still exist. However, as recruitment and training become refined and routinized, such astounding records on the diamond become more and more difficult to replicate, let alone surpass. As systems evolve, loopholes are closed. In the system that concerns us, this translates into fewer and fewer alternative noneducational routes to the center of the social network. We are now left with a handful of celebrity endeavors, primarily in sports and entertainment, as the only noneducational means to a position near the center of the social network.

At the same time, while education is becoming a more and more dominant social sorting mechanism, we are becoming a much more educationally homogeneous society. According to the General Social Survey, the standard deviation around mean years of educational attainment for those 25 years and older has decreased by almost one-half of a year between 1974 and 1994, from about 3.5 to under 3.0 years of formal education. When looked at from the perspective of generational cohorts, the change is even more dramatic. For the gener-

5. Gould, 1985.

ation that reached educational maturity at the end of World War II, the standard deviation around average years of education was 3.5 years. With a mean of a little over 11 years, two-thirds of the population 25 years of age in 1945 had between 8 and 15 years of education. That is, those who ranged from no more than an eighth-grade education to those who ended their education just one year shy of a college degree, a spread of seven years, were within one standard deviation. In contrast, the mean educational attainment for those who reached educational maturity in 1994 was exactly 14 years, with a standard deviation of only slightly more than two years. Two-thirds of 25-year-olds in the mid-1990's have completed between 12 and 16 years of education. This four-year difference represents just over half of the heterogeneity in the 1945 cohort. Meanwhile, the correlations between both absolute and relative educational attainment and various sorted social outcomes have either remained constant or are slowly rising.

Thus, at the same time that we are becoming more educationally homogeneous, we are also sorting more intensively on these smaller and smaller educational differences. If these trends continue, the qualitative aspects of education—*where* the education was received rather than simply the number of relative years attained—will likely be weighted much more heavily. While a Harvard degree has always been worth more than a degree from a less prestigious college or university, these distinctions will surely intensify as the variance around mean years of educational attainment continues to decline. In their recent book, *The Winner Take All Society*, Frank and Cook argue that this process is well underway.[6] And in a more general way, they see in the future a society of greater and greater inequality on the basis of smaller and smaller qualitative shades of differences in talent, performance, or certification.

In addition, economists have argued that the most highly educated segment of society is garnering more and more of the desired outcomes at the expense of the less educated. But these arguments have tended to be overstated. One major reason for their exaggeration is the failure of analysts to take into account the effects of relative educational standing on positional outcomes such as earnings. For example, repeatedly singled out as losing the most earning power since the early 1970's are those who have attained less than a high school diploma.

6. Frank and Cook, 1995, Chapter 8.

However, in 1970, 45% of all of those 25 years and older had not completed high school. As we have defined it, the *relative* education of this group, which accounts for almost half of the adult population, could not be considered especially low. In the mid-1990's, however, only one-fifth of the adult population has not completed four years of high school; therefore, such citizens by definition display far lower levels of relative educational attainment than they did 20 years ago. In 1994, those without a high school education are in the bottom fifth of the adult population, compared with 1970, when they were in the bottom half. Contrasting the decline in earnings among those with less than a high school education with a comparably sized group, defined by their low levels of *relative* education, indicates that considerably more than half of the apparent decline in earnings among those with less than a high school education owes to the fact that lacking a high school diploma in the mid-1990's is indicative of a much lower level of educational standing than was the case 20 years ago, when almost half of the population was similarly educated. To be a high school drop-out in the 1990's is indicative of a far lower relative educational standing than it was 20 years ago. Labor economists may simply be using the wrong frame of reference to index the truly educationally disadvantaged.

The same pattern holds true for political engagement, as it does for most other competitive educational outcomes. And, in the end, there is no compelling evidence for either increasing or decreasing educationally based inequality in political access. What is clear is that competition for scarce resources always produces inequality, and there appears to be no simple recipe for altering the total amont of inequality in political voice and access.

CHANGING THE SHAPE OF INEQUALITY

While total levels of educationally based inequality appear relatively fixed, who attains how much education is clearly susceptible to political initiative and social change. This is exactly what affirmative action in academic admissions and financial aid, for example, is all about. If society perceives that too few women or minority citizens are to be found with the careers, incomes, and organizational positions to place them near the center of the social network in proportion to their numbers, one of the surest ways to rectify this type of inequality is to raise the level of educational attainment in these educationally disadvantaged groups in succeeding generations. However, any politically engineered mechanism for altering the competitive dynamics of attaining ranks in the social network is contentious because the participants soon recognize that a neighbor's gain is his or her own loss. The fact that the changes are deferred over the years, are inherently incremental, and can be claimed to have been earned by the citizen himself or herself makes educational intervention much less conflictual and controversial than almost any other type of intervention in social ranks. The concepts of relative education and positional educational outcomes underscore these social realities and remind us of the zero-sum character of the stakes in a way that the AEM completely misses.

Even after over 30 years of affirmative action policies, educational parity has clearly not been reached. Nevertheless, few would argue that it has not been a profound equalizing force for women and minorities, and such policies have clearly made an enormous difference. There are certainly many more politically engaged and democratically enlightened minority citizens in the mid-1990's than there would have been without educational affirmative action policies in the 1960's, 1970's, and 1980's. But support for affirmative action is clearly on the decline and is so for reasons that our argument would anticipate. First, as parity comes into even distant view, the zero-sum nature of positional outcomes based on differential education becomes more and more obvious to those who perceive that they are being negatively affected by affirmative action. Thus, the more positive progress we make in altering the shape of inequality, the higher the political barriers tend to become. Second, during this very same period when government and society have created special opportunities and supports for minorities, the character of educational competition for the rest of society has been changing in a very different direction.

Since the early 1960's, admissions to institutions of higher learning have become increasingly dependent on performance criteria. Reserved positions for the sons and daughters of alumni have dwindled almost everywhere, along with selection criteria based on the traditionally "socially desirable" student. In their place, instead, are grades received in high school, the quality of the high school attended, and standardized test scores. These changes have been well documented from totally different ideological perspectives by Frank and Cook, and

Herrnstein and Murray.[7] In a liberal state, one might think such changes are to be lauded, for what could be more democratic than admissions based on intellectual achievement and competitive standardized testing? Of all principles of social sorting, none resonates as well, in a society such as ours, as equal opportunity followed by meritocratic selection. However, affirmative action on the one hand, and selection based increasingly on universal achievement criteria, on the other, cannot long be sustained side by side without high political costs. Viewing educational outcomes, as we have in this book, as very often involving competition for scarce resources, where the relatively better educated get more of the goods, leads to a very different view of equality than the traditional model, where education raises the resources of all and can therefore be thought of as a positive-sum commodity leveling the playing field in a Pareto optimal manner.

DOES COMPETITION FOR EDUCATIONAL ADVANTAGE RESULT IN MORE EDUCATION THAN WE CAN AFFORD?

Increasing educational attainment clearly creates a more democratically enlightened citizenry. And a citizenry that is more committed to democratic values, as well as one that has a deeper and more sophisticated understanding of democratic processes, cannot help but provide greater protection for our democratic institutions and practices against whatever anti-democratic forces the future may hold. And while such arguments can be easily overstated, an increasingly educated world would seem likely to exhibit growing support for democratic practices. Beyond fostering a more democratically predisposed citizenry, education appears to have an additive impact on verbal cognitive proficiency and, by extension, on a number of other intellectual skills. The more educated the society, the more intellectually capable and knowledgeable its citizens. There are strong arguments why we need this additional knowledge, both individually and as a society. In an increasingly complex world, more training, both general and specific, will be necessary to deal effectively with the changing environment and to compete with other highly educated societies. Also, the intrinsic worth of education to a citizen's sense of well being may be of incalculable value. In these ways, ever-increasing educational attainment effectively and continuously grows social capital.

7. Frank and Cook, 1995; and Herrnstein and Murray, 1994.

These reasons, however, are not the central factors that are leading to ever-higher rates of educational attainment in the population. Rather, individual citizens attempt to attain as much education as they can because they desire more challenging and prestigious careers, greater wealth, more desirable mates, socially advantaged organizational positions, and perhaps even greater political influence. Attaining more education than those with whom the individual competes is the most effective way to attain the greatest amount of these scarce goods. For the individual, becoming more educated is an entirely rational act. However, when everyone else also behaves in this manner, more education for all leaves everyone in the same place. As Lester Thurow has argued, education has become a defensive expenditure that must be made in order to preserve one's market share.[8] That is, many jobs once filled by high school graduates are now filled exclusively by those with a college degree, not because these jobs require university-level training, but rather because employers can now find college educated applicants who will gladly compete for positions once ably staffed by those with much lower levels of formal educational attainment. Given a choice, employers will typically choose the best-educated person who is willing to take the job. This suggests that the main causal mechanisms pushing rates of educational attainment ever higher may result in little more than *educational inflation*. In this way, individual rationality may be leading to collective irrationality.

Despite all of the positive consequences that accompany aggregate increases in education, the potential costs of such educational inflation are staggering. According to National Center for Education Statistics, one-third of 20- to 24-year-olds are still in school, as compared to about 20% just two decades ago. In addition, almost 10% of those who are between the ages of 25 and 34 are currently still in school, which is up from about 2% as late as the mid-1950's. The combined financial cost to individuals, families, and government of keeping so many in school for so long is enormous. Other costs, such as potential losses in earnings and tax revenue, for example, must also be calculated.[9]

Neither is it at all clear that ever-increasing educational attainment will make us, as we are often told, more competitive in the global econ-

8. Thurow, 1972, 1975, 1980.
9. The prolonging of this dependency surely has other social consequences, perhaps positive as well as negative.

omy. America's problems with international competitiveness would seem to have much more to do with the relatively high cost of our labor rather than with an adequately educated workforce. For example, even in intellectually and educationally demanding areas such as computer software engineering, in which we are the undisputed world leader, it is fundamental wage differentials that are driving increased reliance on offshore development, rather than the shortage of suitably educated domestic labor.

How much formal education is enough or too much in a society is an extraordinarily complex issue for which our research provides no definitive answers. However, the prevailing views in social science are so clearly immersed in the paradigm of education as "social capital," that viewing education from another angle—from the perspective of education as social competition rather than as social growth—is, we believe, very much worth considering.

A

1990 Citizen Participation Study Questions

The analysis in Chapter 2 through Chapter 5 uses data from the follow-up 1990 Citizen Participation Study, conducted by The National Opinion Research Center at the University of Chicago. This appendix presents the exact wording of the questions used to make the variables in our models. The distributions reported are weighted as described in Appendix B and represent only those respondents who are 25 years and older. The total weighted sample size is 1282 for respondents 25 years and older. Unless labeled otherwise, the percentages given are the proportion of the number of valid responses. If missing data exceeds 4% of the sample, total percentages are also presented.

I   INDEPENDENT VARIABLES

I.I   *Age*

Respondents were asked *In what year were you born?* Their age was coded as 1990 minus the year of birth.

AGE	COUNT	PERCENTAGE
25–29	166	12.9
30–34	188	14.6
35–39	216	16.9
40–44	157	12.3
45–49	112	8.8
50–54	92	7.3
55–59	67	5.3
60–64	80	6.3

AGE	COUNT	PERCENTAGE	(Continued)
65–69	77	6.0	
70–74	53	4.1	
75 and older	74	5.7	

1.2 *Education*

Education was measured in years of formal education completed. The basic question used was *What is the highest grade of regular school that you have completed and gotten credit for?* (If necessary: *By regular school, we mean a school that can be counted toward an elementary or high school diploma or a college or university degree.*)

Because this question had an upper limit of 17+ years, a subsequent question was used to fill out years above 17: *What is the highest degree that you have earned?* Respondents who reported receiving a professional degree, such as M.D., J.D. or D.D.S., were assigned a score of 18, and respondents reporting a doctoral degree were assigned a score of 19.

YEARS OF EDUCATION	COUNT	PERCENTAGE
0-7 years	33	2.6
8 years (grammar school)	39	3.0
9-11 years	135	10.5
12 years (high school)	433	33.7
13-15 years	280	21.9
16 years (college)	189	14.7
17 years (1 year post-college)	140	10.9
18+ years (2+ years post-college)	34	2.7

1.3 *Race*

The question was *What is your race?* (or *Which category best describes your racial background?*).

RACE	COUNT	PERCENTAGE
White	1082	84.4
Black	112	8.8
Hispanic/Latino	52	4.0
Alaskan Native	15	1.2
Asian	12	.9
Other	8	.6

1.4 *Gender*

The respondent's gender was coded by the interviewer.

GENDER	COUNT	PERCENTAGE
Male	608	47.4
Female	674	52.6

2 EDUCATIONAL OUTCOME VARIABLES

2.1 *Family income*

Which of the income groups listed on this card includes the total 1989 income before taxes of all members of your family living in your home? Please include salaries, wages, pensions, dividends, interest, and all other income. (If uncertain: What would be your best guess?)

Missing data were filled in with information from the screener: *Now, including yourself and all family members in your household, for all of 1988, what was your total family income?* In each case, a range of choices was offered.

FAMILY INCOME	COUNT	PERCENTAGE
under $10,000	153	11.9
$10,000 – $19,999	219	17.1
$20,000 – $29,999	222	17.3
$30,000 – $39,999	210	16.4
$40,000 – $49,999	167	13.0
$50,000 – $59,999	103	8.0
$60,000 – $79,999	97	7.6
$80,000 – $99,999	51	4.0
$100,000 and over	60	4.7

2.2 *Occupational prominence*

Occupational prominence is a seven-point scale based on six questions. Respondents were given one point each for affirmative responses to the following four questions:

Here is a list of things that people sometimes have to do as part of their jobs. After I read each one, please tell me whether or not you have engaged in that activity in the last six months as part of your job.

Have you...
- *Written a letter?*
- *Gone to a meeting where you took part in making decisions?*
- *Planned or chaired a meeting?*
- *Given a presentation or speech?*

One additional point was assigned if the respondents supervised any employees directly, and another point was assigned if they also supervised employees indirectly:

In your job, about how many other people (do/did) you supervise who (are/were) directly responsible to you or report(ed) directly to you? (If necessary, probe: *On average, what would you say?*)

About how many people (do/did) you supervise indirectly—that is, how many people report(ed) to the people you supervise(d)? (If necessary, probe: *On average what would you say?*)

"Yes" Answers:	Count	Valid Percentage	Total Percentage
Wrote a letter	530	60.3	41.3
Decision-making meeting	627	71.4	48.9
Planned or chaired a meeting	333	38.0	26.0
Gave presentation or speech	374	42.7	29.2
Supervised people directly	486	38.0	37.9
Supervised people indirectly	178	14.0	13.9

Occupational Prominence	Count	Percentage
0 (low)	318	24.9
1	217	17.0
2	182	14.2
3	190	14.9
4	167	13.1
5	131	10.3
6 (high)	71	5.6

2.3 *Membership in nonpolitical organizations*

Respondents were asked a variety of questions about membership in organizations: *Here is a list of organizations. Please read through this list and when you have finished, I'll have some questions.*

We used two of the questions:

- *Are you a member of...*(here type of organization was read)*?*
- *Does this organization sometimes take stands on any public issues—either locally or nationally?*

From a group of 20 organizational types, labeled A through T, we selected those 10 types for whom a majority of the membership said that the organization does *not* take stands on public issues. The membership scale we created is the sum of the number of types of organizations of which the respondent is a member. (Note that he/she could be a member of several organizations of the same type, but that still would count as only one point on our scale.)

A   *Kiwanis or a local women's club or a fraternal organization at school?*

C   *Groups affiliated with your religion such as the Knights of Columbus or B'nai B'rith? (If necessary: Aside from your activity within your own congregation or your contributions to your own congregation.)*

M   *Youth groups such as the Girl Scouts or the 4-H?*

N   *Literary, art, discussion, or study groups?*

O   *A hobby club, sports or country club, or some other group or club for leisure time activities?*

P   *An association related to where you live—like a neighborhood or community association, or a home owners' or condominium association, or a block club?*

   People sometimes give time or money to organizations that don't really have members. Aside from the organizations we have discussed (and aside from any charitable work associated with your (church/synagogue), in the last twelve months have you given time to any other organization that provides social services in such fields as health or service to the needy? For instance, a hospital, a cancer or heart drive, or a group like the Salvation Army that works for the poor.

R   *What about an educational institution—a local school or your own school or college or some organization associated with education such as a school alumni association or a school service organization like the PTA? Do you belong to or give time to any such organization?*

S   *What about some cultural organization that is active in providing cultural services to the public—for example, a museum, the symphony, or public radio or television? Do you give time to any organization that is active in this way?*

T   *Lastly, have I missed any other organization you belong to, give time to, or are associated with?*

	TYPE OF ORGANIZATION	COUNT OF MEMBERS	PERCENTAGE
A	Service/fraternal	172	13.5
C	Religious	118	9.2
M	Youth	102	8.0
N	Literary/art	65	5.1
O	Hobby/sports	265	20.8
P	Neighborhood/home owner	156	12.2
Q	Health/service to needy	203	16.0
R	Educational	254	19.9
S	Cultural	94	7.4
T	Other	38	3.1

NUMBER OF TYPES OF ORGANIZATIONAL MEMBERSHIP	COUNT	PERCENTAGE
0	659	51.4
1	369	28.8
2	161	12.5
3	58	4.6
4 or more	29	2.2

3   INTERVENING VARIABLES

3.1   *Verbal Cognitive Proficiency*

Verbal cognitive proficiency was measured with a 10-item vocabulary test: *Now we would like to know something about how people go about guessing words they do not know. On this card are listed some words—you may know some of them, and you may not know quite a few of them. On each line* (hand card GG), *the first word is in capital letters—for example, BEAST. Then there are five other words. Tell me the number of the word that comes closest to the meaning of the word in capital letters. For example, if the word in capital letters is BEAST, you would say '4,' since 'animal' comes closer to BEAST than any of the other words. If you wish, I will read the words to you. These words are difficult for almost everyone—just give me your best guess if you are not sure of the answer.* Example: *BEAST means... afraid, words, large, animal, separate.*

There are 10 word-definition questions following the introduction, all in the same format as the example. Because the National Opinion Research Center uses this set of words in other surveys, we will not list the specific words here.

NUMBER OF CORRECT RESPONSES	COUNT	PERCENTAGE
0	10	.8
1	14	1.1
2	24	1.9
3	71	5.6
4	119	9.3
5	194	15.2
6	260	20.3
7	218	17.0
8	140	10.9
9	134	10.5
10	97	7.6

3.2 *Social network centrality*

This measure is a simple additive scale of the number of public figures the respondent is known by.

We are interested in whether you are personally acquainted with various kinds of people—that is, if you met or called the person, he or she would recognize you or your name. Here is a list of some kinds of people. Are you personally acquainted with any of them?

- *a current member of Congress (House or Senate).*
- *a current member of the state legislature (either house).*
- *a member of the local elected council in your community.*
- *a member of some other local official board.*
- *someone who works for the local media—a local newspaper or TV station.*
- *someone working for one of the national media.*

MEMBERS OF:	KNOWN BY	PERCENTAGE
Congress	120	9.3
State legislature	206	16.1
Local council	438	34.2
Other local board	397	31.0
Local media	345	26.9
National media	40	3.1

NUMBER OF PUBLIC FIGURES WHO KNOW RESPONDENT	COUNT	PERCENTAGE
0	607	47.7
1	236	18.5
2	174	13.7
3	131	10.3
4	69	5.4
5	44	3.5
6	12	1.0

4 DEPENDENT VARIABLES

4.1 *Political Engagement*

4.1.1 Voting. *In talking to people about elections, we find that they are sometimes not able to vote because they're not registered, they don't have time, or they have difficulty getting to the polls. Think about the presidential elections since you have been old enough to vote. Have you voted in all of them, in most of them, in some of them, rarely voted in them, or have you never voted in a presidential election?*

Now, thinking about the local elections that have been held since you were old enough to vote, have you voted in all of them, in most of them, in some of them, rarely voted in them, or have you never voted in a local election?

For the voting scale, responses to the questions above were coded:

		PRESIDENTIAL ELECTIONS		LOCAL ELECTIONS	
		Count	Percentage	Count	Percentage
Never	0.0	155	12.1	195	15.3
Rarely	0.25	61	4.8	114	8.9
Some	0.5	153	12.0	261	20.5
Most	0.75	303	23.7	432	33.9
All	1.0	607	47.4	273	21.4

The scores added to get a nine-value scale ranging from 0 to 2:

VOTING SCORE	COUNT	PERCENTAGE
0.0	151	11.8
0.25	17	1.4
0.5	54	4.2
0.75	38	3.0
1.0	131	10.3
1.25	121	9.5
1.5	249	19.5
1.75	256	20.1
2.0	257	20.2

4.1.2 *Political attentiveness.* Six questions probed respondents' attention to politics. The four questions on interest and attention to newspapers have a four-point scale, low to high. The two discussion questions have a five-point scale, low to high. When factor analysis was done on the six attentiveness questions, a single and very strong underlying dimension was found. Thus, each question was rescaled on a 0–1 scale, and the resulting scales simply added.

The six questions are as follows:

- *Thinking about your local community, how interested are you in local community politics and local community affairs?*
- *How interested are you in national politics and national affairs?*
- *When you read the newspaper, how much attention do you pay to local politics and community affairs? A great deal, some, very little, or none?*
- *When you read the newspaper, how much attention do you pay to stories on national and world politics and public affairs? A great deal, some, very little, or none?*
- *How often do you discuss local community politics or local community affairs with others?*
- *How often do you discuss national politics and national affairs with others?*

VERY INTERESTED IN:	COUNT	PERCENTAGE
Local community affairs	296	23.1
National affairs	446	34.9
Local news	466	36.5
National news	407	31.9
DISCUSS DAILY OR ALMOST DAILY:		
Local community affairs	242	18.9
National affairs	332	26.0

POLITICAL ATTENTIVENESS	COUNT	PERCENTAGE
0 (low)	26	2.1
1	66	5.2
2	149	11.7
3	341	26.7
4	383	29.9
5	242	18.9
6 (high)	71	5.5

4.1.3 *Knowledge of political leaders.* This measure is an additive measure of the number of correct responses to the following four questions (Note that two correct responses are possible from the first question).

- *We want to know how well known the different governmental leaders are around here. If you happen to know, what are the names of the United States Senators from (state where respondent lives)?*
- *Could you tell me the name of the congressman or congresswoman from this district? Do you happen to know his or her name?*
- *What about the name of the person who is your state representative to the (state where respondent lives) (House of Representatives/ Assembly/House of Delegates)? Do you happen to know your (representative's/assemblyman's or assembly woman's/delegate's) name?*
- *What is the name of the head of the local public school system?*

LEADERS KNOWN	COUNT	PERCENTAGE
One senator only	334	26.4
Both senators	445	35.2
Congressman/woman	476	38.6
State representative	262	20.7
Head of public schools	361	28.5

NUMBER OF LEADERS KNOWN	COUNT	PERCENTAGE
0	332	26.0
1	250	19.6
2	266	20.8
3	230	18.0
4	137	10.7
5	61	4.8

4.1.4 *Participation in difficult political activities.* Our collection of difficult political acts is made up of contacting public officials, working for political campaigns, being a member of or attending meetings of a local board, and other informal political activity. We use a five-point scale valued from 0 to 4; respondents receive one point for each type of political act performed. The questions are as follows:

Contacting public officials:

Now, I want to ask you a few questions about contacts you may have initiated with government officials or someone on the staff of such officials—either in person or by phone or letter—about problems or issues with which you were concerned. Please don't count any contacts you have made as a regular part of your job.

- *In the past twelve months, have you initiated any contacts with a federal elected official or someone on the staff of such an official: I mean someone in the White House or a congressional or senate office?*
- *What about a nonelected official in a federal government agency? Have you initiated a contact with such a person in the last twelve months?*
- *What about an elected official on the state or local level—a governor or mayor or a member of the state legislature or a city or town council—or someone on the staff of such an elected official?*
- *And what about a nonelected official in a state or local government agency or board? Have you initiated a contact with such a person in the last twelve months?*

OFFICIAL CONTACTED	COUNT	PERCENTAGE
Elected federal official	173	13.5
Nonelected federal official	109	8.6
Elected local official	336	26.3
Nonelected local official	178	13.9

Campaign work:

Since January 1988, the start of the last national election year, have you worked as a volunteer—that is, for no pay at all or for only a token amount—for a candidate running for national, state, or local office?

	COUNT	PERCENTAGE
Campaign volunteers	111	8.6

Board membership and meeting attendance:

Now some questions about your role in your community:
- *In the past two years, since (current month, 1988), have you served in a voluntary capacity—that is, for no pay at all or for only a token amount—on any official local governmental board or council that deals with community problems and issues such as a town council, a school board, a zoning board, a planning board, or the like?*
- *Have you attended a meeting of such an official local government board or council in the past twelve months?*

	COUNT	PERCENTAGE
Volunteered in local government in last 2 years	41	3.2
Attended local government meeting in last year	184	14.9

Informal political action:

Aside from membership on a board or council or attendance at meetings, I'd like to ask also about informal activity in your community or neighborhood. In the past twelve months, have you gotten together informally with or worked with others in your community or neighbor-

hood to try to deal with some community issue or problem? (If you have mentioned this activity elsewhere, perhaps in connection with your church or synagogue, or an organization or a local campaign, don't repeat it here.)

	COUNT	PERCENTAGE
Informal political action	272	21.2

NUMBER OF TYPES OF POLITICAL ACTS PERFORMED	COUNT	PERCENTAGE
0	651	50.8
1	344	26.8
2	168	13.2
3	94	7.3
4	25	2.0

4.2 Enlightenment

4.2.1 Tolerance. The tolerance measure is a simple additive scale of the number of tolerant responses to the following four questions.

- *There are always some people whose ideas are considered bad or dangerous by other people. Consider someone who is openly homosexual. If some people in your community suggested that a book that he or she wrote in favor of homosexuality should be taken out of your public library, would you favor removing this book or not?*
- *What about someone who believes that blacks are genetically inferior? If some people in your community suggested that a book he or she wrote arguing that blacks are genetically inferior should be taken out of your public library, would you favor removing this book or not?*
- *Or consider someone who advocates doing away with elections and letting the military run the country. If such a person wanted to make a speech in your community, should he or she be allowed to or not?*
- *And what about someone who is against all churches and religion. If such a person wanted to make a speech in your community, should he or she be allowed to or not?*

TOLERANT RESPONSE TO:	COUNT	PERCENTAGE
Pro-homosexual book	878	68.5
Racist book	895	69.8
Militarist speech	904	70.6
Atheistic speech	916	71.5

NUMBER OF TOLERANT RESPONSES	COUNT	PERCENTAGE
0	125	9.8
1	130	10.2
2	207	16.2
3	211	16.5
4	604	47.3

4.2.2 *Knowledge of principles of democracy.* This measure is an additive scale of the number of correct responses to the following three questions.

- *Does the Fifth Amendment to the American Constitution mainly guarantee citizens protection against forced confessions or mainly guarantee freedom of speech?*
- *When people talk about 'civil liberties,' do they usually mean the right to vote and run for office, or freedom of speech, press and assembly?*
- *Which is the major difference between democracies and dictatorships: that democratic governments allow private property or that democratic governments allow citizens to choose their representatives freely?*

PRINCIPLE	NUMBER WHO KNOW	PERCENTAGE
Fifth Amendment	579	45.3
Civil liberties	1033	81.1
Democracy versus dictatorship	1128	88.4

NUMBER OF PRINCIPLES KNOWN	COUNT	PERCENTAGE
0	62	4.8
1	172	13.5
2	562	44.0
3	481	37.7

4.2.3 *Knowledge of other current political facts.* The measure is an additive scale of the number of correct responses to four questions. The first two listed below are from the 1990 survey, while the third and fourth are from the 1989 screening survey.

- *We are interested in how much people know about American government. On average over the past few years, did the federal government spend more money on the National Aeronautics and Space Administration (NASA) or Social Security?*
- *Who was mainly behind the increased use of primary elections in the United States to choose candidates: party 'bosses' who can use them to control nominations or reformers who want the voters to choose party candidates themselves?*
- *How old do you have to be to vote for president of the United States?*
- *Which party has more members in the United States House of Representatives—the Democrats or the Republicans?*

FACT	NUMBER WHO KNOW	PERCENTAGE
NASA/Social Security $	369	28.8
Primary election reform	580	45.5
Age to vote	1049	81.9
House majority party	871	67.9

NUMBER OF CORRECT RESPONSES	COUNT	PERCENTAGE
0	53	4.1
1	249	19.4
2	460	35.9
3	381	29.7
4	140	10.9

CORRELATION MATRIX

The zero-order correlations among the explanatory variables in our model from the 1990 Citizen Participation Survey are as follows:

Correlations:	Education	Occupational Prominence	Family Income	Organizational Membership	Social Network Centrality	Verbal Proficiency
Education						
Occupational Prominence	.48					
Family Income	.38	.35				
Organizational Membership	.31	.26	.28			
Social Network Centrality	.26	.29	.25	.28		
Verbal Proficiency	.54	.28	.25	.27	.19	

Source: 1990 Citizen Participation Study
N = 1224

B

Weighting Procedures for the 1990 Citizen Participation Study Data

by Martin Frankel, Chief Statistical Scientist

National Opinion Research Center

Whenever disproportionate stratified sampling is used to assure adequate sample sizes for domains of analytical interest, it is necessary to apply case level "weights" for analysis of either the entire sample or combinations of domains. These weights are required in order to avoid estimation bias that may arise as a result of differences between domains with respect to the analytical variables of interest.

In general, the use of weights has an impact on the reliability of estimates. Analytical formulas and other computational procedures are available for determination of the exact impact of weighting. However, when the use of these methods is not feasible, there are approximations that can be used to adjust estimates of reliability (that is, standard errors) for the impact of weighting. One of these adjustments makes use of the rel-variance of the weights as follows: adjusted standard error = standard error based on simple random sampling assumptions times the square root of the quantity 1 plus the rel-variance of the weights, or

$$SE(\text{adjusted}) \; = \; SE(\text{SRS}) + (1 + RV^2)^{\frac{1}{2}}$$

This adjustment is generally considered appropriate for estimates of standard errors for means and proportions. It is generally considered conservative for more analytical estimates, such as differences between means and proportion, correlations, and regression coefficients.

It should be noted that this formula for adjustment may be implemented in certain software packages by adjusting the sum of weights to equal the sample size divided by 1 plus the rel-variance of the weights.

C

Basic Model by Race and Gender

TABLE C.1 Education to intervening and dependent variables:
Standardized coefficients from maximum likelihood LISREL estimation

	Education	Occupational Prominence	Family Income	Organizational Membership	Verbal Proficiency	Social Network Centrality
Occupational Prominence	.48 (5.6)					
Family Income	.37 (3.8)	.18 (1.9)				
Organizational Membership	.14 (1.3)	.13 (1.2)	.08 (0.8)			
Verbal Proficiency	.47 (5.3)			.02 (0.2)		
Social Network Centrality		.25 (2.5)	.14 (1.4)	.06 (0.6)		
Political Engagement Scale	.27 (2.7)		.02 (0.2)	.17 (2.0)	.15 (1.7)	.30 (3.7)
Enlightenment Scale	.30 (2.6)	.06 (0.6)	.11 (1.2)		.18 (1.9)	

Blacks only (n=106)
t values in parentheses below coefficients

TABLE C.2 Education to intervening and dependent variables: Standardized coefficients from maximum likelihood LISREL estimation

	Education	Occupational Prominence	Family Income	Organizational Membership	Verbal Proficiency	Social Network Centrality
Occupational Prominence	.49 (18.3)					
Family Income	.26 (8.0)	.22 (6.8)				
Organizational Membership	.20 (5.7)	.10 (3.1)	.17 (5.4)			
Verbal Proficiency	.51 (18.9)			.10 (3.6)		
Social Network Centrality		.21 (6.6)	.12 (3.9	.19 (6.2)		
Political Engagement Scale	.12 (3.9)		.07 (2.6)	.16 (5.9)	.16 (5.6)	.40 (15.2)
Enlightenment Scale	.29 (8.2)	.08 (2.7)	.06 (2.0)		.26 (8.5)	

Whites only (n=1036)

t values in parentheses below coefficients

TABLE C.3   Education to intervening and dependent variables:
Standardized coefficients from maximum likelihood LISREL estimation

	Education	Occupational Prominence	Family Income	Organizational Membership	Verbal Proficiency	Social Network Centrality
Occupational Prominence	.49 (13.4)					
Family Income	.22 (5.2)	.33 (7.9)				
Organizational Membership	.18 (4.1)	.17 (3.6)	.14 (3.2)			
Verbal Proficiency	.49 (13.4)			.11 (2.9)		
Social Network Centrality		.14 (3.2)	.14 (3.3)	.24 (6.0)		
Political Engagement Scale	.13 (3.1)		.08 (2.2)	.15 (4.2)	.15 (3.9)	.39 (11.0)
Enlightenment Scale	.26 (5.7)	.02 (0.4)	.07 (1.9)		.32 (7.9)	

Men only (n=585)
t values in parentheses below coefficients

TABLE C.4 Education to intervening and dependent variables: Standardized coefficients from maximum likelihood LISREL estimation

	Education	Occupational Prominence	Family Income	Organizational Membership	Verbal Proficiency	Social Network Centrality
Occupational Prominence	.47 (13.5)					
Family Income	.33 (7.8)	.08 (1.9)				
Organizational Membership	.19 (4.4)	.08 (1.9)	.18 (4.6)			
Verbal Proficiency	.52 (15.2)			.11 (3.2)		
Social Network Centrality		.24 (6.2)	.12 (3.0)	.14 (3.5)		
Political Engagement Scale	.14 (3.5)		.05 (1.3)	.17 (5.0)	.20 (5.4)	.38 (11.8)
Enlightenment Scale	.30 (6.7)	.10 (2.8)	.06 (1.6)		.26 (6.8)	

Women only (n=638)

t values in parentheses below coefficients

D

Creating the Political Engagement and Enlightenment Scales

We use principal components analysis with oblique rotation to identify the two underlying dimensions of democratic citizenship. As a check on this solution (which yielded the two components of political engagement and enlightenment in Table 5.1), Table D.1 and Table D.2 present results from two analyses with different extraction methods and oblique rotation. Table D.1 displays the results from a principal axis factoring, and Table D.2 shows the results with maximum likelihood. The table entries correspond to the pattern matrix from the factor analysis. Both extraction methods identify two dimensions, with the same arrangement of loadings of the seven characteristics of voting, political attentiveness, knowledge of political leaders, and participation in difficult political activities loading on one factor, while tolerance, knowledge of the principles of democracy, and knowledge of other political facts load on the second factor.

TABLE D.1 Principal axis factor analysis of citizenship measures

	POLITICAL ENGAGEMENT	ENLIGHTENMENT
Voting	.70	−.13
Political attentiveness	.64	.12
Knowledge of political leaders	.50	.09
Participation in difficult political activities	.50	.05
Tolerance	−.07	.49
Knowledge of principles of democracy	.16	.50
Knowledge of other political facts	.17	.43

Solution rotated with direct oblimin

TABLE D.2 Maximum likelihood factor analysis of citizenship measures

	POLITICAL ENGAGEMENT	ENLIGHTENMENT
Voting	.70	−.13
Political attentiveness	.63	.13
Knowledge of political leaders	.50	.09
Participation in difficult political activities	.50	.05
Tolerance	−.07	.48
Knowledge of principles of democracy	.15	.51
Knowledge of other political facts	.17	.42

Solution rotated with direct oblimin

Our choice of oblique rotation is based on the theoretical assumption that the factors are correlated. In the two factor analyses presented above, the two factors are correlated at 0.50, confirming this assumption. However, as an additional check, Table D.3 presents the results of an analysis using an orthogonal method of rotation. The data in this table show that the general pattern of the identification of the overall political engagement and enlightenment components remains.

TABLE D.3 Principal components analysis of citizenship measures

	POLITICAL ENGAGEMENT	ENLIGHTENMENT
Voting	.76	.00
Political attentiveness	.72	.27
Knowledge of political leaders	.65	.18
Participation in difficult political activities	.66	.13
Tolerance	−.09	.80
Knowledge of principles of democracy	.30	.64
Knowledge of other political facts	.28	.61

Solution rotated with varimax

E

Nonrecursive Specifications

The nonrecursive model estimated to examine the possibility of a reciprocal relationship between social network centrality and participation in difficult political activities is reported in Table E.1. A comparison of the coefficients reported in this table with those presented in Figure 4.4 indicates that there is very little change in the rest of the model when the nonrecursive path is added.

TABLE E.1 Education to participation in difficult political activities: Coefficients from maximum likelihood estimation

	STANDARDIZED COEFFICIENT	UNSTANDARDIZED COEFFICIENT	STANDARD ERROR	*t* VALUE
Education	.08	.03	.01	2.85
Occupational Prominence	.08	.05	.03	1.64
Family Income				
Organizational Involvement	.19	.20	.05	4.26
Verbal Proficiency				
Social Network Centrality	.40	.28	.12	2.23
Difficult Political Acts back to Social Network Centrality	−.02	−.03	.32	−.10

The results of the estimation of the nonrecursive model with knowledge of political leaders as the dependent measure are reported in Table E.2. Comparing these results to those reported in Table 4.3 reveals that the paths from education and organizational involvement to knowledge of political leaders are slightly stronger when the pathway from leadership knowledge to social network centrality is included.

TABLE E.2 Education to knowledge of political leaders: Coefficients from maximum likelihood estimation

	STANDARDIZED COEFFICIENT	UNSTANDARDIZED COEFFICIENT	STANDARD ERROR	t VALUE
Education	.11	.06	.02	3.32
Occupational Prominence				
Family Income				
Organizational Involvement	.11	.16	.05	3.33
Verbal Proficiency	.18	.13	.02	5.96
Social Network Centrality	.18	.18	.08	2.12
Knowledge of Political Leaders back to Social Network Centrality	.14	.14	.08	1.66

F

Educational Environment and
Relative Education Measures

by Jean G. Jenkins

Central to our hypotheses about the effects of education on democratic citizenship are the concepts of educational environment and relative education. Educational environment has been defined as the mean educational level in the population when an individual reaches educational maturity (age 25). Relative education is the ratio of the individual's educational level to the educational environment. This appendix documents the creation of these two measures with the pooled data from the General Social Survey (GSS) and the National Election Study (NES). The SPSS code used to create these measures can be obtained from the authors.

Both data sets contain a variety of demographic information about the respondents, including year of birth and years of education, from which we create the educational environment and relative education measures. GSS data were obtained each year between 1972 and 1994 except for 1979, 1981, and 1992, when surveys were not taken. In the GSS data, there are a total of 32,380 cases. (The surveys of 1982 and 1987 were oversampled for African-Americans, and the cases from those two surveys were weighted to bring the sample representation into agreement with actual population distributions while not changing the total sample size.) The NES data included 12 samples taken in national election years between 1972 and 1994. The total unweighted sample size for these years is 24,509. Cases were weighted in 1974, 1976, 1992, and 1994 to produce a representative sample of the U.S. adult population, and the weighted sample size is 26,060. Because we use only respondents age 25 and older, our weighted GSS sample size is 28,495 and our weighted NES sample size is 22,681 for a total of 51,176 cases.

The GSS and NES data were then combined into a single data file in order to create the educational environment and relative education measures. Educational levels across this time period in the NES and GSS data sets are very similar to each other in level and pattern. Figure F.1 documents the similarity in years of educational attainment by year of birth for the GSS and NES data separately.

FIGURE F.1 **Mean years of education by year of birth**

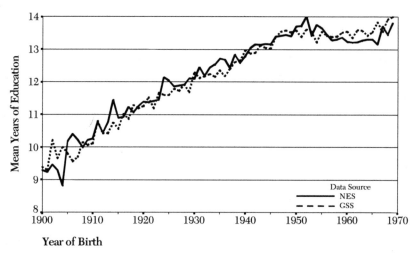

Year of Birth

Source: GSS, 1972–1994; NES, 1972–1994

In order to create measures of educational environment and relative education, measures of cohort and individual educational attainment were standardized between the GSS and NES data. The respondent's year of birth was used as the cohort indicator. The GSS year-of-birth measurement was used directly. For the NES data, the year of birth was constructed as the survey year minus the respondent's age. In both of the data sets, the respondent's year of birth ranged between 1874 and 1969, and the educational environment measure was calculated for all of those birth cohorts. However, because the number of respondents born before 1900 is small (1,311, or 2.6% of the sample), their mean educational levels varied greatly from year to year. We omitted these early birth cohorts from the figures and tables so that they would not obscure the patterns for the bulk of the sample.

Both the GSS and NES measure the number of years of school completed. The GSS scale ranges between 0 and 19 years, with the top category being 20 and more years. The NES scale ranges between 0 to 16 years, with a top category of 17 and more years. An auxiliary NES question about educational degrees earned enabled us to expand the NES scale to 20+ years. Master's degrees were recoded as 18 years, law degrees were recoded as 19 years, and all forms of doctor's degrees were recoded as 20+ years.

CREATING THE MEASURES OF EDUCATIONAL ENVIRONMENT AND RELATIVE EDUCATION

The measure of relative education is simply the ratio between an individual's years of education and the mean years of education of the total adult population—what we call the educational environment.

Consistent with the U.S. Bureau of the Census, we have adopted age 25 as an approximation of the age at which formal education is completed. In addition, we theorize that at this time of educational maturity, citizens are in competition primarily with individuals between the ages of 25 and 50. Adults over 50 are unlikely to be competing for the same occupational and organizational positions that are sought by citizens 25 years their junior. Thus, our operational definition of relative education for any given individual is the ratio of his or her educational attainment and the educational environment. The educational environment is defined as the mean educational level of all adults 25 to 50 years old in the population at the time the citizen reached eductional maturity.

The equation below specifies the educational environment (E_c) for a given birth year or cohort (c) as the ratio between the sum of years of education (e_i) for all individuals of the same birth cohort, or the preceding 25 birth cohorts, and the total number of individuals (n) in those 26 birth cohorts (c–25 to c).

$$E_c = \frac{\sum_{i=1}^{n} e_i}{n}$$

The next equation defines the measure of relative education, where relative education (re$_i$) is the ratio between the actual years of education (e$_i$) for an individual, and the educational environment (E$_c$) for persons in that individual's birth cohort (c).

$$re_i = \frac{e_i}{E_c}$$

AGE DISTRIBUTION BIAS

The educational environment measure was calculated from the combined GSS and NES data sets, with data collection spanning the years 1972 to 1994. While the survey organizations responsible for data collection did their best to assure that the demographic characteristics of each sample were representative of the population as a whole, lumping the samples together as we did introduces bias in the sizes of the year of birth cohorts. Figure F.2 shows the number of respondents for each year of birth in the pooled sample of GSS and NES data. Members of the older cohorts are underrepresented, since many of their members died before or during the 23-year data collection span. The younger cohorts are underrepresented, since they were only gradually added to the sample as they turned 25. Cohorts with birth years from approximately 1930 through 1947 were eligible for all samples and probably suffered few losses from death, as the oldest of them would be just 64 in 1994.

These distributional biases may cause the educational environment measures computed from the sample to vary less over time than do the true values for the population. Recall that the pool of candidates for the educational environment measure for all cohorts includes all persons who are aged 25 through 50 when the members of the given cohort are 25 years old. For the early cohorts the available respondents in our sample were disproportionately closer to 25 when the cohort was 25 since more of those who would have been closer to 50 had already died. Because educational levels were steadily rising, that distributional bias would cause the educational environment measure to be larger than the true figure for the early cohorts. Conversely, for the cohorts born after 1947 the respondents falling in the pool were disproportionately older, closer to 50 when the cohort was 25, since the older cohorts were old enough to be interviewed during more of the 23 years of data collection. Such a bias would cause the educational environment measure for the later cohorts to be somewhat smaller than the true figure.

FIGURE F.2 Size of birth cohorts in pooled GSS and NES data

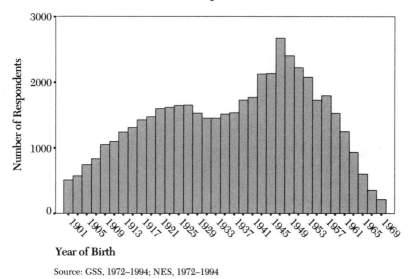

Year of Birth

Source: GSS, 1972–1994; NES, 1972–1994

We investigated these biases in the educational environment measure by calculating an alternative measure based on respondent educational level but weighting the contribution of each cohort using approximate age distribution figures from U.S. Bureau of the Census population tables. Figure F.3 shows both the educational environment from the GSS and NES data used in our analysis and the alternate measure created with census age distribution approximations. Notice that the bias for the later cohorts is extremely small. This is due to the lessening of the rate of educational increase later in the twentieth century.

FIGURE F.3 Mean educational environment by year of birth from sample and census age distributions

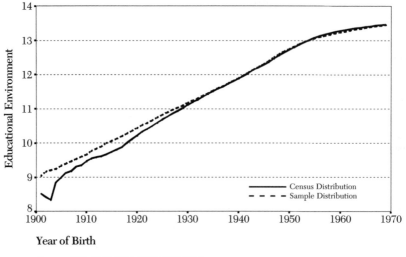

Source: GSS, 1972–1994; NES, 1972–1994

Would eliminating the age distribution bias in the educational environment measure have made a difference in the analysis of the effects of relative education versus absolute education on enlightenment and political engagement? To test this hypothesis, we substituted the relative education measure created with the census age distribution and replicated the analysis presented in Table 8.1. Table F.1 below shows the comparison between the two versions of relative education. The results show that the impact of the two versions of relative education on political engagement and tolerance are almost identical. (The census age distribution covers birth years between 1900 and 1969. Both equations in Table F.1 were run for these birth years and therefore do not match Table 8.1 exactly.)

TABLE F.1 Comparison of two versions of relative education: Impact on political engagement and tolerance

POLITICAL ENGAGEMENT	STANDARDIZED COEFFICIENT	t VALUE	ADJUSTED R^2
Sample relative education	.44	71.1	.22
Census relative education	.44	71.0	.22
TOLERANCE			
Sample relative education	.33	44.5	.12
Census relative education	.31	41.7	.11

Standardized OLS regression coefficients
Source: NES, 1972–1994; GSS, 1976–1994

G

Documentation of the Over Time Data

TABLE G.1 Percentage of tolerant responses by year

	1976	1977	1980	1982	1984	1985	1987	1988	1989	1990	1991	1993	1994
TEACH COLLEGE													
Atheist	39	36	44	45	45	45	47	45	53	52	54	53	54
Communist	40	28	41	45	47	45	47	49	53	55	56	60	57
Homosexual	52	49	56	56	60	58	58	59	66	65	65	71	72
Militarist	35	31	40	39	40	40	40	37	41	43	45	48	47
Racist	41	40	45	44	42	43	45	43	48	47	45	45	44
KEEP BOOK IN LIBRARY													
Atheist	58	58	61	61	64	62	67	65	69	69	71	70	71
Communist	55	54	58	58	60	58	61	60	64	66	69	69	68
Homosexual	56	56	58	57	61	57	58	62	66	65	70	69	70
Militarist	55	54	59	58	60	57	59	58	62	62	68	69	65
Racist	60	62	66	63	65	62	66	64	68	67	68	68	68
MAKE SPEECH													
Atheist	62	60	65	64	68	66	69	70	72	73	73	72	73
Communist	53	55	55	57	60	58	59	61	65	66	69	70	68
Homosexual	62	63	67	67	71	69	70	72	79	77	77	81	81
Militarist	53	49	57	55	57	55	57	56	59	58	63	65	64
Racist	60	59	63	61	59	58	63	64	64	64	65	62	62

Source: GSS, 1976–1994

For each of the 13 years in which the tolerance questions were asked, a principal components analysis was run. Table G.2 presents the results of these analyses. The first row of the table displays the percentage of variance explained by the first principal component, and the rows below present the loadings of the individual items on this first principal component. The last row of the table reports the reliability (Alpha) of this set of 15 items in each of the years. In addition to the principal components analysis, a factor analysis was performed using the maximum likelihood method. The results were virtually identical to those from the principal components analysis in terms of the stability of the loadings and the variance accounted for by the first factor. These results underscore the findings that all of the tolerance questions are related to a single underlying dimension, and that this relationship is stable over time.

TABLE G.2 Dimensionality of tolerance items by year: Factor loadings for the first principal component

	1976	1977	1980	1982	1984	1985	1987	1988	1989	1990	1991	1993	1994
% Variance First PC	51	48	53	52	50	52	49	48	45	48	47	47	47
TEACH COLLEGE													
Atheist	.71	.69	.71	.74	.69	.73	71	.67	.70	.71	.69	.69	.70
Communist	.60	.65	.68	.65	.66	.69	.66	.64	.58	.64	.58	.61	.58
Homosexual	.72	.67	.71	.69	.68	.69	.69	.67	.65	.63	.63	.65	.62
Militarist	.67	.64	.69	.70	.66	.70	.70	.68	.64	.71	.68	.66	.67
Racist	.62	.54	.61	.64	.57	.59	.55	.51	.56	.59	.59	.56	.59
KEEP BOOK IN LIBRARY													
Atheist	.76	.75	.76	.78	.77	.75	.72	.72	.71	.73	.73	73	.73
Communist	.79	.76	.82	.80	.80	.79	.78	.77	.73	.75	.76	.75	.75
Homosexual	.77	.75	.78	.76	.76	.77	.73	.74	.72	.71	.72	.71	.70
Militarist	.73	.76	.78	.75	.76	.78	.76	.75	.75	.78	.74	.75	.73
Racist	.70	.66	.72	.74	.65	.72	.68	.64	.66	.68	.69	.66	.67
MAKE SPEECH													
Atheist	.75	.72	.74	.73	.72	.72	.71	.71	.69	.71	.71	.71	.71
Communist	.76	.75	.75	.74	.75	.75	.72	.76	.72	.72	.73	.73	.74
Homosexual	.75	.70	.74	.72	.72	.72	.70	.70	.66	.66	.66	.66	.67

TABLE G.2 Dimensionality of tolerance items by year: Factor loadings for the first principal component (Continued)

	1976	1977	1980	1982	1984	1985	1987	1988	1989	1990	1991	1993	1994
MAKE SPEECH (Continued)													
Militarist	.69	.69	.73	.72	.70	.74	.74	.73	.69	.71	.70	.74	.70
Racist	.67	.64	.65	.65	.61	.62	.62	.58	.57	.63	.62	.64	.66
Reliability (Alpha)	.93	.92	.94	.93	.93	.93	.92	.92	.91	.92	.92	.92	.92

Source: GSS, 1976–1994

The tolerance measure used in the analysis was constructed by counting the number of tolerant responses across the fifteen questions. This measure is correlated with an index of tolerance created with principal components analysis at 0.996.

The measure of overall political engagement was created using the PRINCALS technique, which is a form of principal components analysis that employs an alternating least squares approach. PRINCALS has a number of features that distinguish it from traditional principal components analysis including the capability to combine similar categories of variables and requantifying the underlying scale of a variable. In the analysis reported below, however, none of these features were used. It was the missing value imputation feature of PRINCALS that made it an attractive alternative to standard principal components analysis. Typically, an observation that has missing information on any of the original variables used in a principal components analysis is assigned a missing factor score on the newly created dimensions identified in the analysis. PRINCALS produces exactly the same results as principal components analysis when there is no missing data. However, when missing data are present, it iterates to optimize the category quantifications. The category quantification times the component loading for the variable is used to derive the initial scores for each case. These scores are divided by the square root of the number of nonmissing scores per subject. Once this adjustment is made, the scores are normalized so their sum of squares is equal to the number of variables times the number of subjects. These normalized scores are divided again by the square root of the number of nonmissing variables for the case to produce the final scores. This approach utilizes weights for both the variables and the cases. The component loadings provide the weights for the variables as they do in standard principal components analysis. The number of nonmissing values across the set of variables provides the weights for the cases. To minimize the potential impact of missing data on the results, we included in the PRINCALS analysis only cases that had valid scores on three of the four component variables. Approximately 2,000 cases out of the 21,000 cases used in the analysis were missing on one of the four variables used to measure engagement in the NES data. When we compared the engagement scores produced by PRINCALS from the NES data with those generated using standard principal components analysis, the two measures correlated at 0.996 for the 19,000 cases that were assigned a score by both methods.[1]

The four measures used to create the overall political engagement scale had similar component loadings on the dimension created from PRINCALS, although the campaign participation measure was slightly lower than the other variables. Table G.3 presents the component loadings produced by PRINCALS.

TABLE G.3 PRINCALS loadings for political engagement

ENGAGEMENT COMPONENT	LOADING
Campaign activity	.56
Vote	.71
Following politics	.74
Knowledge of House candidates	.71

Source: NES, 1972–1994

1. We would like to thank Jacqueline Meulman from the University of Leiden for her assistance is preparing this appendix on the PRINCALS technique.

H

Documentation of Unreported Coefficients

TABLE H.1 Unstandardized regression coefficients for Table 8.1

YEAR OF SURVEY (1972 EXCLUDED)	POLITICAL ENGAGEMENT WITH ABSOLUTE EDUCATION		POLITICAL ENGAGEMENT WITH RELATIVE EDUCATION	
	β	STANDARD ERROR	β	STANDARD ERROR
1974	−8.17	.68	−7.64	.66
1976	−2.38	.68	−1.57	.67
1978	−5.08	.69	−3.62	.68
1980	−1.95	.79	−.32	.77
1982	−8.43	.78	−6.49	.76
1984	−3.92	.72	−1.23	.70
1986	−12.17	.70	−8.97	.68
1988	−6.04	.73	−2.69	.71
1990	−11.54	.71	−7.77	.69
1992	−4.90	.69	−.79	.67
1994	−6.58	.73	−2.36	.70
EDUCATION	2.79	.04	36.30	.51
Adj. R^2	.17		.21	
N	20940		20939	

TABLE H.1 Unstandardized regression coefficients for Table 8.1 (Continued)

YEAR OF SURVEY (1976 EXCLUDED)	TOLERANCE WITH ABSOLUTE EDUCATION		TOLERANCE WITH RELATIVE EDUCATION	
	β	STANDARD ERROR	β	STANDARD ERROR
1977	−.15	.17	−.07	−.18
1980	.26	.18	.50	.19
1982	.13	.17	.46	.18
1984	.29	.18	.77	.19
1985	−.03	.17	.48	.18
1987	.19	.17	.82	.18
1988	.13	.20	.79	.21
1989	.58	.19	1.28	.20
1990	.53	.20	1.25	.21
1991	.80	.20	1.62	.21
1993	.79	.19	1.73	.20
1994	.68	.16	1.69	.17
EDUCATION	.71	.01	6.08	.14
Adj. R^2	.22		.12	
N	15952		15952	

TABLE H.2 Unstandardized regression coefficients for Table 8.3

YEAR OF SURVEY (1972 EXCLUDED)	VOTING IN NATIONAL ELECTIONS		KNOWLEDGE OF ELECTED OFFICIALS	
	β	STANDARD ERROR	β	STANDARD ERROR
1974	−16.32	1.33	−27.51	1.37
1976	.41	1.35	−1.04	1.25
1978	−14.65	1.38	16.18	1.26
1980	.11	1.58	21.50	1.39
1982	−11.20	1.58	1.07	1.39
1984	3.29	1.47	13.94	1.33
1986	−16.37	1.46	.42	1.32
1988	−.05	1.54	16.25	1.37
1990	−19.00	1.54	9.35	1.37

TABLE H.2 Unstandardized regression coefficients for Table 8.3 (Continued)

1992	6.90	1.53	16.13	1.37
1994	–8.48	1.63	24.89	1.43
AGE AND GENERATION				
Age 25–29	–3.58	1.05	–1.26	.82
Age over 75	–7.11	1.50	–5.80	1.19
Pre-New Deal generation	–5.23	1.46	–1.00	1.19
New Deal consolidation	.23	.74	2.29	.59
Vietnam war and after	–2.22	1.06	–3.33	.82
EDUCATION				
Years of education	3.99	.10	3.60	.08
Educational environment (years)	–5.90	.49	–4.14	.39
DEMOGRAPHICS				
Female	–2.98	.60	–11.00	.47
African-American	–1.92	.99	–8.79	.76
Other nonwhite	–13.73	2.05	–6.00	1.57
FAMILY AND COMMUNITY				
Married	6.10	.67	2.83	.52
Retired	1.67	1.05	1.44	.82
Home owner	8.73	.72	5.15	.56
Recently moved	–10.60	.79	–2.54	.61
Never attend church	–7.75	.82	–1.15	.64
Attend church weekly	6.64	.70	2.99	.55
Reside in rural area	–2.54	.63	.34	.49
PARTISANSHIP				
Independent of party affiliation	–7.99	.91	–4.99	.71
Strong party affiliation	13.40	.68	6.12	.53
Adjusted R^2	.21		.30	
N	20866		18948	

TABLE H.2 Unstandardized regression coefficients for Table 8.3 (Continued)

YEAR OF SURVEY (1972 EXCLUDED)	POLITICAL ATTENTIVENESS		CAMPAIGN ACTIVITY	
	β	STANDARD ERROR	β	STANDARD ERROR
1974	2.42	.97	−.00	.54
1976	.34	.98	1.00	.52
1978	−10.64	1.00	2.81	.56
1980	−8.03	1.14	−1.34	.62
1982	−7.41	1.14	.30	.64
1984	−7.06	1.08	−1.37	.58
1986	−7.62	1.06	−.44	.59
1988	−9.88	1.12	−1.34	.61
1990	−5.37	1.11	−1.19	.62
1992	−3.47	1.11	−1.57	.61
1994	−4.54	1.18	−1.67	.66
AGE AND GENERATION				
Age 25–29	−.28	.76	−.69	.43
Age over 75	−6.05	1.08	−.67	.60
Pre-New Deal generation	−3.67	1.05	−1.35	.59
New Deal consolidation	1.35	.53	.53	.30
Vietnam war and after	−1.21	.77	−1.55	.43
EDUCATION				
Years of education	3.42	.07	1.31	.04
Educational environment (years)	−4.63	.36	−.68	.20
DEMOGRAPHICS				
Female	−9.68	.44	−1.14	.25
African-American	.08	.72	−.68	.40
Other nonwhite	−5.04	1.49	−.74	.83

TABLE H.2 Unstandardized regression coefficients for Table 8.3 (Continued)

YEAR OF SURVEY (1972 EXCLUDED)	POLITICAL ATTENTIVENESS		CAMPAIGN ACTIVITY	
	β	STANDARD ERROR	β	STANDARD ERROR
FAMILY AND COMMUNITY				
Married	2.08	.48	.37	.27
Retired	4.15	.76	.01	.42
Home owner	2.10	.52	.93	.29
Recently moved	.65	.57	−1.19	.32
Never attend church	−3.08	.59	−1.62	.33
Attend church weekly	1.24	.50	.46	.28
Reside in rural area	−1.05	.45	.27	.26
PARTISANSHIP				
Independent of party affiliation	−2.05	.66	.57	.37
Strong party affiliation	11.37	.49	5.22	.28
Adjusted R^2	.19		.08	
N	20581		22443	

TABLE H.3 Unstandardized regression coefficients for Figure 8.1 and Figure 8.2

AGE AND GENERATION	MODEL WITH EDUCATIONAL ENVIRONMENT (FIGURE 8.1)		MODEL WITHOUT EDUCATIONAL ENVIRONMENT (FIGURE 8.2)	
	β	STANDARD ERROR	β	STANDARD ERROR
Age 25–29	−.39	.91	−5.06	.76
Age over 75	−5.14	1.09	−3.58	1.09
Pre-New Deal generation	−3.52	.96	.52	.86
New Deal consolidation	1.66	.56	.98	.55
Vietnam war and after	−.35	1.46	−1.34	1.46

TABLE H.3 Unstandardized regression coefficients for Figure 8.1
and Figure 8.2 (Continued)

	MODEL WITH EDUCATIONAL ENVIRONMENT (FIGURE 8.1)		MODEL WITHOUT EDUCATIONAL ENVIRONMENT (FIGURE 8.2)	
AGE AND GENERATION	β	STANDARD ERROR	β	STANDARD ERROR
EDUCATION				
Years of education	2.96	.07	2.81	.07
Educational environment (years)	−3.32	.35	(not in model)	
DEMOGRAPHICS				
Female	−6.48	.46	−6.44	.46
African-American	−2.18	.81	−2.81	.81
Other nonwhite	−3.59	1.79	−4.08	1.80
FAMILY AND COMMUNITY				
Married	3.29	.53	2.90	.53
Retired	4.53	.81	6.13	.80
Home owner	3.75	.54	4.05	.54
Recently moved	−3.97	.60	−4.59	.60
Never attend church	−2.91	.67	−2.90	.67
Attend church weekly	2.42	.52	2.71	.52
Reside in rural area	−1.00	.47	−1.01	.47
PARTISANSHIP				
Independent of party affiliation	−4.54	.68	−4.91	.69
Strong party affiliation	9.27	.53	9.68	.53
ACCOUNTING VARIABLE				
Presidential election year	4.97	.44	5.41	.44
Adjusted R^2	.30		.29	
N	7878		7878	

TABLE H.4 Unstandardized regression coefficients for Figure 8.3

EDUCATION	β	STANDARD ERROR
Years of education	.42	.02
Educational environment (rounded years)	.64	.16
Education of parents (years)	.16	.02
DEMOGRAPHICS		
Female	−.27	.12
RELIGION AND IDEOLOGY		
Frequency of church attendance	−.25	.02
Religious liberal	.96	.16
Protestant	−.70	.13
Conservative views	−.23	.05
TYPE AND LOCATION OF RESIDENCE		
In rural area at age 16	−.69	.14
In suburbs at age 16	.58	.22
Now reside in rural area	−.75	.15
In South at age 16	−.45	.20
In foreign country at age 16	−.72	.28
Now reside in South	−.78	.20
AGE AND GENERATION		
Educational maturity after 1979	−1.04	.32
Decade of educational maturity	.16	.12
Adj. R^2	.38	
N	5090	

TABLE H.5 Unstandardized regression coefficients for Table 8.7: Equation for income

YEAR OF SURVEY (1974 EXCLUDED)	β	STANDARD ERROR
1975	−1261	717
1976	−72	732
1977	2269	686

TABLE H.5 Unstandardized regression coefficients for Table 8.7: Equation for income (Continued)

Year of Survey (1974 excluded)	β	Standard Error
1980	2423	706
1982	–548	631
1984	–511	688
1985	614	669
1987	117	616
1988	–12	676
1989	–240	675
1990	742	698
1991	–257	695
1993	2290	659
1994	1419	536
Education		
Years of education	1870	54
Educational environment	–2541	175
Education of parents (years)	213	48
Demographics		
African-American	–1562	480
Female	–11966	287
Hours worked	251	8
Married	2674	297
Type and Location of Residence		
Reside in rural area	–1587	416
Reside in South	–1594	302
Reside in suburbs	2602	363
Reside in urban area	1933	400
Age and Generation		
Quadratic fit of age	1	0
Adj. R^2	.32	
N	15252	

TABLE H.6 Unstandardized regression coefficients for Table 8.7: Equation for organizational membership

YEAR OF SURVEY (1974 EXCLUDED)	β	STANDARD ERROR
1975	−.06	.06
1977	.07	.05
1980	−.26	.06
1984	−.09	.06
1987	−.18	.05
1988	−.07	.06
1989	−.04	.06
1990	−.06	.07
1991	−.14	.06
1993	.01	.06
1994	−.01	.09
EDUCATION		
Years of education	.20	.01
Educational environment (years)	−.22	.02
Education of parents (years)	.04	.00
DEMOGRAPHICS		
Female	−.30	.03
Hours worked	.01	.00
Married	.09	.03
Has household members 13–17 years old	.11	.02
Has household members 6–12 years old	.17	.02
RELIGION AND IDEOLOGY		
Frequency of church attendance	.17	.01
AGE AND GENERATION		
Educational maturity after 1975	−.13	.05
Age 70 or older	−.12	.06
Adj. R^2	.21	
N	15887	

TABLE H.7 Unstandardized regression coefficients for Table 8.7: Equation for verbal proficiency

YEAR OF SURVEY (1980 EXCLUDED)	β	STANDARD ERROR
1982	−.13	.06
1984	−.06	.06
1987	−.23	.06
1988	−.32	.07
1989	−.23	.07
1990	−.12	.07
1991	−.08	.07
1993	−.11	.07
1994	−.12	.06
EDUCATION		
Years of education	.32	.01
Educational environment	−.19	.02
Education of parents (years)	.07	.01
DEMOGRAPHICS		
African-American	−.92	.05
Other nonwhite	−1.00	.10
Female	.23	.03
TYPE AND LOCATION OF RESIDENCE		
In rural area at age 16	−.43	.04
In South at age 16	−.36	.03
In foreign country at age 16	−1.02	.08
AGE AND GENERATION		
Educational maturity after 1975	−.23	.05
Age 25–29	−.28	.05
Age 75 or older	−.36	.08
Adj. R^2	.35	
N	13218	

Bibliography

Abramson, Paul R., and John H. Aldrich. 1982. The Decline of Electoral Participation in America. *American Political Science Review* 76:502–521.

Abramson, Paul R., and Ronald Inglehart. 1995. *Value Change in Global Perspective*. Ann Arbor: University of Michigan Press.

Aldrich, John H. 1993. Rational Choice and Turnout. *American Journal of Political Science* 37:246–278.

Almond, Gabriel A., and Sidney Verba. 1963. *The Civic Culture: Political Attitudes and Democracy in Five Nations*. Princeton: Princeton University Press.

Alwin, Duane F. 1991. Family of Origin and Cohort Differences in Verbal Ability. *American Sociological Review* 56:625–638.

Alwin, Duane F., and Jon A. Krosnick. 1991. Aging, Cohorts, and the Stability of Sociopolitical Orientations over the Life Span. *American Journal of Sociology* 97:169–182.

Barber, Benjamin. 1984. *Strong Democracy: Participatory Politics for a New Age*. Berkeley: University of California Press.

Barnes, Samuel H., Max Kaase, et al. 1979. *Political Action: Mass Participation in Five Western Democracies*. Beverly Hills, Calif.: Sage Publications.

Baumgartner, Frank R., and Jack L. Walker. 1988. Survey Research and Membership in Voluntary Associations. *American Journal of Political Science* 32:908–928.

Becker, Gary. 1993. *Human Capital: A Theoretical and Empirical Analysis with Special Reference to Education*, 3rd ed. Chicago: University of Chicago Press.

Becker, Gary, and B. R. Chiswick. 1966. Education and the Distribution of Earnings. *American Economic Review* 56:358–369.

Beiner, Ronald, ed. 1995. *Theorizing Citizenship*. Albany: The State University of New York Press.

Bell, Daniel. 1972. On Meritocracy and Equality. *Public Interest* 29:29–68.

Berelson, Bernard R., Paul F. Lazarsfeld, and William N. McPhee. 1954. *Voting: A Study of Opinion Formation in a Presidential Campaign*. Chicago: University of Chicago Press.

Bianchi, Robert. 1989. *Unruly Corporatism: Associational Life in Twentieth-Century Egypt*. New York: Oxford University Press.

Blalock, Hubert M., Jr. 1961. *Causal Inferences in Non-experimental Research*. Chapel Hill: University of North Carolina Press.

Blau, Peter M., and Otis Dudley Duncan. 1967. *The American Occupation Structure*. New York: Wiley.

Bourdieu, Pierre. 1987. *Distinction: A Social Critique of the Judgment of Taste*. Trans. Richard Nice. Cambridge: Harvard University Press.

———. 1990. *Reproduction in Education, Society and Culture*, 2nd ed. Beverly Hills, Calif.: Sage Publications.

Bowles, Samuel, and Herbert Gintis. 1976. *Schooling in Capitalist America: Educational Reform and the Contradictions of Economic Life*. New York: Basic Books.

Brody, Richard. 1978. The Puzzle of Political Participation in America. In *The New American Political System*, ed. Anthony King. Washington, D.C.: American Enterprise Institute.

Burnham, Walter Dean. 1970. *Critical Elections and the Mainsprings of American Politics*. New York: Norton.

———. 1996. Realignment Lives: The 1994 Earthquake and its Implications. In *The Clinton Presidency: First Appraisals*, ed. Colin Campbell and Bert A. Rockman. Chatham, N.J.: Chatham House Publishers.

Burt, Ronald S. 1982. *Toward a Structural Theory of Action*. New York: Academic Press.

Campbell, Angus, Philip E. Converse, Donald E. Stokes, and Warren E. Miller. 1960. *The American Voter*. New York: Wiley.

Campbell, Angus, Gerald Gurin, and Warren E. Miller. 1954. *The Voter Decides*. Evanston, Ill.: Row, Peterson.

Cassell, Carol A., and Robert C. Luskin. 1988. Simple Explanations of Turnout Decline. *American Political Science Review* 82:1321–1330.

Chong, Dennis. 1993. How People Think, Reason, and Feel about Rights and Liberties. *American Journal of Political Science* 37:867–899.

Christman, John. 1988. Constructing the Inner Citadel: Recent Work on the Concept of Autonomy. *Ethics* 99:109–124.

Cole, Mike, ed. 1988. *Bowles and Gintis Revisited: Correspondence and Contradiction in Educational Theory*. New York: Falmer Press.

Coleman, James S. 1973. *The Mathematics of Collective Action*. Chicago: Aldine.

Collins, Randall. 1979. *The Credential Society: An Historical Sociology of Education and Stratification*. New York: Academic Press.

Conover, Pamela Johnston, Ivor M. Crewe, and Donald D. Searing. 1991. The Nature of Citizenship in the United States and Great Britain: Empirical Comments on Theoretical Themes. *Journal of Politics* 53:800–832.

_____. 1993. Citizen Identities in the Liberal State. Paper presented at the annual meeting of the American Political Science Association, Washington, D.C.

Converse, Philip E. 1972. Change in the American Electorate. In *The Human Meaning of Social Change*, ed. Angus Campbell and Philip E. Converse. New York: Russell Sage Foundation.

Dahl, Robert A. 1961. *Who Governs? Democracy and Power in an American City*. New Haven: Yale University Press.

———. 1971. *Polyarchy: Participation and Opposition*. New Haven: Yale University Press.

Daminco, Alfonso. 1978. *Individuality and Community: The Social and Political Thought of John Dewey*. Gainesville: University Presses of Florida.

Davis, James A. 1975. Communism, Conformity, Cohorts, Categories: American Tolerance in 1954 and 1972–73. *American Journal of Sociology* 81:491–513.

Dawson, Michael. 1995. Desperation and Hope: Competing Visions of Race and American Citizenship. Unpublished manuscript.

Delli Carpini, Michael X., and Scott Keeter. 1993. Measuring Political Knowledge: Putting First Things First. *American Journal of Political Science* 37:1179–1206.

———. 1996. *What Americans Know about Politics and Why It Matters*. New Haven: Yale University Press.

Dewey, John. 1916. *Democracy and Education: An Introduction to the Philosophy of Education*. New York: Macmillan.

Dietz, Mary. 1992. Context Is All: Feminism and Theories of Citizenship. In *Dimensions of Radical Democracy: Pluralism, Citizenship, Community*, ed. Chantal Mouffe. New York: Verso.

Downs, Anthony. 1957. *An Economic Theory of Democracy*. New York: HarperCollins.

DuBois, William Edward Burghardt. 1989 [1903]. *The Souls of Black Folk*. New York: Bantam Books.

Duncan, Otis Dudley. 1968. Ability and Achievement. *Eugenics Quarterly* 15:1–11.

Duncan, Otis Dudley, David L. Featherman, and Beverly Duncan. 1972. *Socioeconomic Background and Achievement*. New York: Seminar Press.

Durkheim, Emile. 1961. *Moral Education: A Study in the Theory and Application of the Sociology of Education*. New York: The Free Press of Glencoe.

Dworkin, Ronald. D. 1977. *Taking Rights Seriously*. Cambridge: Harvard University Press.

Easton, David, and Jack Dennis. 1969. *Children in the Political System: Origins of Political Legitimacy*. New York: McGraw-Hill.

Eckland, Bruce K. 1965. Academic Ability, Higher Education, and Occupational Mobility, *American Sociological Review* 30:735–746.

Eckstein, Harry. 1961. *A Theory of Stable Democracy*. Princeton: Center of International Studies, Princeton University.

Elster, Jon. 1989. *The Cement of Society: A Study of Social Order*. Cambridge: Cambridge University Press.

————. 1990. Selfishness and Altruism. In *Beyond Self-Interest*, ed. Jane J. Mansbridge. Chicago: University of Chicago Press.

Ethics. 1995. Vol. 105. Chicago: University of Chicago Press.

Etzioni, Amitai, ed. 1995. *New Communitarian Thinking: Persons, Virtues, Institutions, and Communities*. Charlottesville: University of Virginia Press.

Ferejohn, John A., and Morris P. Fiorina. 1975. Closeness Counts in Horseshoes and Dancing. *American Political Science Review* 69:920–925.

Filer, John E., Lawrence W. Kenny, and Rebecca B. Morton. 1993. Redistribution, Income, and Voting. *American Journal of Political Science* 37:63–87.

Fiorina, Morris P. 1976. The Voting Decision: Instrumental and Expressive Aspects. *Journal of Politics* 38:390–415.

Foner, Eric. 1988. *Reconstruction: America's Unfinished Revolution, 1863–1977*. New York: Harper & Row.

Frank, Robert H., and Philip J. Cook. 1995. *The Winner–Take–All Society*. New York: The Free Press.

Freeman, Linton C. 1979. Centrality in Social Networks: Conceptual Clarification. *Social Networks* 1:215–239.

Friedkin, Noah E. 1991. Theoretical Foundations for Centrality Measures. *American Journal of Sociology* 96:1478–1504.

Galston, William. 1991. *Liberal Purposes: Goods, Virtues, and Duties in the Liberal State*. New York: Cambridge University Press.

Gibson, James. 1992. Alternative Measures of Political Tolerance: Must Tolerance Be "Least-Liked"? *American Journal of Political Science* 36:560–577.

Gibson, James L., and Richard D. Bingham. 1982. On the Conceptualization and Measurement of Political Tolerance. *American Political Science Review* 76:603–620.

_____. 1985. *Civil Liberties and Nazis: The Skokie Free-Speech Controversy.* New York: Praeger.

Gould, Stephen Jay. 1981. *The Mismeasure of Man.* New York: Norton.

_____. 1985. *The Flamingo's Smile: Reflections in Natural History.* New York: Norton.

Gutmann, Amy. 1987. *Democratic Education.* Princeton: Princeton University Press.

_____. 1995. Civic Education and Social Diversity. *Ethics* 105:557–579.

Hanchard, Michael G. 1990. Identity, Meaning and the African–American. *Social Text* 8:31–42.

Hansen, John Mark. 1985. The Political Economy of Group Membership. *American Political Science Review* 79:79–96.

Hansen, Mogens Herman. 1991. *The Athenian Democracy in the Age of Demosthenes: Structure, Principles, and Ideology.* Cambridge, Mass.: Blackwell Publishers.

Hanson, Russell L. 1993. Deliberation, Tolerance and Democracy. In *Reconsidering the Democratic Public,* ed. George E. Marcus and Russell L. Hanson. University Park: Pennsylvania State University Press.

Haworth, Lawrence. 1986. *Autonomy: An Essay in Philosophical Psychology and Ethics.* New Haven: Yale University Press.

Heclo, Hugh. 1977. *A Government of Strangers: Executive Politics in Washington.* Washington, D.C.: Brookings.

Heise, David R. 1975. *Causal Analysis.* New York: Wiley.

Helliwell, John F., and Robert D. Putnam. 1996. Correction. *PS* 29:138.

Herrnstein, Richard J. 1971. *IQ in the Meritocracy.* Boston: Little Brown and Company.

Herrnstein, Richard J., and Charles Murray. 1994. *The Bell Curve: Intelligence and Class Structure in American Life.* New York: The Free Press.

Hirsch, Fred. 1976. *Social Limits to Growth.* Cambridge: Harvard University Press.

Huckfeldt, Robert. 1983. Social Contexts, Social Networks, and Urban Neighborhoods: Environmental Constraints on Friendship Choice. *American Journal of Sociology* 89:651–669.

Huckfeldt, Robert, Paul Allen Beck, Russell J. Dalton, and Jeffrey Levine. 1995. Political Environments, Cohesive Social Groups, and the Communication of Public Opinion. *American Journal of Political Science* 39:1025–1054.

Huckfeldt, Robert, and John Sprague. 1987. Networks in Context: The Social Flow of Political Information. *American Political Science Review* 81:1197–1216.

————. 1991. Discussant Effects on Vote Choice: Intimacy, Structure, and Interdependence. *Journal of Politics* 53:122–158.

————. 1992. Political Parties and Electoral Mobilization: Political Structure, Social Structure, and the Party Canvass. *American Political Science Review* 86:70–86.

Jencks, Christopher S. 1990. Varieties of Altruism. In *Beyond Self-Interest*, ed. Jane J. Mansbridge. Chicago: University of Chicago Press.

Jencks, Christopher S., M. Smith, H. Acland, M. J. Bane, D. Cohen, H. Gintis, B. Heyns, and S. Michelson. 1972. *Inequality: A Reassessment of the Effects of Family and Schooling in America*. New York: Basic Books.

Jennings, M. Kent, and Gregory B. Markus. 1988. Political Involvement in the Later Years: A Longitudinal Survey. *American Journal of Political Science* 32:302–316.

Jennings, M. Kent, and Richard G. Niemi. 1974. *The Political Character of Adolescence: The Influence of Families and Schools*. Princeton: Princeton University Press.

————. 1981. *Generations and Politics: A Panel Study of Young Adults and Their Parents*. Princeton: Princeton University Press.

Jensen, Arthur Robert, 1969. How Much Can We Boost IQ and Scholastic Achievement? *Harvard Educational Review* 39:1–123.

Jones, Kathleen B. 1990. Citizenship in a Woman–Friendly Polity. *Signs* 15:781–812.

Kant, Immanuel. 1900. *Kant on Education*. Trans. Annette Churton. Boston: D. C. Heath and Co.

Key, V. O. 1961. *Public Opinion in American Democracy*. New York: Alfred A. Knopf.

Knoke, David. 1986. Associations and Interest Groups. *Annual Review of Sociology* 12:1–21.

————. 1990a. Networks of Political Action: Toward Theory Construction. *Social Forces* 68:1041–1063.

————. 1990b. *Organizing for Collective Action: The Political Economy of Associations*. Hawthorne, N.Y.: Aldine de Gruyter.

Kotler, Neil G. 1974. *Politics and Citizenship in New England Towns: A Study of Participation and Political Education*, Ph.D. dissertation, University of Chicago.

Krausz, Tadeusz, and Kazimierz M. Slomczynski. 1985. How Far to Meritocracy? Empirical Tests of a Controversial Thesis. *Social Forces* 63:623–642.

Kuklinski, James H., Daniel S. Metlay, and W. D. Kay. 1982. Citizen Knowledge and Choices on the Complex Issue of Nuclear Energy. *American Journal of Political Science* 26:615–642.

Kymlicka, Will, and Wayne Norman. 1994. Return of the Citizen: A Survey of Recent Work on Citizenship Theory. *Ethics* 104:352–381.

Lane, Robert E. 1959. *Political Life: Why People Get Involved in Politics.* Glencoe, Ill.: Free Press.

Lash, Scott, and John Urry. 1994. *Economics of Signs and Space.* Beverly Hills, Calif.: Sage Publications.

Laumann, Edward O. 1966. *Prestige and Association in an Urban Community.* Indianapolis: Bobbs-Merrill.

———. 1973. *Bonds of Pluralism: The Forms and Substance of Urban Social Networks.* New York: Wiley.

Lazarsfeld, Paul, Bernard Berelson, and Hazel Gaudet. 1944. *The People's Choice: How the Voter Makes Up His Mind in a Presidential Campaign.* New York: Columbia University Press.

Lippmann, Walter. 1927. *The Phantom Public.* New York: Macmillan.

Lipset, Seymour Martin, and Rinehart Bendix. 1959. *Social Mobility in Industrial Society.* Berkeley: University of California Press.

Locke, John. 1965. *Two Treatises of Government.* Ed. Peter Laslett. New York: New American Library.

———. 1989. *Some Thoughts Concerning Education.* Ed. John W. Yolton and Jean S. Yolton. New York: Oxford University Press.

Lockridge, James A. 1970. *A New England Town the First Hundred Years: Dedham, Massachusetts, 1636–1736.* New York: Norton.

Luskin, Robert. 1987. Measuring Political Sophistication. *American Journal of Political Science* 31:856–899.

Macedo, Stephen. 1990. *Liberal Virtues: Citizenship, Virtue, and Community.* Oxford: Oxford University Press.

MacKinnon, Catharine A. 1993. *Only Words.* Cambridge: Harvard University Press.

Mansbridge, Jane J. 1980. *Beyond Adversary Democracy.* New York: Basic Books.

———., ed. 1990. *Beyond Self-Interest.* Chicago: University of Chicago Press.

Marsden, Peter V. and Noah E. Friedkin. 1993. Network Studies of Social Influence. *Sociological Methods and Research* 22:127–151.

Mascie-Taylor, C. G. N., and A. J. Boyce, eds. 1988. *Human Mating Patterns.* New York: Cambridge University Press.

Mason, William M., and Stephen E. Fienberg, eds. 1985. *Cohort Analysis in Social Research: Beyond the Identification Problem.* New York: Springer-Verlag.

Matsuda, Mari J., ed. 1993. *Words That Wound: Critical Race Theory, Assaultive Speech, and the First Amendment.* Boulder, Colo.: Westview Press.

McClosky, Herbert, and Alida Brill. 1983. *Dimensions of Tolerance: What Americans Believe about Civil Liberties.* New York: Russell Sage Foundation.

McClosky, Herbert, and John Zaller. 1984. *The American Ethos: Public Attitudes Toward Capitalism and Democracy.* Cambridge: Harvard University Press.

Merriam, Charles E. 1931. *The Making of Citizens: A Comparative Study of the Methods of Civic Training.* Chicago: University of Chicago Press.

———. 1934. *Civic Education in the United States.* New York: Scribner's.

Meyer, John W. 1977. The Effects of Education As an Institution. *American Journal of Sociology* 83:55–77.

Meyer, Michael J. 1987. Stoics, Rights, and Autonomy. *American Philosophical Quarterly* 24: 267–71.

Michael, Robert T. 1972. *The Effect of Education on Efficiency in Consumption.* New York: National Bureau of Economic Research.

Mill, John Stuart. 1958. *Considerations on Representative Government.* Ed. Currin V. Shields. Indianapolis: Bobbs-Merrill.

Miller, Warren E. 1992. The Puzzle Transformed: Explaining Declining Turnout. *Political Behavior* 14:1–46.

Mincer, Jacob. 1958. Investment in Human Capital and Personal Income Distribution. *Journal of Political Economy* 66:281–302.

———. 1970. The Distribution of Labor Incomes: A Survey with Special Reference to the Human Capital Approach. *Journal of Economic Literature* 8:1–16.

———. 1974. *Schooling, Experience, and Earnings.* New York: Columbia University Press for National Bureau of Economic Research.

Mueller, John. 1992. Democracy and Ralph's Pretty Good Grocery: Elections, Equality, and the Minimal Human Being. *American Journal of Political Science* 36:983-1003.

Nie, Norman H., Sidney Verba, and John Petrocik. 1976. *The Changing American Voter.* Cambridge: Harvard University Press.

Nunn, Clyde R., H. J. Crockett, and J. A. Williams. 1978. Tolerance for Nonconformity. San Francisco: Jossey-Bass.

Olneck, Michael R., and James Crouse. 1979. The IQ Meritocracy Reconsidered: Cognitive Skill and Adult Success in the United States. *American Journal of Education* 88:1–31.

Olson, Mancur, Jr., 1965. *The Logic of Collective Action: Public Goods and the Theory of Groups.* Cambridge: Harvard University Press.

Pateman, Carole. 1992. Equality, Difference, Subordination: The Politics of Motherhood and Women's Citizenship. In *Beyond Equality and Difference: Citizenship, Feminist Politics, and Female Subjectivity*, ed. Gisela Bock and Susan James. New York: Routledge.

Phillips, Anne. 1993. *Democracy and Difference.* University Park: Pennsylvania State University Press.

Pocock, J. G. A. 1992. The Ideal of Citizenship since Classical Times. *Queen's Quarterly* 99:35–55.

Powell, G. Bingham, Jr. 1984. *Contemporary Democracies: Participation, Stability, and Violence.* Cambridge: Harvard University Press.

———. 1986. American Voting in Comparative Perspective. *American Political Science Review* 80:23–37.

Przeworski, Adam. 1991. *Democracy and the Market: Political and Economic Reforms in Eastern Europe and Latin America.* New York: Cambridge University Press.

Putnam, Robert D. 1995a. Bowling Alone: America's Declining Social Capital. *Journal of Democracy* 6:65–78.

———. 1995b. Tuning In, Tuning Out: The Strange Disappearance of Social Capital in America. *PS* 28:664–683.

Quattrone, George A., and Amos Tversky. 1986. Self-deception and the Voter's Illusion. In *The Multiple Self*, ed. Jon Elster. New York: Cambridge University Press.

Rawls, John. 1971. *A Theory of Justice.* Cambridge: Belknap Press of Harvard University Press.

———. 1993. *Political Liberalism.* New York: Columbia University Press.

Riker, William H., and Peter C. Ordeshook. 1968. A Theory of the Calculus of Voting. *American Political Science Review* 62:25–42.

Roethlisberger, Fritz Jules, and William J. Dickson. 1939. Management and the Worker. Cambridge: Harvard University Press.

Rosenstone, Steven J., and John Mark Hansen. 1993. *Mobilization, Participation, and Democracy in America.* New York: Macmillan.

Rousseau, Jean Jacques. 1964. *The First and Second Discourses.* Ed. Roger D. Masters. New York: St. Martin's Press.

———. 1979. *Emile: Or, On Education.* Trans. Allan Bloom. New York: Basic Books.

Sandel, Michael J. 1984. *Liberalism and Its Critics*. New York: New York University Press.

Schlozman, Kay Lehman, and John T. Tierney. 1986. *Organized Interests and American Democracy*. New York: Harper & Row.

Schlozman, Kay Lehman, Sidney Verba, and Henry Brady. 1995. Participation's Not a Paradox: The View from American Activists. *British Journal of Political Science* 25:1–36.

Schmitter, Philippe C. 1986. Neo-Corporatism and the State. In *The Political Economy of Corporatism*, ed. Wyn Grant. London: Macmillan.

Schultz, Theodore W. 1960. Capital Formation by Education. *Journal of Political Economy* 68:571–583.

———. 1961. Investment in Human Capital. *American Economic Review* 51:1–17.

———. 1971. *Investment in Human Capital: The Role of Education and of Research*. New York: The Free Press.

Scott, John. 1991. *Social Network Analysis: A Handbook*. Newbury Park, Calif.: Sage Publications.

Sewell, William H., and Robert M. Hauser. 1975. *Education, Occupation, and Earnings*. New York: Academic Press.

Sewell, William H., Robert M. Hauser, and David L. Featherman, eds. 1976. *Schooling and Achievement in American Society*. New York: Academic Press.

Shaffer, Stephen D. 1981. A Multivariate Explanation of Decreasing Turnout in Presidential Elections, 1960–1976. *American Journal of Political Science* 25:68–95.

Shklar, Judith N. 1991. *American Citizenship: The Quest for Inclusion*. Cambridge: Harvard University Press.

Smith, Rogers M. 1988. The American Creed and American Identity: The Limits of Liberal Citizenship in the United States. *Western Political Quarterly* 41:225–251.

———. 1993. Beyond Tocqueville, Mrydal, and Hartz: The Multiple Traditions in America. *American Political Science Review* 87:549–566.

Smith, Tom W. 1995. Some Aspects of Measuring Education. *Social Science Research* 24:215–242.

Sniderman, Paul M., Richard A. Brody, and James H. Kuklinski. 1984. Policy Reasoning and Political Values: The Problem of Racial Equality. *American Journal of Political Science* 28:75–94.

Sniderman, Paul M., Richard A. Brody, and Philip Tetlock. 1991. *Reasoning and Choice: Explorations in Political Psychology*. New York: Cambridge University Press.

Sniderman, Paul M., Philip E. Tetlock, James M. Glaser, Donald Philip Green, and Michael Hout. 1989. Principled Tolerance and the American Mass Public. *British Journal of Political Science* 19:25–45.

Snyder, Thomas D., ed. 1993. *120 Years of American Education: A Statistical Portrait*. National Center for Education Statistics, U.S. Department of Education. Washington, D.C.: U.S. Government Printing Office.

Somjee, A. H. 1968. *The Political Theory of John Dewey*. New York: Teachers College Press, Columbia University.

South, Scott J. 1991. Sociodemographic Differentials in Mate Selection Preferences. *Journal of Marriage and the Family* 53:928–940.

Statistical Abstract of the United States. 1972–1994. Volumes 93–114. United States Department of Commerce, Economics and Statistics Administration, Bureau of the Census. Washington, D.C.: United States Government Printing Office.

Steiner, David M. 1994. *Rethinking Democratic Education: The Politics of Reform*. Baltimore: Johns Hopkins University Press.

Stevens, Jacqueline. 1995. Beyond Tocqueville, Please! *American Political Science Review* 89:987–990.

Stouffer, Samuel. 1955. *Communism, Conformity, and Civil Liberties*. New York: Doubleday.

Sullivan, John L., James Piereson, and George E. Marcus. 1979. An Alternative Conceptualization of Political Tolerance: Illusory Increases 1950s–1970s. *American Political Science Review* 73:781–794.

_____. 1982. *Political Tolerance and American Democracy*. Chicago: University of Chicago Press.

Sunstein, Cass R. 1993. *Democracy and the Limits of Free Speech*. New York: The Free Press.

Takaki, Ronald T. 1990. *Iron Cages: Race and Culture in Nineteenth Century America*. New York: Oxford University Press.

Tarcov, Nathan. 1984. *Locke's Education for Liberty*. Chicago: University of Chicago Press.

Taylor, Charles. 1989. Cross-Purposes: The Liberal-Communitarian Debate. In *Liberalism and the Moral Life*, ed. Nancy Rosenblum. Cambridge: Harvard University Press.

Teixeira, Ruy. 1987. *Why Americans Don't Vote: Turnout Decline in the United States, 1960–1984*. Westport, Conn.: Greenwood Press.

_____. 1992. The Disappearing American Voter. Washington, D.C.: Brookings.

Thompson, Dennis F. 1970. *The Democratic Citizen: Social Science and Democratic Theory in the Twentieth Century*. London: Cambridge University Press.

―――. 1976. *John Stuart Mill and Representative Government*. Princeton: Princeton University Press.

Thorndike, Robert L. 1942. Two Screening Tests of Verbal Intelligence. *Journal of Applied Psychology* 26:128–35.

Thorndike, Robert L., and George H. Gallup. 1944. Verbal Intelligence of the American Adult. *Journal of General Psychology* 30:75–85.

Thurow, Lester. 1972. Education and Economic Equality. *Public Interest* 28:66–81.

―――. 1975. *Generating Inequality: Mechanisms of Distribution in the U.S.* New York: Basic Books.

―――. 1980. *The Zero Sum Society: Distribution and the Possibilities for Economic Change*. New York: Basic Books.

Uhlaner, Carole J. 1989. Rational Turnout: The Neglected Role of Groups. *American Journal of Political Science* 33:390–422.

Verba, Sidney, and Norman H. Nie, 1972. *Participation in America: Political Democracy and Social Equality*. New York: Harper & Row.

Verba, Sidney, Norman H. Nie, and Jae-on Kim. 1978. *Participation and Political Equality: A Seven-Nation Comparison*. New York: Cambridge University Press.

Verba, Sidney, and Gary R. Orren. 1985. *Equality in America: The View from the Top*. Cambridge: Harvard University Press.

Verba, Sidney, Kay Lehman Schlozman, and Henry E. Brady. 1995. *Voice and Equality: Civic Voluntarism in American Politics*. Cambridge: Harvard University Press.

Walker, Jack L. 1991. *Mobilizing Interest Groups in America: Patrons, Professions, and Social Movements*. Ann Arbor: University of Michigan Press.

Walzer, Michael. 1984. *Spheres of Justice*. New York: Basic Books.

―――. 1989. Citizenship. In *Political Innovation and Conceptual Change*, ed. Terence Ball, James Farr, and Russell L. Hanson. Cambridge: Cambridge University Press.

―――. 1992. *What It Means to Be an American: Essays on the American Experience*. New York: Marsilio Publishers.

Warner, W. Lloyd, and Paul S. Lunt. 1941. *The Social Life of a Modern Community*. New Haven: Yale University Press.

―――. 1942. *The Status System of a Modern Community*. New Haven: Yale University Press.

We the Americans: Our Education. 1993. United States Department of Commerce, Economics, and Statistics Administration, Bureau of the Census. Washington, D.C.: United States Government Printing Office.

Wellman, Barry, and Stephen D. Berkowitz, eds. 1988. *Social Structures: A Network Approach*. New York: Cambridge University Press.

Wolfe, Tom. 1980. *The Right Stuff*. New York: Bantam Books.

Wolfinger, Raymond E., and Steven J. Rosenstone. 1980. *Who Votes?* New Haven: Yale University Press.

Wuthnow, Robert, ed. 1991. *Between States and Markets: The Voluntary Sector in Comparative Perspective*. Princeton: Princeton University Press.

Young, Iris Marion. 1989. Polity and Group Difference: A Critique of the Ideal of Universal Citizenship. *Ethics* 99:250–274.

_____. 1990. *Justice and the Politics of Difference*. Princeton: Princeton University Press.

Zaller, John. 1992. *The Nature and Origins of Mass Opinion*. New York: Cambridge University Press.

Index